THE ELGIN AFFAIR

BOOKS BY THEODORE VRETTOS

Hammer on the Sea

A Shadow of Magnitude

Origen

Birds of Winter

Lord Elgin's Lady

The Elgin Affair

THE ELGIN AFFAIR

The

Abduction of Antiquity's Greatest Treasures

and the

Passions It Aroused

THEODORE VRETTOS

ARCADE PUBLISHING • NEW YORK

For John Fowles

FIRST EDITION

Library of Congress Cataloging-in-Publication Data

Vrettos, Theodore
     The Elgin affair : the abduction of Antiquity's greatest treasures and the passions it aroused / Theodore Vrettos.
         p. cm.
     Includes bibliographical references and index.
     ISBN 1-55970-386-5
     1. Elgin marbles—Public opinion. 2. Art thefts—Greece—Athens. 3. Elgin, Thomas Bruce, Earl of, 1766–1841—Ethics. I. Title.
NB92.V7   1997
733'.3'09385—dc21   97-12442

Published in the United States by Arcade Publishing, Inc., New York

Distributed by Little, Brown and Company

10 9 8 7 6 5 4 3 2 1

Designed by API

BP

PRINTED IN THE UNITED STATES OF AMERICA

$\mathcal{C}$ONTENTS

Author's Note

*T*HE LONG, COMPLEX, AND BYZANTINE STORY of the Elgin Marbles has fascinated and preoccupied me for many years. Among my friends and fellow writers, there are those who would say that the proper term is "obsessed."

Almost twenty-five years ago I published a book entitled *A Shadow of Magnitude*, in which I described Lord Elgin's grand adventure, based on the best research then available. Later, I wrote a novel entitled *Lord Elgin's Lady*, which was based on the same story, but told this time from the viewpoint of his Scottish bride, Mary Nisbet, whom Elgin married in 1799 when Mary was only twenty-one.

Two reasons compelled me to take up the elements of the early books and retell the story: For one thing, the issue of the ownership of the marbles, which are arguably among the most precious and stunning sculptures of ancient Greece, once again came to the fore. Increasingly, various voices not only from Greece but from around the world were calling for the return of the marbles to their original home. So great was the outcry that thirty-three British MPs introduced into the House of Commons — at their political risk and peril, it must be said — a draft resolution urging the British government to take that heroic step, citing a recent television poll that showed 92.5 percent of the 100,000 viewers polled in favor of the move. The Greek authorities for their part were threatening to take the case to the international court. Thus by the mid-1990s, the Elgin Marbles had become a burning moral issue of international interest.

My second and more important reason was that considerable additional material has come to light over the past two and a half decades, which offers important new insights about Lord Elgin's picaresque adventure and needed absolutely to be incorporated into the story, both for accuracy and currency. Further, the earlier book on the subject was embarrassingly filled with misspellings, typographical errors — even missing pages — and I have long felt the need to correct it. Thus, though *The Elgin Affair* follows roughly the same structure as *A Shadow of Magnitude*, the new book, which contains at least thirty-five percent new material, completely supersedes it.

THEODORE VRETTOS
JULY 1997

Acknowledgments

I AM GRATEFUL TO THE STAFF of Greek and Roman Antiquities at the British Museum; also to the trustees of the British Museum for permission to reproduce their photographs. I am equally indebted to the trustees and the librarians of the National Library of Scotland for their patient help in tracking down elusive documents, particularly the court records on the adultery trial against Lady Elgin and Robert Fergusson in Edinburgh. I owe additional thanks to the staff of the Scottish Records Office in Edinburgh.

I wish to thank John Murray (Publishers) Ltd., London, for permission to quote from *The Letters of Mary Nisbet, Countess of Elgin*, and Oxford University Press, for permission to quote from *Lord Elgin and the Marbles*, by William St. Clair.

I received much help from the Gennadios Library in Athens, the Library of Lambeth Palace in London, and Widener Library at Harvard University. Dr. David Mitten of Harvard's Fogg Art Museum was especially cooperative, as were the staffs of the Victoria and Albert Museum in London, the Greater London Council, the National Archaeological Museum at Athens, and the Archeological Museum at Olympia.

I am deeply grateful to Richard Seaver, president and publisher of Arcade Publishing, for his astute editorial counsel and support; also to Katherine Balch, Timothy Bent, and Calvert Barksdale.

Further gratitude is owed to Dr. Michael L. Dertouzos and his staff at the Massachusetts Institute of Technology, chiefly Mark Pearrow and Kyle Pope. Barbara Harrison offered generous and gracious assistance, as did Jeff Snyder and Olga Pelensky.

Above all, my greatest debt of gratitude is to my wife, Vas, whose invaluable labor and love provided the necessary encouragement to complete the task.

Principal Characters

Napoleon Bonaparte (1769–1821), emperor of France

Thomas Bruce, seventh earl of Elgin and eleventh of Kincardine, (1766–1841), British diplomat, art collector, and ambassador to Turkey under King George III

George Gordon Byron (1788–1824), English romantic poet

Joseph Dacre Carlyle (1760–1804), professor of Arabic at Cambridge and classical scholar attached to Lord Elgin's embassy

Vicomte François-August-René de Chateaubriand (1768–1848), diplomat, traveler, and author, one of the first romantic writers in France

Comte de Choiseul-Gouffier, French collector and antiquarian

Edward Daniel Clarke (1769–1822), English mineralogist, traveler, and writer

George Cruikshank (1792–1878), English artist, caricaturist, and illustrator

Robert Fergusson of Raith, Scotland (1777–1846), second husband of Lady Elgin and subject of the scandalous trial for adultery.

John Flaxman (1755–1826), English sculptor and draftsman

John Galt (1779–1839), Scottish novelist and traveler

King George III (1738–1820), king of Great Britain and Ireland

William Wyndham Grenville (1759–1834), British foreign secretary under King George III

Lady Emma Hamilton (1765–1815), wife of Sir William Hamilton and famous as the mistress of Lord Nelson

Sir William Hamilton (1730–1803), British diplomat, archaeologist, and notable collector

William Richard Hamilton (1777–1859), Lord Elgin's first private secretary; studied at Oxford and Cambridge

Thomas Hardy (1840–1928), English novelist and poet

Benjamin Robert Haydon (1786–1846), English historical painter and writer

John Cam Hobhouse (1786–1869), close friend of Lord Byron, and fellow traveler

Rev. Philip Hunt (1771–1867), chaplain of Lord Elgin's embassy in Constantinople

John Keats (1795–1821), one of England's greatest poets

Richard Payne Knight (1750–1824), English patron of the arts and writer

Leonidas Logothetis, British consul in Athens

Giovanni Battista Lusieri, court painter for the king of Naples and supervisor of all the artists employed by Lord Elgin in Athens

Hector McLean (1762–1801), physician to Lord Elgin's embassy in Constantinople

John Philip Morier (1777–1857), Lord Elgin's second private secretary

Viscount Horatio Nelson (1758–1805), British naval commander

Mary Nisbet (1777–1855), Lord Elgin's wife

William Nisbet, Lady Elgin's father

Mrs. William Nisbet, Lady Elgin's mother

Joseph Nollekens (1737–1823), neoclassical sculptor whose work made him the most fashionable English portrait sculptor

William Pitt the Younger (1759–1806), British prime minister under King George III

Sir Joshua Reynolds (1723–1792), the most prominent figure in the English school of painting and its leading portrait painter; the first president of the Royal Academy

Comte Horace François Sébastiani (1772–1851), marshall of France and ambassador to Turkey and Egypt under Napoleon

Selim III (1761–1808), sultan of Turkey

Joseph Severn (1793–1879), English portrait and subject painter

Percy Bysshe Shelley (1792–1822), English poet

Charles Maurice de Talleyrand-Périgord (1754–1838), French diplomat and statesman, foreign minister under Napoleon

J. M. W. Turner (1775–1851), one of England's greatest painters

John Tweddell (1769–1799), classical scholar, traveler, and writer

Benjamin West (1738–1820), American historical and portrait painter under the special patronage of King George III

Significant Dates

1766   July 20. Lord Elgin is born in Dunfermline, Scotland.

1792   Elgin is appointed envoy to Brussels.

1795   Elgin serves as envoy extraordinary to Berlin.

1798   August 1. Napoleon and the French fleet suffer a crushing defeat by Lord Nelson in the Battle of the Nile.

1799   March 11. Elgin marries Mary Nisbet of Dirleton, Scotland.

1799   September 3. Lord and Lady Elgin set sail from Portsmouth.

1799–1802   Lord Elgin serves as ambassador extraordinary to Constantinople.

1800–1802   Under Lusieri's supervision, shiploads of sculptures, friezes, and metopes are removed from the Athenian Acropolis and dispatched to England.

1803   January 16. Lord Elgin closes down the embassy at Constantinople.

1803   August 28. While detained by the French in Barèges, Lord Elgin is sent to prison at Lourdes.

1805   February 2. Lady Elgin is permitted to leave France while her husband is still in prison. On the voyage to England, she is accompanied by Robert Fergusson.

1808   March 11. The trial of R. J. Fergusson, for adultery with Lady Elgin, is held in Edinburgh. Elgin wins the case.

1816   August 15. Lord Elgin's collection of Parthenon marbles is sold and transferred to the British Museum.

1821   May 15. Lord Elgin marries Elizabeth Oswald of Dunnikeir and leaves Scotland to live in Paris, where he dies on November 14, 1841.

1821   July 8. Lady Elgin marries Robert Fergusson. After his death in 1846, she returns to her family home in Dirleton, remaining there until her death in 1855.

Prologue

E ARLY IN 1798, the government of France appointed the brilliant young general Napoleon Bonaparte commander in chief of the "Army of England," a huge force already assembled on the Channel coast of France for the invasion of Great Britain. After some deliberation, Bonaparte suggested that these forces should be used to invade Egypt, not England, and the decision was at once adopted.

In May of that year, a powerful armada under Bonaparte's command set sail from Toulon and successfully eluded the British fleet in the Mediterranean, capturing Malta and incorporating the island into the French Republic.

Toward the middle of June, the armada set sail from Malta, and after again escaping the British warships in the Mediterranean, it arrived safely in Egypt.

At this time, Egypt was under the control of the Ottoman Empire, along with most of the Balkan countries, the Middle East, and the North African coast. But this was a pretense of Turkish authority because the real control of Egypt was in the hands of the Mamluks. Nevertheless the nebulous authority of the Turks was somehow maintained, and whenever a new pasha of Egypt was appointed by the Porte, he was received by the Mamluks with an impressive formal ceremony and then escorted to the citadel, where he lived in virtual imprisonment until his term of office expired.

Understandably, the Turkish government nourished a deep hatred for the Mamluks, and although France had been Turkey's oldest and safest ally up until this time, the invasion of Egypt by Napoleon came as a complete surprise. Indeed, almost at the precise moment that Bonaparte was seizing Egypt, French foreign minister Talleyrand was in Constantinople persuading the Turks that France was occupying Egypt only in Turkey's interest.

On August 6, Henri Ruffin, the French chargé d'affaires at Constantinople, was summoned to the seraglio by the Turkish minister and reprimanded harshly: "The Sublime Porte was pained to see an allied power seize without warning Turkey's most precious province, the navel of Islam."[1] Before Ruffin could respond, he was quickly escorted out of the seraglio by a military guard and taken to the prison of the Seven Towers. The next day, Sultan Selim III issued a formal declaration of war against France.

Even while Ruffin was being led to prison, the British admiral Horatio Nelson had already destroyed the French fleet in the Battle of the Nile. The victory, and subsequent declaration of war on France by the Turks, gave the British government the opportunity not only to secure Turkey as an ally in their war against the French, but also to become the most favored nation in the Ottoman Empire.

It was into these turbulent events that Thomas Bruce, seventh earl of Elgin, was thrust when he accepted the post of ambassador extraordinary to the Sublime Porte and set sail in 1799 for Constantinople with his beautiful young wife. Up until this time, England had regarded Turkey as a remote and unimportant country and hadn't even bothered to maintain an official embassy at Constantinople, leaving all relations with Turkey in the hands of the Levant Company, an English chartered firm that had been given exclusive rights in all British trade with the eastern Mediterranean. Its official title, incorporated by royal charter, was the Governor and Merchants of England Trading to the Levant Seas. Moreover it had the statutary right to appoint all British ambassadors, consuls, and deputies in the Levant, and to lay charges on its very own members. It also had the power to impose fines and send home any member who voiced dissent against the company. At various times, it even maintained its own fleet of warships.

Lord Elgin's appointment as ambassador to the Porte was first presented by King George III to the governor and trustees of the Levant Company before it was approved. The last member of the Levant Company to assume the role of ambassador was Robert Liston. He left in 1794, and Sir William Sydney Smith temporarily took the post and refused to relinquish it, even after Lord Elgin arrived in Constantinople.

Part 1

Sicily

*T*HE SICILIAN SKY was on fire when HMS *Phaeton* dropped anchor off Palermo at noon. Inside the stifling bowels of the
frigate's only stateroom, the young bride trickled more vinegar into her silk handkerchief and dabbed it weakly over her face and
wrists. A glass of Portuguese brandy lay untouched on the small oak
table beside the bunk where her husband had placed it before leaving
the cabin earlier that morning. She had been stricken by the sea from
the very moment she stepped on board the *Phaeton* at Portsmouth. "A
fortnight in Lisbon offered no relief, nor the vinegar now."[1] Indeed, its
obnoxious fumes augmented her misery, and in desperation she fled
once again to her beloved Archerfield, forcing her tortured brain to
conjure a picture of peaceful Scottish woods protecting her father's
house from the western wind as fields of autumn grass frolicked along
the golden sands of Aberlady Bay. In her wildest dreams, she still found
it hard to believe that she was the wife of Thomas Bruce, seventh earl
of Elgin and eleventh of Kincardine.

Lord Elgin was born on July 20, 1766, of noble and ancient an-
cestry. The Bruce name of Culross in the kingdom of Fife was traced
directly from Robert de Brus, a knight of Normandy, who accompanied William the Conqueror into England. From this same lineage
was born the famous Robert the Bruce, first king of Scotland
(1306–1329), whose heart is buried in Melrose Abbey, and whose
sword still hangs at Broomhall, the palatial estate of the Elgin family.
Lord Elgin's mother was in particular favor at court as the countess of
Elgin and was governess at one time to the young princess Charlotte
of Wales, the only daughter of George IV.

Elgin inherited the earldom in his boyhood. After an education at
Harrow, Westminster, Saint Andrew's, and Paris, he was commissioned
an ensign in the Foot Guards, passing swiftly through the lower ranks,
and eventually was given command of his own regiment, the Elgin

Highland Fencibles. He was elected to the House of Lords in 1790, and the next year, at the age of twenty-five, was granted his first diplomatic assignment by Britain's prime minister William Pitt. It came at short notice, and within twenty-four hours Elgin set off for Vienna as envoy extraordinary to the newly crowned emperor Leopold II.

For almost a year, he accompanied Leopold on long trips to the Austrian territories in Italy and tried repeatedly to persuade the emperor to bring Austria into alliance with England. Although his long months of labor and dedication proved unsuccessful, Elgin nevertheless managed to establish a sound diplomatic reputation and was subsequently rewarded by Lord William Wyndham Grenville, Britain's foreign secretary, with a second appointment: envoy to Brussels, where he remained for two years, mostly as a liaison officer between the Belgian and Austrian armies. Henry Dundas, who for many years had regulated all the parliamentary elections in Scotland and was instrumental in getting Elgin elected to the House of Lords, once again came to Elgin's assistance and wrote a strong letter of recommendation to Lord Grenville:

> Although not very rich, he is easy in his circumstances and would not with a view to emolument alone wish for employment. But if he can be creditably to himself employed in the public service, it would give him pleasure to be so. He thinks himself perfectly safe in that respect in the hands of the present government. He will never urge you to anything; nor will he ever bring forward any pretentions, but you will at any time find him ready to obey any call made upon the grounds I have stated.[2]

Elgin was assigned to the court of Prussia at Berlin, and as British minister plenipotentiary he became involved for the first time in his life with the many intrigues of foreign diplomacy, which he found distasteful. Furthermore, as a gentleman nurtured in the old school, he was firmly entrenched in outdated principles and old-fashioned conceptions of honor and tradition. He was far from naive, however, and although he remained in Berlin until his thirty-second year without being married, he was by no means unacceptable to women. A steady visitor to the embassy house at Berlin was a certain "fair favourite,

Madame Ferchenbeck,"[3] but nothing came of the relationship, and Elgin returned to England in 1798, stopping first at the office of the foreign secretary before continuing to Brighton for a well-earned holiday.

A few days later, while dancing with the princess Augusta at a ball given by the fleet at Weymouth, Elgin was drawn aside by King George III and told that he should apply at once for the post of ambassador to Turkey, but with the stipulation that he find himself a wife, since his prolonged bachelorhood was considered a distinct disadvantage for an ambassador, particularly in the Levant.

There were countless young ladies on both sides of the firth, attractive and of sound family fortune, but Elgin chose Mary Nisbet, who lived in Dirleton, a small village ten miles east of Edinburgh. William Nisbet's estates brought in eighteen thousand pounds annually, and Elgin certainly was aware of this when he made his heralded appearance at Archerfield, the Nisbet home, on the raw morning of March 11. It was not an easy victory for him. William Nisbet did not favor the discrepancy in age; his daughter was only twenty-one and Elgin thirty-three. Aside from this, some of Edinburgh's wealthiest young men had already expressed their desire to marry his only child. Furthermore, he also knew that Elgin had recently incurred heavy debts restoring Broomhall. Nevertheless, he was attracted by the idea of marrying his daughter to a member of the nobility, and he gave his consent.

Soon after Elgin's application for ambassador was accepted, he selected a sizable staff for his embassy. The men were youthful, well qualified, and dedicated. Foremost among them was Professor Joseph Dacre Carlyle, who previously held the chair in Arabic at Cambridge. He had just turned thirty-nine and already had several important books published. He also had a weakness for poetry and "kept beleaguering everyone on the staff with his poor verses."[4] His chief purpose in joining the embassy was to fulfill a sincere desire to convert the natives of Asia and Africa by distributing an Arabic version of the Bible, over which he had labored for several years. Lord Elgin had no objection to this as long as Carlyle was able to fortify the embassy with his knowledge and scholarly achievement.

The Reverend Philip Hunt was twenty-eight and had been for a short time a clergyman under the patronage of Lord Upper Ossory. A meticulous scholar, he could dissect the history of many archaeological sites in Europe and Asia and had a sound knowledge of Greek. The opportunity to join Lord Elgin's embassy excited him:

> As the Turks have now made a common cause with us to stop the progress of the French, it has been thought expedient by our court to send a splendid Embassy to Constantinople in order to enter into certain treaties for the mutual advantage of both countries. The Earl of Elgin is appointed Ambassador Extraordinary etc., to the Porte, and by the interest of my worthy and excellent friend, the Reverend Mr. Brand, Rector of Maulden, the situation of chaplain and private secretary to the Ambassador will most probably be filled by me. I have consulted Lord Ossory and my other friends here, and they all concur in describing it as a most brilliant opportunity of improving my mind and laying the foundation of a splendid fortune. I need only add that it is a situation by which the young son of a Nobleman might aspire; that it will be certainly attended with great present advantages and most probably lead to an independent fortune.[5]

Elgin's two other secretarial assistants were both twenty-two. John Morier knew about the East, having been born in Smyrna, where his father was consul. This was his first diplomatic assignment, and he religiously supplied his diary with many details of the voyage, particularly Lord Elgin's coldness of manner and frugality. Even during their first day at sea, Morier noticed

> a great indifference on the part of Lord Elgin towards those most immediately dependent upon him. However, part of this can be attributed to His Lordship's chronic indisposition. He suffers constantly from rheumatism and is susceptible to catching cold, which is a deep source of vexation for Her Ladyship. Everyone under employment has very quickly discovered that His Lordship does not intend to pay one penny of the salary agreed upon until the Embassy is closed by order of the government. He has even stood by and allowed all in the party to pay their own expenses and studiously avoids any mention of money.[6]

Elgin's first personal secretary, William Richard Hamilton, was also on his first assignment. He had studied at Oxford and Cambridge, and when his sponsor wrote to Elgin, the letter brimmed with hyperbole: "He has much good sense and great activity of mind. He is industrious and in the highest degree anxious to render himself useful. His manners are most pleasing and his principles perfectly good, so you may use him at once as your companion and your confidant."[7]

Dr. Hector McLean was the embassy physician. "An esteemed medical authority,"[8] he was at his wit's end in effecting a cure for Lady Elgin's mal de mer and with great exasperation finally decided that the *Phaeton* should stop briefly at selected ports of call to afford her some measure of relief. McLean had a weakness for alcohol and confined himself in his compartment throughout most of the voyage.

Lady Elgin unabashedly regarded her husband's desire for the post at Constantinople as vain and senseless. The world was already spinning into the nineteenth century, yet Turkey still remained a barbarous country, her plague-infested towns swelling with harems and dens of hashish. To seek such an embassy at a time when England was at war with Bonaparte seemed even more absurd, but Elgin, refusing to be dissuaded, continually reminded her of Constantinople's ancient beauty and fame, the matchless splendor of Haghia Sophia,* the Gardens of Pera, the Bosporus, the seraglio.†

But more importantly, Elgin had a deeper reason for seeking the post at Constantinople. From the time he was a young student at Westminster, he had developed a fond affection for art, and especially sculpture. Largely through the influence of Thomas Harrison, the architect he had engaged to restore Broomhall, Elgin learned that the best models of classical art were to be found in Greece, not Rome. Harrison further suggested that while Elgin was at Constantinople he could make periodic visits to Athens, where excellent opportunities for improving his knowledge of Greek sculpture and architecture were agelessly present. Although many publications had been recently

---

*The Church of Saint Sophia was Emperor Justinian's greatest achievement. Begun in A.D. 532, it marks the highest development of Byzantine architecture.
†The palace of the sultans.

written by English and German scholars, Harrison insisted that books could not truly inspire. Far more important were plaster casts of the actual objects, as well as paintings and drawings done in situ under the brilliance of the Grecian sky.

Harrison's words stirred Lord Elgin. It was the opportunity he had long been seeking, the chance to restore the entire position of the fine arts in Great Britain and to improve British architecture, painting, and sculpture. Moreover, classical designs could be used everywhere, even on furniture and household items, and consequently the embassy could very well benefit the whole advancement of the arts in England. It was a grandiose scheme, and immediately after Elgin learned that he had been accepted for this much-desired post, he put his ideas to Lord Grenville. After requesting sufficient money to support such an important undertaking, Elgin furthermore asked for painters, artists, architects, draftsmen, and formatori. These demands, however, exceeded Grenville's authority, and he suggested that Elgin present them in person to the prime minister, William Pitt. Pitt's response was disheartening: "His Majesty's Government cannot equip your Embassy with such grand ideas. If you choose to embark upon this venture you must do so at your own expense."[9]

Elgin's salary had already been fixed at only six thousand pounds per year. Nevertheless he was determined to carry his scheme forward, and soon the best painters of England offered themselves at Broomhall. First to arrive was the watercolor painter Thomas Girtin. He waited two hours in the great hall before being interviewed, only to learn that Elgin could offer him thirty pounds annually, which was half the salary of an English valet. In addition to his main task as artist of the embassy, Girtin "was also expected to assist Lady Elgin in the decoration of fire screens, worktables, and other household duties requiring artistic knowledge."[10]

Next came Richard and Robert Smirke. Robert was the more famous of the two brothers. At the age of thirteen, he was apprenticed in London to a heraldic painter, and seven years later, he studied in the schools of the Royal Academy. His works were usually small, humorous, graceful, and accomplished in draftsmanship. He also executed many clever and popular book illustrations. With each of the brothers, Elgin was forced to adjust his price, but the basic terms remained unacceptable, and further negotiations broke down.

William Daniell, another artist to be interviewed, was the nephew of the great English painter Thomas Daniell. William had accompanied his uncle on a voyage to India when he was only fourteen, and shortly after this, his many sketches engraved in aquatint had been published. However, he, too, balked at Elgin's terms and reluctantly refused the proposal.

In the weeks that followed, Elgin had the same results with the rest of the artists that presented themselves at Broomhall. Shortly before embarking on the *Phaeton* with his young bride, he called upon Benjamin West* for advice, and the venerable painter suggested the name of J. M. W. Turner, who was only twenty-four but had already gained stature in London art circles.

Turner seemed quite willing at first, but when Elgin demanded sole possession of all paintings and added that Turner's leisure hours were to be devoted to drawing lessons for Lady Elgin, "the young artist retaliated with a salary demand of four hundred pounds, at which point the interview was brought to a sharp halt by Elgin."[11]

HMS *Phaeton* had now covered more than half the way to her destination, yet Elgin was still without an artist who would supervise his grand scheme. Seized by a heavy melancholy, he became even crankier with the members of his staff, and although Lady Elgin tried to lift his sagging spirits, she, too, had her own discomfort to consider.

While the *Phaeton* strained at her anchor, the ship's courier Charles Duff was sent into Palermo to secure lodgings. He returned with the discouraging news that it was impossible to get on shore that night. In the next breath, however, Duff revealed that Sir William Hamilton had learned of their arrival and was offering the use of his house.

---

*Benjamin West (1738–1820) was born in Springfield, Pennsylvania. He executed his first painting at the age of seven while sitting by the cradle of his sister's child. The infant happened to smile in its sleep, and young Benjamin drew its portrait. West settled in Philadelphia as a portrait painter at the age of eighteen, and two years later he moved to New York. In 1760, he traveled to Europe, visiting Italy for three years before settling in London. King George III took him under his special patronage, from which many commissions resulted. He died in London and was buried in Saint Paul's Cathedral.

At first Lady Elgin balked at the thought of living under the same roof with Lord Nelson's notorious mistress Emma Hamilton, but she had been one whole month on the high seas, confined in a damp cabin that was divided into six insufferable compartments by a hideous green curtain. To make matters worse, not one day had passed without listening to the constant complaints of the Reverend Philip Hunt: "How can I be expected to share this molecular compartment with four other gentlemen? It is twelve feet long, six broad, and six high. It has five beds, thirteen trunks, six basins, hats, dressing gowns, boat cloaks, a cabin-boy brushing our shoes, servants preparing our shaving apparatus, five foul clothes bags, four portmanteaux, brooms, blankets, quilts, an Eighteen-Pounder with carriage tackles, iron crow, balls and grapeshot!"[12]

Despite these annoyances, Hunt managed to perform his ministerial duties on board the *Phaeton* and also to conduct services on deck every Sunday morning, even in bad weather.

Fortunately, the lodging problem was solved the following morning, when Duff succeeded in his search for a private palazzo. It was not far from Sir William Hamilton's residence, and it overlooked the Bay of Palermo. The drawing room was so enormous Hunt paced it off: "seventy-six foot long and twenty-five wide!"[13] The ceiling was lavishly decorated with a pastoral scene that painfully reminded Lady Elgin of her Archerfield. A huge French window led onto a balcony, from which every ship in the harbor was plainly visible. Her mal de mer found instant relief here, and during the noon meal she even exchanged puns with Captain Morris of the *Phaeton*. Later in the afternoon, they received an invitation for dinner at Sir William's, and quite surprisingly Lady Elgin raised no objection.

The entire party chose to walk to the Hamilton house, climbing leisurely up the narrow cobbled street that coursed asymmetrically through rows of white stucco houses with green tile roofs. Elgin, still dispirited about not having a painter to supervise his project in Athens, avoided all conversation, but Duff quickly remedied this with a boisterous account of what had happened to him on the previous day, when he called upon Lord Nelson at Sir William's house: "I was met at the door by a little old woman in a white bedgown and black petticoat.

'What do you want, Sir?' says she. 'Lord Nelson,' I reply. 'And what do you want with his Lordship?' again says she. I rebuked her on the spot and warned that she should look after her own business, at which point a male servant appeared and escorted me into the hall. 'You have inquisitive housekeepers,' says I to him. He coughed behind his hand then replied: 'But she is not a housekeeper, Sir. That is Lady Hamilton's mother!'"[14]

It was unfortunate that the world knew Sir William Hamilton only as the aged husband of the famous Emma. Elgin, however, was very much aware that Sir William had already achieved a well-deserved reputation as an antiquary. "While serving as ambassador at Naples, Sir William developed a passion for collecting many works of art, particularly vases, and was one of the first to appreciate the true origin of Greek vases, which up to that time were erroneously called Etruscan because they were found in southern Italy."[15] His treasures were innumerable: hundreds of vases and priceless gems, a splendid thesaurus of valuable coins, and many fine pieces of sculpture. Quite often he had to pay exorbitant prices and eventually, finding himself at the point of financial ruin, was forced to sell his entire collection at a great loss. Most of his treasures were bought by the British Museum.

Two male servants escorted the Elgin party into the front hall, where the walls and floor were of marble. On the wall beyond the foyer was a sweeping mural that Elgin regarded as a poor example of Italian art: pudgy little angels with pouting lips hovering around an equally pudgy youth, while above them loomed the enormous muscular presence of God.

Inside the drawing room, they were greeted by Lady Hamilton and Sir William. A middle-aged naval officer in full dress stood rigidly by the bay window, his right arm severed at the elbow, a brown leather patch over his right eye: Viscount Horatio Nelson! British admiral and naval hero whose genius reached its greatest height at the Battle of the Nile, one of the most brilliant naval battles in history. Soon after this great victory, Nelson arrived at Naples and fell headlong into an affair with Lady Hamilton, whose husband was the British ambassador at Naples. Strikingly beautiful and the subject of much gossip throughout Europe, Lady Hamilton quickly wasted most of Lord Nelson's money, dragged him around "like a bear,"[16] and forced him to incur heavy gambling debts. Nelson had no children by his wife, Frances, the daughter of a West Indies physician, but Lady Hamilton bore him a daughter, Horatia.

Throughout dinner Elgin was struck by Lady Hamilton's beauty. "Now that is a fine woman for you," he whispered to his wife, "good flesh and blood. A whapper!"[17]

Lady Elgin was immersed in thought. She could not understand why a fine gentleman like Sir William allowed such a "sick goat to roam freely in his house for more than a year. Nelson had no upper teeth, and there was an ugly wound on his forehead. Indeed, he seemed to be quite dying."[18]

Sir William graciously toasted their health, then wished Elgin success in Constantinople. The drink was anisette, and it encouraged Lady Elgin's appetite for dinner: lamb swimming in thick tomato sauce, summer squash, okra, broccoli, cheese pie, small puffs of fried meats, and a wide variety of wines. Later, during tea, they were all amused by Nelson's remarks about "that lean and sallow little man whose boots and hat were much too large for him." Yet in the very next breath, Nelson readily admitted to Napoleon's genius.

Before leaving England, Elgin had been well briefed on Napoleon and the French invasion of Egypt. His instructions ran to twenty-six pages and concluded with the stern warning that "not only was he to keep vigilant watch over the interests of His Majesty, promote commerce, maintain British privileges, persuade the Turks to open the Black Sea to English trade, establish a postal station at Suez, but above all, he was to assist in every possible way to expel the French from Egypt and thus keep the Ottoman Empire on friendly terms with Great Britain."[19]

Only a few months before he accepted his embassy in 1799, Elgin learned that Napoleon had amassed a powerful force on the Channel coast for the purpose of invading England, but in the final hour he changed his mind and reported to his government that the plan was impossible, and instead suggested that these same forces, which numbered over 54,000 men, be used in an invasion of Egypt. As he himself remarked, "Europe is a molehill. Everything here wears out. We must go to the Orient, where the greatest glories have always been acquired."[20]

When the French armada lifted anchor at Toulon, "the sea turned choppy and almost to the man, the army became seasick."[21] But Napoleon quickly buoyed their spirits by reminding them that when he took command of the forces on the Ligurian coast, they were in the greatest want, lacking everything and having sold even their family possessions to provide for their daily needs. He promised them an end to their privations and then led them successfully into Italy, where all was given them in abundance. Immediately thereafter, he made a solemn promise that if they would now follow him into Egypt, they all would be given enough money to purchase six acres of land when they returned to France. And thus, in May of 1799, this great force set sail from Toulon. The Admiralty, and Lord Nelson in particular, never expected such a move. Moreover, the Egyptians, who had been under the control of the Mamluks* for five centuries, soon realized they were no match for the French and offered little resistance.

Bonaparte boasted that "the Battle of the Nile was a general's dream: decisive victory, few casualties, enormous booty, and hardly a prisoner."[22] Elgin, however, strongly disagreed. Napoleon's victory was far from decisive, since a large part of the enemy force escaped intact with its commanders; and it was to this force that Elgin would have to direct his attention as soon as he arrived in Constantinople.

The dinner at Sir William's had almost drawn to an end, when Lady Hamilton walked to the glass doors of the drawing room and loudly clapped her hands. Several musicians appeared with cellos and violins. They seated themselves quietly in the center of the room and waited for Lady Hamilton's nod. A medley of songs was rendered by her in a strong and melodic voice, and although Lady Elgin listened

---

*First introduced into Egypt by the sultans in the thirteenth century, these fierce warriors from the Caucasus took control of the country within a few years. They kept replenishing their forces by bringing in a steady flow of young soldiers from the Caucasus. When Napoleon invaded Egypt, the Mamluks, although they had a powerful army of ten thousand men, were soundly defeated by the modern weapons of the French.

intently, deep down she winced at Lady Hamilton's pretentious mannerisms.

Precisely at noon the next day, a servant of Lady Hamilton came to the palazzo with an invitation to lunch at two o'clock, after which they were to watch a rowing match at four, where the king and queen of Naples would be present, and following this, a grand ball in the evening: a gala fete to celebrate the birthday of the royal son and heir to the throne. Lady Elgin wore her choicest pink gown with white lace cloak.

After tea, Sir William suggested a stroll through Palermo's streets. Lady Hamilton hastened to her bedchamber and returned in a dress of white silk with matching gloves and hat. Most of her bosom was exposed, which bothered only Lady Elgin, who was determined by this time not to enter into a degrading competition "with such a fickle woman, who changed clothes and jewelry at the twinkle of an eye."[23]

As they walked in leisure down the sharp hill leading to the bay, Sir William unveiled much of Palermo's history: how it had been built originally on a tongue of land between two inlets, resulting in the creation of two excellent harbors that eventually joined into one and formed the small bay facing entirely to the east, where Palermo now lay. A few more yards brought them before the porch of the ancient cathedral. Sir William remarked that it had been built by the English archbishop Walter, who was sent to Sicily by Henry II as tutor to the king. At this point Lady Hamilton complained of a sudden fatigue and took leave of them, but with the assurance that she would recover for the rowing match later in the afternoon.

The harbor was strangely deserted. Palermo's museum stood only a short distance away, and Elgin's eyes instantly came alive when he beheld the abundant collection of Etruscan sarcophagi, the sepulchral urns, the numerous bas-reliefs, and the large assortment of Greek vases. Along with these were many oil paintings and an extensive array of Sicilian majolica.

Sir William was genuinely pleased to find someone who shared his love for antiquities, whereupon Elgin seized the opportunity to say that Sir William's book of engravings not only had inspired him while at Westminster, but in fact had brought about several altercations with a classmate who refused to accept that "Josiah Wedgwood the potter was thoroughly influenced by Sir William's inspiring text."[24]

This was an excellent opportunity for Elgin to tell Sir William about his real reason for seeking the post at Constantinople and how he had to abandon his plans when he couldn't find a capable artist to supervise the project. Sir William was sympathetic to Elgin's plight and regretted that he could be of no assistance, especially since Palermo was no substitute for Naples. There was also the unpleasant situation in his house. Lady Hamilton was at that age in life that demanded insatiable attention. Aside from this, Sir William's health had begun to deteriorate, and he suffered constantly from bilious fevers. It was this rapid approach to dotage, he explained, that accounted for his devotion to Lady Hamilton, and his complaisance in her relationship with Nelson.

A few minutes later, Lady Elgin drew her husband aside. "I never saw three people make such thorough dupes of themselves as Lady Hamilton, Sir William, and Lord Nelson!"[25] she said quietly but firmly.

Before leaving the museum, Sir William mentioned with a muffled sigh that he understood Nelson was planning to set sail for Minorca in a few days. Under his breath Elgin repeated the information to his wife, adding in a whisper, "But many people are laying bets that Nelson will not go."[26]

On the long climb up another hill, Elgin reiterated his ardent desire to send professional artists, architects, and molders to Athens. Sir William urged him to persist, then suddenly stopped walking, and exclaimed, "I have just the man for you, the ideal person for your project in Athens. He is the first painter in Italy: Giovanni Battista Lusieri. He lives in Messina and is fondly called Don Tita. I first heard of him when he served as court painter for the King of Naples."[27]

Elgin's interest was piqued even more when he learned that Lusieri was not one to quibble over money. Sir William went on to explain that Don Tita devoted himself almost entirely to large panoramas:

They are upon a considerable scale in length, not less than seven or eight feet, and generally they embrace the eighth of a circle. He even has one, a view of Constantinople, eighteen feet by three feet high, which comprehends the fourth of a panorama. These drawings are merely careful outlines done with a hard pencil or crow-pen. No attempt is made at light or shade. He takes an incredible amount of time in doing them; the outline of Constantinople alone was a study of three months. On examining the subjects from which several of his outlines have been made, I confess that I could not perceive the minutiae described in them, and I am thus led to suppose that he must have used a telescope.[28]

The rowing match proved to be a dull performance, and when it was finished the Elgins were brought back to their palazzo in Sir William's carriage. Lady Elgin was in a quandary over what she would wear for the ball that evening, since Lady Hamilton upon several occasions during the rowing match had tried to make light of the matter by calling it "a silly little birthday party,"[29] and advising Lady Elgin to wear only a common dress. After being forewarned that it was a constant trick of Lady Hamilton "to make everyone she can, go undressed,"[30] Lady Elgin chose her blue-and-silver gown, to which she added her pearl necklace and diamond bracelet. At quarter past seven they were summoned outside, where Sir William's carriage again awaited them. They sat in the front seat, while Lady Hamilton sat between her husband and Nelson in the rear seat. She wore a gold silk gown studded with jewels and a tiara of glittering diamonds!

Soon after their arrival at the palace, there was a thunderous display of fireworks, and while the air still lay heavy with smoke, a large platform was cleared and the dancing commenced. As the men cast lingering looks toward Lady Hamilton and the women whispered into each other's ears, servants in Chinese dress moved through the crowd serving wine and morsels of fried meat. Only a few couples chose to dance. Lady Hamilton took this moment to proclaim that "Her Majesty had spent more than six thousand pounds for this affair, which Elgin considered an extravagant waste."[31]

Their table rested alongside a Japanese bridge that spanned an artificial pond. A covey of ducks swam peacefully in one corner, while rows of brightly lit lamps cast their reflection on the water. In time, the food was served, and under the soft hue of the swaying lamps, Nelson cleared his throat and asked Elgin if he realized what exactly awaited him at Constantinople. Elgin assured him he was very much aware that Sir Sydney Smith would never live down his sudden removal from the embassy post in Constantinople.

Smith had made captain at sixteen and fought in several battles of the American Revolutionary War, but soon thereafter, finding life rather dull, he disobeyed Admiralty orders and "accepted an invitation from the King of Sweden to be his naval advisor in a war against Russia and conducted his naval operations from the King's yacht."[32] The Admiralty eventually sent him on a fact-finding tour of Turkey, but as soon as war broke out with France, Sir Sydney purchased a ship at his own expense, collected a crew of unemployed sailors at Smyrna, and set off to join the English Mediterranean fleet. To show its gratitude, His Majesty's government rewarded him with the post at Constantinople, which he was to serve jointly with his brother, John Spencer Smith. Nelson strenuously fought this appointment, claiming it was a hazardous risk assigning political duty to an active service officer, let alone to a man who had attained his reputation through disobedience. It galled him to envision Sir Sydney on the bridge of his *Tigre*, laying siege to Acre with drawn sword and puffed chest, while the treacherous Turks praised him to Allah.

Although Elgin had been previously apprised of all this, Nelson's words nevertheless disturbed him. He never expected to encounter a mess like this: "one Smith brother, an employee of the Levant Company, in charge of British affairs in Constantinople; the other, a national hero, holding both naval and diplomatic rank, cruising off the coast of Egypt in his *Tigre*."[33] With Nelson now about to embark for Minorca, Bonaparte was firmly anchored in Egypt, defying both the British and the Turks to throw him out.

After dinner, Sir William introduced them to the king and queen of Naples. Their Highnesses conversed only in French. Standing beside her obese and ornately decorated husband, the queen looked tiny and fragile. Her purple gown was adorned with jewels, and two fingers of each hand sagged under the weight of huge diamond rings as she explained, in a soft and charming voice, that she was the sister of Marie Antoinette. Tearfully, she revived each frightful moment of the French conquest of Naples, ending with the sad announcement that half of their kingdom was now lost to Bonaparte.

The king (Ferdinand I, a Spanish Bourbon) suddenly fell silent, but his face lit up when Lady Elgin conveyed her polite assurance that this was indeed the most gala day in her life — what with the rowing match, the fireworks, the music, and the absolutely delicious food. Elgin joined in and, lifting his wineglass, drank to Lord Nelson, upon which "Lady Hamilton actually greeted [Scottish for *wept*]!"

Three days later, the Elgins traveled by carriage to Messina for a meeting with Giovanni Battista Lusieri. It was a tedious journey over bad mountain roads, requiring frequent stops, and although their guide claimed to know the way blindfolded, it took them almost a week before they finally arrived at Messina, where they were directed down a narrow cobblestone street, to the heart of the old city. Lusieri's house was a two-story structure whose white stucco walls were cracked at many places. The inner staircase shook under their weight.

Lady Elgin was surprised to find Lusieri so tall. He had deeply set brown eyes, a full black mustache, and a short pointed black beard. Elgin became immediately impatient when he discovered that Lusieri did not speak English. He had a fair comprehension of French, however, and Elgin carefully explained the purpose of their visit: "Lusieri was to supervise an artistic commission, which was to include an architect who would take notes of buildings and temples; also to employ several formatori who would make casts of such sculptures and works of art that were found to be accessible. All drawings, pictures, and sketches were to remain in Lord Elgin's possession and be his sole property."[34]

This was not an uncommon practice in the nineteenth century. Many men of nobility and station were often accompanied in their travels by famous painters: Jacques Carrey was in the suite of the Marquis de Nointel, Lord Charlemont took Richard Dalton on a tour through Egypt, and Lord Elgin's predecessor at Constantinople, Sir Robert Ainslie, had employed Ludwig Mayer for a similar purpose.

Lusieri's salary was set at two hundred pounds sterling per year, and when he insisted that it be in writing, Elgin obliged by drawing up the contract in French:

It is agreed between Lord Elgin and Signor Lusieri that the latter must accompany his Lordship in his embassy to Turkey as a painter and especially to employ his time and his art under the direction of his Excellency. It is understood that all works which Signor Lusieri shall do during this time will be at the disposal of his Excellency, in consideration of which he will receive two hundred pounds sterling per year, living always at the expense of his Excellency.

In case Signor Lusieri wishes to make copies of some works done during his employment for his own use, it is agreed that the choice will be made through the consideration of both parties. Signor Lusieri will also be at liberty to return to his country before the expiration of the term of his employment should unexpected circumstances oblige him.

> Made in Messina in the presence
> of Lord and Lady Elgin[35]

After both parties signed the document, Elgin promptly informed Lusieri that he was to travel at once with Elgin's secretary, William Hamilton, into Rome and Naples with the following instructions: "(1.) To engage a man for casts. A painter of figures to work with Lusieri. All work to be entirely Elgin's property and the salaries fixed at the second table (fifty pounds per annum); (2.) Also to procure all necessary materials for the painters, and casts for the moulders."[36]

Here, Lady Elgin made a request for herself: "A Caro of Vertioso"*[37] similar to those employed by Lady Hamilton — a cellist or two, a violinist, and someone to accompany the pianoforte. Elgin, of course, hardly felt inclined to burden his embassy with such luxury, and he assented only after Lady Elgin hinted that good musicians could be engaged in Italy at the second table of salary, for which they might even be induced to wear livery and act occasionally as servants.

At any other time, such extravagance might have bothered Elgin, but on this warm October day he had found a new joy, knowing that at last he had taken the first real step toward achieving the fondest goal of his life. Hamilton and Lusieri were in Rome a full month before Elgin finally received word from them:

---

*Lady Elgin should have written "Carro of Virtuosi" (a cartload of musicians).

My dear Lord:

Please be advised that many Italian artists have found it necessary to quit Rome because of the French. Those who have remained are generally of a suspicious nature and we have been forced to inquire about their political principles as well as their professional ability. Aside from this, those who have offered to sign on with us have presented various objections as to character, age, line of life and talent. But after many weeks of extensive search, and largely through the influence of Signor Lusieri's acquaintances here, I am able to report that I have completed all arrangements according to your Lordship's instructions.

The first to be engaged was a draftsman for figures and sculpture. We had been told that he was trained at Carlsruhe. He has great skill and his concise drawings indicate taste and mind. We are led to believe that he is the only man of culture his nation has ever produced, for he is a Tartar and a native of Astracan! We have fixed his salary at one hundred pounds per annum.

Upon Signor Lusieri's insistence, we secured the services of two architects, since it is impossible for one man to cope with such a great undertaking as this. The chief architect is an extremely deformed humpback, but your Lordship must remember that only his head and hands were the object of our search. He shall take with him a young man who has been accustomed to study under him as a scholar. We have fixed their total salary at five hundred Roman piastres, or one hundred and twenty-five pounds.

We have also recruited two men for making plaster moulds. Each shall receive one hundred pounds per annum. I need not remind your Lordship that we were indeed fortunate to avail ourselves of their employ, since there are only six moulders in all of Rome, the rest having gone to France. Her Ladyship will be pleased to hear that I had the good fortune to procure at Naples a Maître de Chapelle with all the qualities her Ladyship desired, except the inclination to appear occasionally as groom of the chamber. As he is a very well-mannered young man, I did not think it proper to press this added burden upon him, particularly as I learned from every quarter that persons of his profession would, with natural vanity, rather starve than stoop to such imaginary degradation.

He is bringing two other musicians with him: one plays the clarionet and the other, the violincello. I believe it will be possible though difficult to prevail upon these to wear livery, or at least a separate uniform, which would answer fully to her Ladyship's request.

Because of the war, we have been completely excluded from communication with the rest of the world, and although we are but a short distance from each other, I fear this message may not reach Palermo until after your Lordship's departure for Constantinople, in which event I shall await your Lordship's further instructions.

> Believe me to be,
> Your most humble servant etc.
> William Richard Hamilton[38]

Surprisingly, Hamilton's lavish distribution of money did not upset Elgin. Early the next morning, he was awakened by the Reverend Hunt and Professor Carlyle, who wanted him to accompany them "on an exploration of the ruins at Taormina; also to fulfill Elgin's great desire to investigate Homer's account of the phenomenon at Scylla and Charybdis,* and perhaps climb Etna too."[39]

They were gone five days, and during their absence, Lady Elgin kept busy with afternoon teas and nightly soirees. One evening she attended the opera with the queen of Naples and was the honored guest at a reception that followed. Lady Hamilton was there, and Lady Elgin made several efforts at conversation, but Emma seemed quite distracted. Nelson indeed must have gone to Minorca!

Elgin returned looking rested and in rapture over their visit to Scylla and Charybdis. At dinner that night, Captain Morris announced it was imperative that they sail immediately for the Aegean, since wind and sea were now favorable. Elgin elatedly dispatched a message to his secretary Hamilton at Rome, ordering him to embark at once for Constantinople with Lusieri and the party of artists. The Elgins then called upon Sir William and Lady Hamilton for the last time. Sir William was sorry to learn they were leaving and assured them he would be at the docks in the morning to see them off. Emma still looked downcast, presumably because of Lord Nelson's departure.

At dawn the next day, October 19, they were transported to the

---

*Scylla is the rock on the Italian side of the Strait of Messina opposite the whirlpool Charybdis, personified by Homer (*Odyssey*, XII, 104) as a female sea monster who devoured sailors.

docks, where they exchanged sad farewells and endless toasts with Sir
William and Emma. The sea may have been favorable, as Captain
Morris had said, but strong winds swept the *Phaeton* across the Aegean
and into the archipelago. "The tossing was dreadful," complained
Lady Elgin. "I was all but dead from the contrary winds and great
rolling of the waves."[40]

On the last day of October, the wind failed, and they had to drop anchor off the isle of Tenedos at the entrance to the Dardanelles. Within
an hour, they were met by a Turkish vessel and, after a loud exchange
of salutes, invited on board and brought before a pompously dressed
young Turkish officer, whose raven beard and thick eyebrows consumed most of his face. A red turban rested proudly on his head. He
introduced himself as Capitan Pasha, then took Lady Elgin's hand and
kissed it. Turning to Elgin, he joyously declared that Turkey had just
entered into a treaty of alliance with England and that the treaty had
been negotiated by Sir Sydney Smith and his brother, Sir John Spencer
Smith. It infuriated Elgin to hear that "provisions were also made to
open the Black Sea to British shipping, an assignment that had been
his primary objective."[41]

   When they returned to the *Phaeton*, Captain Morris feared they
could be forced to lay anchor off Tenedos for an indefinite period,
since the wind generally remained contrary at that time of year. Elgin
did not agree, insisting they would be in Constantinople by Thursday
of that week. Fortunately for Lady Elgin, the sea turned calm by late
afternoon, and she managed to catch a few hours of needful sleep. She
was awakened by the sound of voices above, and climbing onto the
deck, she saw Captain Morris conversing with Capitan Pasha. Elgin
was nowhere in sight. Captain Morris relieved her anxiety, saying that
Elgin had gone ashore with the Reverend Hunt immediately after the
noon meal but had given not the slightest hint as to their destination.
Before leaving the *Phaeton*, Capitan Pasha kissed Lady Elgin's hand
and extended a dinner invitation for that evening on board his ship, *Selim III*.

   Throughout the rest of that afternoon, Lady Elgin and her maid
Masterman searched all the trunks in the hold of the *Phaeton* for an ap-

propriate gown to wear, together with jewelry, evening slippers, and hat. Shortly before dusk, Elgin returned to the ship with Hunt. At first he voiced objection about dining with the Turk, but since his wife had already dressed for the occasion, he relented. Putting on his white uniform with sword attached, he explained that Hunt had wanted him to look at something in Yenicher, a small village just off the shore from Tenedos. Lady Elgin did not press the matter further.

They climbed into the pasha's small boat and boarded *Selim III*, where Capitan Pasha, alongside his crew, stood at rigid attention in full uniform with red fez and white plume. There was a deafening sound of cannons, and as they passed along the deck, the Turkish crewmen saluted.

It was a lavish dinner. Elgin was still aggravated over the news of the Smith brothers' treaty with the Turks, but after a few glasses of Samian wine, he mellowed, then accepted Capitan Pasha's invitation to sit on floor cushions while Turkish coffee was served in fragile demitasse cups. Eventually the narghile, a Turkish water pipe, was brought out and passed from hand to hand. Elgin, eager to please the young Turkish officer, puffed several times, coughed, then helped himself to more coffee. During a momentary silence, Elgin reached into his coat pocket and withdrew an official message handed to him by Capitan Pasha the moment they had stepped onto the *Selim III*. It was from the grand vizier and disclosed an unsettling bit of information relating to Elgin's appointment as ambassador to the Sublime Porte:

> When Sir Sydney Smith first announced Your Lordship's appointment, I was much grieved on my friend being displaced and asked: "But why should there be any change? We went on very well together; things went on very well." Sir Sydney proceeded to say that Your Lordship was a great landed proprietor in Scotland, that Your Lordship had great influence there, and that the English Government were in the habit of conciliating such people as Your Lordship by the appointment to high situations. I turned to Sir Sydney, and said: "Ah, then I understand that your government have also got their mountain chiefs to conciliate, just as we here in Turkey." At this point, I asked what the new ambassador was called, what Your Lordship's name was. Upon Sir Sydney's pronounciation of the name, I cried: "Oh, but Elkin is very bad. It

means evil genius, the Devil! How could the English Government send us such a person!"[42]

Early the next morning, Elgin, still excited by what he had seen the previous day, suggested they all go on a picnic to a place that the natives claimed to be the actual site of Troy.

The weather was unseasonably warm, and the servants prepared a basket of cold meats, oranges, grapes, bread, cheese, and wine. Captain Morris and Dr. McLean chose to remain on board, but everyone else eagerly went along, including Masterman, who at first was apprehensive about the choppy ride in the captain's barge. As soon as they crossed the channel, they encountered a swift current and could not land on the Asia Minor coast until noon. The crewmen were ordered back to the *Phaeton*, and Elgin made arrangements with them to be picked up precisely at dusk. Hunt volunteered to carry the basket of food, while Professor Carlyle armed himself only with his worn-out text of the *Iliad*, determined to prove to the doubting Hunt his own theory about the exact location of Troy. Lady Elgin had her own book to read: Plato's *Republic*.

They proceeded at a slow pace and came eventually into a village, where Elgin bargained for a guide and half a dozen asses. Putting her book away, Lady Elgin felt awkward sitting on her beast, but she soon accustomed herself to its swaying gait, and within an hour they arrived at the desolate village of Sigeum. They stopped beneath a large plane tree to eat and rest, and once more she opened her book and continued reading until Elgin commanded them to move on again across a barren plateau, where herds of camels grazed under the watchful eyes of fierce-looking shepherds in long cloaks of burlap. "Along the way, Carlyle frequently consulted Homer, much to the dismay of Hunt, who had his own theories about the actual site of Troy."[43]

The asses labored up a long slope and at last reached the summit. Below them lay Yenicher, sprawled against the bleached sand like a crumpled white blanket. The guide quickly led his beasts to the well for water, while Elgin hastened toward a small white church directly across the dust-filled street. Only a few inhabitants were in sight. At the entrance to the church, and on each side of the door, rested two marble seats. One was a sculptured relief of mothers with their children; the other bore an ancient Greek inscription that momentarily perplexed Hunt, until he discovered that it read from right to left to prevent any attempt to alter or corrupt it.

Elgin had known about these seats for a number of years. "They were first discovered by Lady Montagu* in 1718, and she could have had them for the price of a small bribe, but the captain of her ship did not have the proper tackle to remove them."[44] When she offered to purchase them from the townspeople, they objected vehemently because, as Hunt declared, they regarded the seats as a sure remedy for all forms of sickness: "To explain this," he added,

> it may be necessary to mention that during the winter and spring a considerable part of the neighbouring plain is overflowed, thus afflicting the inhabitants with agues; and such is the state of superstition at present among the Greek Christians, that when any disease becomes chronic or beyond the reach of common remedies, it is attributed to daemoniacal possession. The priest is then called in to exorcise the patient, which he generally does in the porch of the church by reading long portions of Scripture over the sufferer, sometimes the whole of the four gospels. In addition to this, the custom is to roll the patient on the marble stone which contains the Sigean inscription, the characters of which never having been deciphered by any of their teachers, are supposed to contain a powerful charm. This long-standing practice, however, has nearly obliterated the inscription.[45]

Since nothing of further interest was at Yenicher, the party headed back for Sigeum, arriving there just before dusk. The crewmen from the *Phaeton* had yet to appear, and the travelers were obliged to seek shelter from the night's dampness inside a deep cave, where Hunt lit a fire and the rest of the food was consumed.

---

*Lady Mary Wortley Montagu (c. 1689–1762), author, traveler, and collector, whose wit and beauty made her a prominent figure at court, was a voracious letter writer and corresponded with such notables as Alexander Pope, Horace Walpole, the painter George Romney, and others. One of her letters to Pope contained a parody on his "Epitaph on the Lovers Struck by Lightning."

Huddled with her husband under the same blanket in the raw wind-blown evening, Lady Elgin haltingly broke the news to him that she was pregnant. Elgin was overjoyed and instantly proclaimed it would be a boy: "Lord Bruce, the Eighth Earl of Elgin and the Twelfth of Kincardine!"[46]

When the crewmen at last arrived, Elgin did not admonish them for their tardiness, but instead slapped each of them on the backside and was the first to leap onto the captain's barge.

The next morning, Lady Elgin awoke from a deep sleep and found a note on the table beside her bunk, saying that Elgin had gone off with Captain Morris and the crew, and would return before night-fall. After a light breakfast, she and Masterman again busied themselves with the trunks in the hold of the *Phaeton*, getting everything in readiness for their arrival in Constantinople. Just before the noon meal, Hunt went ashore with Carlyle and came back laden with baskets of bread, fruit, and casks of wine. Lady Elgin spent the rest of the afternoon strolling leisurely along the deck and tossing morsels of bread to the shrieking gulls in the channel.

Elgin and the others returned to the *Phaeton* around three in the afternoon. He had a wild look in his eyes, and with impassioned words, declared that he had gone to Capitan Pasha and asked if he could have the two marble seats from the church at Yenicher. "Permission was duly granted," he exclaimed, "and I dispatched the full complement of the *Phaeton* to Yenicher. At first, the Greek priests wailed and tried to prevent the crewmen from taking away the seats, but when they realized that I had received permission from Capitan Pasha, they withdrew in tears."[47]

Turkey

A THOUSAND MINARETS jabbed at the cloudless sky, while in the bustling harbor of Constantinople vessels of all sizes and description surrounded the *Phaeton* and saluted her with steady cannon fire. The Elgin party was accorded official greetings from the highest dignitaries of the Porte and given flowers, fruits, and sweets by a long line of servants assembled in brilliant costumes along both sides of the quay. Speeches were made, after which Elgin passed out gold watches and chains to the young Turkish officers. For the older officers, he had English pistols and rings set in diamonds. Even the servants were included, each receiving some manner of gift or token. At the conclusion of the formal ceremony, Elgin and his wife were carried in golden chairs to the British Palace, an aged structure of white stone, whose facade was pockmarked with holes and ugly cracks. A crowd of Turks in bright-colored robes flocked around them, blocking the way, and they had to seek the assistance of janissaries, the elite guard of the sultan, to get inside.

While Elgin was driven to the seraglio for an audience with the sultan, Masterman drew a warm bath for Lady Elgin, and later in the afternoon, as she was about to catch a nap, Elgin returned to announce they were invited to the official ceremony of welcome by the sultan himself. Since Turkish custom forbade the presence of women at such affairs, the sultan, with great reluctance, agreed to allow Lady Elgin to come, provided she dressed as a man.

The idea fascinated her. Duff was immediately dispatched to obtain the necessary costume: blouse, vest, pantaloons, and fez. The red satin slippers were too large for her feet, and she had to stuff the toes with cotton. Elgin put on his full-dress uniform and sparkling black boots, and as they stepped out of the British Palace, they discovered several hundred janissaries lined in parade formation on both sides of

27

the street. They got into the carriages and were quickly escorted to the Tophana docks, from where they crossed the Golden Horn by boat, to the seraglio.

Suddenly Lady Elgin began to feel uncomfortable. The pantaloons were hot and sticky, and to aggravate her distress, the janissaries kept stopping for no apparent reason, making the long ride unendurable.

The procession lasted two full hours, and when they were finally introduced to the sultan, he personally conducted them into the audience room, which was protected by rows of eunuchs and guards.

The sultan's golden throne glistened with sparkling stones of various cuts and sizes. On a damask-covered table rested a glass case containing a large cluster of diamonds, and in his turban, he wore the famous jeweled aigrette. His robe was of yellow satin trimmed with black sable. In a cabinet nearby, there were two more turbans covered with diamonds.

The sultan, Selim III, did not cast his eye even once toward Lady Elgin during his formal address. When he finished, Elgin stepped forward and presented him with a gold chandelier, a bezoar stone, and several hundred yards of satin and damask. Later, during the formal introductions, the sultan's eyes again avoided Lady Elgin when she was introduced as "Lord Bruce, a young gentleman." The weight of her pantaloons was now unbearable, and hot perspiration began pouring down her face. Elgin mercifully came to her rescue, making hasty apologies to the sultan, then helping her out of the room. As soon as they reached their carriage, she flung off the vest and fez and was about to do the same with the pantaloons when Elgin stopped her, warning that the janissaries had already encircled the carriage and were forming ranks for the march back to the boat in the Golden Horn and the climb up the sharp hill to the British Palace.

Moving off at last down the narrow cobbled street toward the docks, Elgin let loose a tirade of epithets against His Majesty's government for refusing to give him one penny to improve the fine arts of an entire country, "yet here was King George, throwing seven thousand pounds away on idiotic gifts for treacherous Turkish hands!"

* * *

The preconceived notions that Lady Elgin had entertained about Constantinople rapidly melted away in the happy months that followed. From her bedroom window on the second story of the palace she could see almost every corner of the city. The domes and mosques seemed to rise up from the sea, while the multicolored houses clashed under the sharp rays of the winter sun and sent a splash of beauty into the sky. Elgin was a patient teacher and called many things to her attention, even how "the dwellings of the Turks were painted in the brightest colors, whereas those of the Greeks, Armenians, and Jews were subjected to morbid shades of black and brown."[1] An enormous garden surrounded the palace, and through it coursed a network of walks, all leading to a high gate overlooking the Bosporus.

What impressed her most, however, was the elegant dress of the Turks. Each class had its appropriate costume: the janissaries wore an upright white felt cap with a broad flap that hung halfway down the back; the officers had long rolls of coarse linen over their heads that were carefully crossed and intertwined until they made their heads appear even wider than their shoulders; the merchants wore thick white turbans with long flowing red robes; and the hamals, who plied the docks at Tophana, although bare chested and destitute, found a great source of pride in their soiled baggy white pantaloons. To Lady Elgin, "the Turkish youths were uncommonly handsome, and dressed in the same manner as their fathers." Every corner of the city had its mendicant dervishes. Wild-looking, half-naked, heads crowned with wreaths of flowers, they wound their way through the dense crowds, shoving their tin cups at every strange face and calling frantically for alms in Allah's name.

The Gardens of Pera were the favorite haunts of the Turkish women, and each evening they flocked there in shapeless white cloaks and black veils of silk, which concealed everything but their brilliant black eyes. They seemed to possess a winsome gait, a delicate shuffling of the feet. Those who preferred to ride came in small tilted wagons drawn by four oxen gaily decorated from head to hoof. Lady Elgin had never before witnessed such merriment and lightheartedness among women. This same mood proved contagious for her, and along with the joyful awareness of new life inside her womb, her days overflowed with rapturous feelings of pleasure and fulfillment.

* * *

The cold winter rains caused Elgin to complain constantly, blaming the bad weather for his persistent attacks of rheumatism, although his wife suspected that his agitation came from a deeper cause. He hadn't heard from his secretary, William Hamilton, in several months and was about to send him a blistering letter, when finally the long spell of silence was broken. Hamilton had posted the letter at Palermo:

My dear Lord:

The long anxiety to hear from your Lordship at Constantinople has at last been relieved by the sight of your letter dated 15th January 1800, however the pleasure I received from reading it was lessened by the sad account you gave of your health. The bad weather we have long had here gives me little room to hope that it has been more favourable with your Lordship. I was greatly astonished at your Lordship's saying that you had received none of my letters from Messina, Naples, and Rome. I trust that the letter I wrote on the first day of January (the first day of the new century), from Messina will have been more fortunate. I am confident that your Lordship will attribute your not hearing from me rather to a failure of the Post than to my neglect.

From the time I arrived at Messina on 30th December, I have been continually prevented from proceeding on my voyage by the most pro-voking circumstances of dilatory merchants and captains, contrary winds and bad weather. At Messina, the only ship in which I could hope to proceed to Constantinople was a Greek Polacca [a three-masted merchant vessel], which was loaded with corn for Malta. To accommo-date me, the captain offered to direct his ship (after leaving her cargo at the Isle of Malta), go thence to Girgenti, and there take in a cargo of sulphur for Constantinople — but this on the condition that I consent to advance money for half the lading, since he would not embark in a new speculation to a lesser amount. For the object of dispatch, I con-sented to his offer and have advanced on my own account the necessary sum — but instead of leaving Messina in four days, we were detained three weeks by strong winds that continued to persecute us in a voyage to Malta of nine days, and from there to Girgenti of eight days. Here fine weather would have permitted us to load and sail in four days, but winds still contrary and violent, and the intervening of three idle holi-days on which no Sicilian would work, even to procure his bread, again assured us of another delay. I therefore determined to come over to

Palermo for a few days, where I shall procure a collection of antiques, which I hope to present to your Lordship safe at Constantinople.

In the meantime, I have left employed among the temples and sarcophagi of Girgenti our architects and painters. I trust that their work will in some degree supply the inconvenience your Lordship cannot but feel in their absence from Constantinople.

> I am,
> Your Most humble servant,
> William Richard Hamilton[2]

The good news from Hamilton only partially alleviated Elgin's melancholy. There was the unsolved problem of the Smith brothers too. Sir Sydney continued to behave as though he was still the ambassador to the Porte, refusing to maintain a file of official papers, dealing directly with the Turkish diplomats without informing Elgin, and even ordering British representatives in the Levant not to correspond with Elgin. Each irregularity brought a sharp reprimand from Elgin, and although Sir John Spencer promised never to allow such incidents to occur again, it now became quite evident that Smith was trying deliberately to sabotage Elgin's efforts and restore the old monopoly of the Levant Company, which was in charge of all trade in the eastern Mediterranean.

Soon after Egypt had capitulated, Bonaparte was forced to make several overtures toward a term of peace with the Turks. At that time, Sir Sydney was cruising the *Tigre* off the coast of Egypt. Grasping the opportunity to bring about a peace settlement on his own, he invited the French representatives on board his ship without saying a word to Elgin, and even led the French to believe that he was negotiating on behalf of both Turkey and England. This infuriated the Turks, and they cast the full blame for this unacceptable treaty on Elgin as soon as he arrived in Constantinople.

Finally, and most annoyingly, Elgin had to deal with the aggravating problem concerning General George Frederic Koehler, commander of British military operations in the Levant. Elgin's first task in Constantinople was to call back Koehler's small force from repairing the Dardanelles forts and place it instead on more active service. Koehler had an inflated ego, Elgin noted, adding that Koehler daily introduced himself as "General Officer Commanding His Majesty's Land Forces in the Ottoman Empire."³ These so-called forces numbered only seventy-six men, most of whom were already depleted by disease.

At any rate, Elgin submitted a full account of his difficulties to Lord Grenville, urging him to remove Sir John Spencer Smith and to reprimand Sir Sydney, but the foreign secretary, answering curtly, reminded Elgin that England was at war and there were more important matters requiring his attention.

Then came El Arish.

In this small town of Syria, Sir Sydney Smith, without Elgin's knowledge, concluded the terms of peace, under which the French were to leave Egypt as neither victors nor conquerors and to be conveyed to France in British warships, provided they never again lifted up arms against England or Turkey. That Sir Sydney negotiated these terms was yet another humiliation for Elgin; nevertheless he put his anger aside and hastily wrote to Lord Grenville: "I have infinite satisfaction in informing your Lordship that on 24th ult. a capitulation was signed in the Grand Vizier's camp at El Arish, in consequence of which the French are to evacuate Egypt within the space of three months."⁴

More determined than ever that Sir Sydney not take credit for the treaty of El Arish, Elgin then wrote to Lord Nelson and ordered him "to provide ships for the evacuation of the captured French troops."⁵ Finally, he undertook the long and arduous task of issuing passports for the safe conduct of every French soldier from Egypt into France.

Grenville's reply came quickly, instructing Elgin not to enter in an arrangement with Bonaparte under any condition, except that Bonaparte surrender himself and his troops as prisoners of war. The Treaty of El Arish was thus rendered null and void, and Elgin had the unpleasant duty of invalidating the passports. Crushed with mortification, he called upon the sultan and strongly suggested that the Turks arrange a graceful withdrawal from the treaty. Selim III refused: "In the eyes of Turkey, Sir Sydney Smith acted as Minister Plenipotentiary and the Treaty of El-Arish was valid!"⁶

Within a fortnight, Elgin received still another message from Grenville: "The British Government has been informed of the Treaty at El-Arish, and although it is quite contrary to the policy laid down in our last dispatch to you, we have decided to accept its terms after all."[7] By this time, however, the grand vizier was in Egypt with his sad collection of soldiers and had prepared to take over Cairo in accordance with the treaty. Bonaparte, on the other hand, had been duly notified by Elgin that the English could not assent to any other terms but unconditional surrender. It was a terrible muddle. Countermanding all previous orders for evacuation, Bonaparte notified the grand vizier that the armistice was over, and a few days later, he attacked the Turks at Heliopolis and soundly defeated them. Elgin felt some measure of relief when the hurt feelings of the Turks eventually abated, but there was one man who did not exonerate him. Napoleon Bonaparte became convinced that the Treaty of El Arish and its subsequent disavowal was an elaborate plot engineered by Elgin to deceive the French and seize them on their passage to France. There was even a story that the French were to be massacred as soon as they came under British power. Bonaparte formed a strong personal hatred for Elgin, whom he later described as one of the greatest enemies of the nation. He convinced himself that it was Elgin who had caused the ill treatment of the French prisoners in Constantinople, and he blamed Elgin for all the reverses of his Egyptian policy.

In the weeks that followed, the French recovered from their crushing defeat in the Battle of the Nile, and in time gained full possession of Egypt. Despite all this, Elgin managed to vindicate himself with the Turks, who now looked upon him as their true champion, whereas the brothers Smith, being solely responsible for the fiasco at El Arish, soon lost all favor and were officially scorned by the Porte.

With his spirits rejuvenated, Elgin again wrote to Lord Grenville, imploring him to remove Sir John Spencer Smith at once from Constantinople and to terminate Sir Sydney Smith's affiliation with the Levant Company. This time his request was heard. A meeting of the British cabinet was called, and its decision was unanimous: "Sir John Spencer Smith was dismissed, and Sir Sydney Smith was relieved of all diplomatic rank!"[8]

Lady Elgin, who had to endure these disturbing events day and night, now settled back into her previous mode of life, resuming her daily strolls through the Gardens of Pera, then reading before dinner. She also accepted invitations to attend teas and concerts. Since the

Smiths had drained Elgin's energy, she decided that another ambassadorial assistant was needed and even volunteered to make the choice herself: "A very pleasant and lively chap named Alexander Stratton, and a most capital whist player!"[9]

With the Smiths at last out of the Levant, Elgin was able to give full attention to the prime purpose of his mission, especially after Hamilton sent further word from Mykonos Isle and reported that "he had hoped in a few days to present himself and his artist companions to Elgin in Constantinople."[10] Almost overnight, Elgin became a changed man. Quite remarkably, he even enjoyed a period of relief from the rheumatism that had plagued him throughout the winter, although Dr. McLean claimed it was his treatment that effected the cure: "Seven leeches on the temples each night for two weeks."[11]

As it turned out, however, Elgin's euphoria was short-lived. During the late days of spring a dreadful disease swept over Constantinople, and in his weakened state he contracted a mysterious fever that produced a disastrous effect on his face, and particularly his nose. Dr. McLean did his utmost to curb the infection, but it was futile. Within a matter of six weeks, most of the nose was eaten away, and by the end of May, nothing remained of it but a raw blotch of skin whose open wounds refused to respond to treatment. McLean maintained that Elgin's affliction had resulted from an ague, a fever characterized by successive attacks of cold and hot fits, much sweating and shaking chills, together with intense pain in the bones and joints. McLean, however, was unable to explain why the disease should confine itself so catastrophically to the nose.

Later, George Gordon, Lord Byron, would cruelly attribute Elgin's disfigurement to venereal disease:

Noseless himself, he brings here noseless blocks
To show what time has done and what the pox.*[12]

---

*Perhaps Byron was on the right track. In his *Treatise on Venereal Disease*, published in London in 1786, the renowned physiologist and surgeon John Hunter discovered conclusive evidence that the most characteristic forms of a particular infection were de-

Lady Elgin was shattered by this development. She tried hard to ignore it, though at times she couldn't bear to look directly into her husband's face. One morning, in an effort to free him from his despair, she suggested a tour of the city. Both Carlyle and Hunt thought it an excellent idea and urged Elgin to comply. He agreed, but only after Hunt added that he had struck an acquaintanceship with the sultan's gardener, a German, who had offered upon several occasions to guide Hunt through the deepest secrets of the seraglio. His was a unique position. Although he was employed chiefly in the sultan's gardens, he often joined in the many receptions given for the different foreign ministers, through whom he eventually came to know a large number of influential people.

They found him in his cottage, taking his midday nap. He was gruff and discourteous when they awoke him. Hunt apologized for the intrusion, then prevailed upon the gardener to conduct them on a personal tour of the gardens. Lady Elgin was permitted to accompany them, again disguised as "Lord Bruce."

They came out of the cottage, climbed into the gardener's special carriage, and after reaching Pera, were escorted into a gondola for Tophana, where another carriage took them to a gate of the seraglio facing the southern side of the Bosporus. A contingent of janissaries stood guard by the main portal, but at the gardener's curt nod, they stepped aside and permitted the party to enter. It was the season of Ramadan, the Moslem holy period, and not a soul could be seen within the grounds. Hunt explained that the Turks imposed strict privations upon themselves from sunrise to sunset during this time, extending even to the use of tobacco, but on the night of the last day of Ramadan they gorged themselves on food, wine, and raucous merriment.

At this point, and after much prodding from Hunt, the gardener agreed to undergo an even greater risk by showing them the harem.

---

posits called gummata, which were of tenacious appearance, ulcerous and oozing with discharge, and attacking specifically one organ of the body: the nose. According to Hunter, the disease constituted the tertiary manifestations of syphilis.

He pointed to a long, gloomy avenue that led from the gate of the courtyard and ran parallel to the high double walls of the seraglio. In a tremulous voice, he described how the sultanas passed through there every morning to take their air. With a restrained grin, he pointed toward the right to a sun lodge, where on overcast days he ventured to hide and watch the women, even though it was strictly forbidden, under penalty of death. He went on to explain,

First to appear are the black eunuchs. They examine the entire garden, running before the Sultanas and warning all persons in the vicinity to avoid approaching or beholding them. Three of the four Sultanas are Georgian, with dark smooth complexions and very long black hair. The fourth is fair and has flaxen hair. Not one of them dyes her teeth black as do other Turkish women. Their dress is rich beyond imagination: long spangled robes, open in front, with silk pantaloons embroidered in gold and silver, and adorned with large pearls and precious stones so heavy as to impede their movements. Their hair hangs loosely and in very thick tresses on both sides of the face, completely covering their shoulders and reaching down as far as the waist. The tresses too are studded with diamonds, but in a haphazard manner, as though scattered at random. On top of their heads, and leaning to one side, they wear a small circular diadem. Their faces and necks, even their breasts, are quite exposed.

Countless rows of white trelliswork burdened with jasmine and other flowering vines lined the walk, while sparrows frolicked in the fountains nearby. After they proceeded down the long gravel path, past a small grove of orange trees in full bloom, they climbed a sharp marble staircase and stepped finally into the upper gardens of the seraglio. From this height they were able to see the long stretch of the Asia Minor coast and the mouth of a winding canal, through which moved a steady flow of gondolas, fishing vessels, and merchantmen.

At that moment, Lady Elgin felt a painful cramp and doubled over. Her husband instantly became alarmed.

"Lord Bruce!" she whispered reassuringly.

* * *

Bouyouk Dere*

My very dear Mother:

I must tell you of my sublime joy as I sit here on the sofa in the parlor while the Greek Paramana† is rocking Bruce to sleep. I still find it difficult to believe that it is almost two years since I held you and my loving father in loving embrace.

On Tuesday we plan to go to Belgrade.‡ Elgin has been there several times and has found some measure of relief from his rheumatism. He says the spa lies in the middle of a forest and consists of many fruit trees and a vast number of fountains. The springs are known for their therapeutic value and hundreds of visitors go there. It has many elegant walks and endless gardens of flowers, all within view of the Black Sea. Elgin was quite struck by the beauty and dress of the women there, and brashly claims they resemble the ancient Greek nymphs. Pshaw!

Mr. Hamilton and his cartload of artists have been hard at work in Athens for many weeks. The musicians, however, remain with us and I can truly say that I have never heard anything to equal the first violin. You will be pleased to know that he once led the orchestra at the opera in Naples. I did not tell you that the artists in Athens are under the supervision of Signor Lusieri, who is a handsome devil but quite taken to moods.

And now for some sad news: Doctor Hector McLean is dead. He was stricken with the palsy, and although he never let on to us the gravity of his illness, the poor man never recovered. He was an excellent scholar, a skillful physician, and a warm friend. We shall all miss him dearly.

---

*A suburb on the outskirts of Constantinople.
†The Greek nurse.
‡A summer resort about fifteen miles from Constantinople. Lady Mary Montagu, in a letter of June 17, 1717, described Belgrade as a village that perfectly deserved the description of the elysian fields. "I am," she wrote, "in the middle of a wood consisting chiefly of fruit trees watered by a vast number of fountains famous for the excellence of their water, and divided into many shaded walks with short grass, all within view of the Black Sea, from which we perpetually enjoy the refreshment of cool breezes that make us insensible to the heat of summer. The village is only inhabited by the richest amongst the Christians, who meet every night at the fountain less than forty paces from my house, to sing and dance." (*The Letters of Mary Nisbet*, p. 79.)

Only yesterday I learned from Elgin that McLean had received the approval of the Duke of York to embark with us for the East, so that he could investigate and make further studies on plagues.

The strange illness that has devoured most of Elgin's nose shows no sign of abating. I have the darkest fear that it is leprosy, although Doctor McLean repeatedly assured me to the contrary. In fact, these were his dying words. Meanwhile we expect Doctor Scott, his replacement, to be here shortly. I trust that he will be better prepared to help poor Elgin.

By the bye, you would be entertained if you could see Elgin at whist. I pique myself amazingly upon having made him play two or three rubbers, and uncommonly well he does it. I have also given a general invitation to young Stratton, our new ambassadorial assistant. He comes every evening, so that it is more like a party. Our expenses here are astronomical. Imagine having sixty people to feed every day, independent of the company at our own table! It seems to get worse with each passing month.

I cannot wait to get to Belgrade and thus be rid of them.

> Your own Mary,
> AMBASSADRESS VERY EXTRAORDINARY![13]

In February 1801, Elgin persuaded the Turks to allow General Koehler to join the grand vizier's army in Syria. Carlyle requested permission to accompany Koehler, hoping that this would afford him the long-awaited opportunity of visiting the monasteries in the Holy Land. At first, Elgin did not favor the idea, but when Carlyle reminded him of his sincere desire to search for ancient manuscripts, and of his goal for their eventual publication, from which he hoped to derive a satisfactory source of income, Elgin gave his wholehearted approval. It was necessary, however, to have the party leave Constantinople secretly. Koehler was to take only a few of his staff and make the journey as far as possible by land, after which it could be concluded by the much easier sea route. In addition to Koehler and Carlyle, the party consisted of two officers, a military draftsman, and thirty attendants. Dressed as Turks and well-armed, they devised a plan to head straight across Asia Minor, something no other European had done in more than a hundred years, since the route took them through the territories of many fierce pashas. A few, however, were reported to be friendly, depending on their current status with the Porte. To preserve the party's safety, Elgin laid down certain rules, and to make certain they would not be forgotten, he insisted that Hunt write everything down:

PREPARATIONS FOR A
TOUR FROM CONSTANTINOPLE

The best night quarters are in the Greek monasteries, which are to be found almost everywhere. On your departure, pay the full value of the provisions which you have consumed, and leave a few piastres as a present to the church. In default of a monastery, a peasant's cottage neatly swept out is infinitely preferable to a Turkish Konak, for in the former you will be protected from the night air and will feel no inconvenience from fleas; in the latter, you will be exposed to the wind and devoured by bugs.

Immediately upon your arrival at a new village, visit the chief, whether Greek or Turk, and present your firman. He then becomes responsible for your safety and good treatment. A Turkish guard is an encumbrance and attended with much expense, although frequently expedient by way of protection from insult and robbery.

Presents of money are always expected by the attendants of persons whom you visit. These in fact constitute their wages. It is best to distribute this money yourself instead of employing a deputy. At every house, you will be treated after the fashion of the country, with pipes and coffee; and when you retire, the attendants will be at the door expecting their fee.

When you travel through a village suspected of harbouring the plague, make every effort to leave it instantly. You will, of course, be told there is no plague, but Truth and Turk rarely mix. In most cases, they will concede there is a feverish complaint in the village, but will assure you a thousand times it is not the plague. Needless to say, this makes the place suspect and you should suffer no intercourse whatsoever with such people.

As to dress, the Tartarian or Polish costume will be found the most convenient. In this case, a defense for the eye will be needed; and the best is made with a piece of paste board cut into the shape of a crescent, covered with green silk and bound around the front of the cap by means of a silk ribbon. The best European dress consists of a white hat with a broad rim, a light-coloured broadcloth great-coat, silk and cotton mixed waistcoat, trousers or loose pantaloons of Manchester or Nanking, and strong roomy half boots. A large Venetian mantle or German Cloak would prove a useful and salutary companion at night. Furthermore, a portable bed frame would conduce much to comfort in a country so full of vermin, particularly if furnished with a mosquito curtain.

On the mode of conveyance by land, horses are to be hired in most places, but if the country is very rocky and mountainous, it would be advisable to choose mules. In the Isles of the Archipelago, you must be contented with asses. The usual rate of travel is about three geographical miles per hour. The horse hire varies from two to three piastres a day for each beast, including all expenses. There is usually a man to every two horses, who accompanies them on foot and receives a backshish or gratuity of twenty paras a day.

Finally, if you should be questioned about the motives of your tour, you may reply that it is the custom of your country and that you have read much of Greece in ancient books, as well as of Egypt and the Holy Land. The most current notion is that you are in search of hidden treasure, since it is impossible for Turks and Egyptians to conceive that you merely travel to examine the mouldering ruins of ancient towns and temples.[14]

The party was gone a little over a week, when Elgin received the first news from Carlyle. Several times during the long journey, General Koehler had become annoyed with Carlyle's many diversions at ancient ruins, but Carlyle was not to be dismayed and kept to his numerous notes. He had the draftsman draw all interesting ruins and fallen temples, and also made a rough map of the entire route, noting points of geographical interest and identifying modern villages with ancient names. After another two weeks, Carlyle sent many other dispatches, supplying Elgin with much information about the modes and customs, and even the political thoughts of each village along the way. From the monastery of Saint Saba in Jerusalem, he wrote: "The library here contains nothing valuable except twenty-nine copies of the Gospels and one of the Epistles. I was permitted by the Superior to bring along with me six of what I judged the oldest manuscripts. These include two copies of the Gospels, one of the Epistles, two books of Homilies and Apostolic Letters, and a copy of the sophist Libanius. I expect the Patriarch will allow me to convey them to England."[15]

Carlyle also hounded General Koehler and the party with his poor verses:

Nicaea hail! renown'd for fierce debate,
    For synods bustling o'er yon silent spot,
For zealous ardour — for polemic hate —
    For truth preserv'd, and charity forgot,
Those scenes are fled — those domes are swept away —
    Succeeding domes now totter to their fall,
And mouldering mosques on moulder'd fanes decay,
    While desolation bends to grasp them all.[16]

Elgin's patience was eventually rewarded by what he wanted to hear most from Carlyle: a detailed military report from the grand vizier's headquarters at Jaffa:

Bonaparte is not idle. He has turned his full attention on the French forces in Egypt and has decided to send an army from Toulon to reinforce them. Meanwhile his commander in Egypt* is more interested in the colonization of the country rather than the military aspects of his assignment. He was warned repeatedly by Bonaparte that an invasion was imminent, yet he did nothing to strengthen his units stationed near the coast. The relief forces from Toulon under the command of Admiral Gauteaume behaved equally as bad. No sooner did they set sail for Egypt, when they swung abruptly around and returned to port, without making any contact with Nelson. Enraged, Bonaparte ordered Gauteaume to sea again, but the admiral, more afraid of Nelson than of Bonaparte, hastened once more to Toulon. And fortunately for us. The British Expeditionary Force under the command of your Lordship's trusted friend, General Abercrombie, landed at Aboukir

---

*General Menou, who had succeeded General Kleber.

Bay, and although they were vigorously opposed by shore artillery and musket fire, their fine training at Marmoris, which they owe largely to your Lordship's labours, enabled them to make a good account of themselves. Those in the Expeditionary Force admiringly say that your Lordship exerted yourself, and at your own expense, securing vast quantities of stores for this Force, scouring the whole of Asia Minor for horses, building special shipyards, sending grain ships to every port in the Mediterranean, and much more. When our beachhead was finally established, it was here that the French commander proved himself inept in military affairs. He procrastinated while we consolidated our forces on shore, and when he at last chose to attack, the results were disastrous. He was soundly defeated and had to escape to Alexandria.

General Abercrombie was then able to bring in more reinforcements by sea; also to consolidate plans with the Grand Vizier's army which was drawn up outside Cairo. At this point, the ancient dykes around Alexandria were breached, and as the sea poured in around the outside of the city, our forces were able to put it under siege. Thus we had the French blocked in two places. On the side of the Turks, surprisingly stood fifteen hundred Mamlukes, which so shocked the French commander in Cairo, he submitted to an immediate surrender. However, when the French forces at Alexandria heard of this, they declared they would fight to the last man for the honour of the Republic. Not so however. Seven days later, they too surrendered.

It therefore is my most pleasant duty to inform your Lordship that the last French resistance in Egypt has come to an end, and the British Expedition under your Lordship's supervision shall be recorded by history as a great military victory.

Unfortunately, I must add one note of sadness to this dispatch: General Abercrombie has died of wounds inflicted upon him during the assault at Aboukir Bay. Koehler too was lost, but not in battle. He died of a severe contagion that is spreading rapidly over Egypt.

I expect to reach Constantinople within two fortnights, depending, of course, on favourable sea passage. If I am forced to travel by land, it may require longer.

> Believe me to be,
> Your obliged servant,
> Joseph Dacre Carlyle[17]

For a whole week, Constantinople was delirious with joy, each celebration lasting into the early hours of morning. There were firework displays, music, dancing in the streets, and endless cannon volleys. In the harbor, Turkish warships reenacted scenes from the triumph at Aboukir Bay. Elgin eagerly joined in by hiring a special ship, over which a gigantic star and crescent were to be hung, but the celebrations had resulted in a complete depletion of all lamps in the city, and he was forced to cancel his plans. Lady Elgin accompanied him to Seraglio Point on the first night of the celebrations. It was raining, but this did not deter the Turks from proceeding with the festivities. The fireworks did not go off well, and the man in charge was immediately replaced by another whose luck was better, since by this time the storm clouds had vanished and the Turkish sky gave birth to a new full moon and millions of stars, which of course the Turks took as a good omen from Allah. Young girls in masquerade danced before Elgin in long lines, shouting gleefully: "Elkin! Elkin!" while both sides of the Bosporus reverberated from the steady blast of rockets, guns, and cannons. The following day, Lady Elgin wrote to her mother, "Indeed, the Turks might have conquered Egypt without Elgin's help had they but fired half the number of cannons in earnest that they are now firing in joke!"[18]

The next morning, they were taken by the sultan's carriage and conveyed to the seraglio, where Elgin was accorded the highest honor of the Porte: an aigrette from the sultan's turban presented to Elgin by Selim III himself. He was also given the Order of the Crescent set in diamonds, a full-length pelisse (a fur cloak bestowed by the Turks as a special mark of honor), and a superbly caparisoned horse. Lady Elgin, too, was granted an unprecedented honor: "She was carried in a gold chair by an escort of black eunuchs and brought to the Valida, the Sultan's mother."[19] From there, they all proceeded to the Greek Kiosk of the Seraglio, where the sultan showed his face to the people. The Moslem priests immediately touched off the cry: "Selim the Conqueror!" and every Turkish woman in the throng responded by loudly wishing him a son.

Later in the afternoon, while Elgin conferred with the Turkish ministers, Lady Elgin rowed about Seraglio Point as the sultan watched from under his canopy on shore. When the gondola pulled up alongside the sultan, he made no acknowledgment, but as soon as it glided away, Lady Elgin glanced back and caught him peering at her through his telescope. She also noticed the sultanas waving from the window of the harem challenging the vigilant eyes of the black eunuchs in the garden below.

At dinner that night, Elgin reported that they were not the only ones to benefit from the sudden love of the Turks. "All British warships were to be granted free provisions and immediate refitting privileges in any Turkish port; and each English officer who took part in the Egyptian campaign, eighteen hundred in all, was to be given a gold medal and pelisse."[20] As long as the Turks were in this benevolent mood, Elgin persuaded them to release the French subjects imprisoned in every part of the Ottoman Empire, impressing upon them that it was contrary to the customs of civilized nations to imprison civilians. He then made still another request: a new structure to house his embassy. Surprisingly, the Turks agreed, bestowing upon him a site of land not too distant from the seraglio. "Wasting no time, Elgin commissioned an architect to begin work on a design for a building that would closely resemble his beloved Broomhall in Scotland."[21]

The final concession from the Turks was totally unexpected: the eventual release of all Maltese slaves who had for centuries been subjugated and maltreated by the Porte while confined in chains at the terrible prison of Bagnio. These expressions of gratitude from the Turks vaulted Elgin to a high pinnacle of diplomatic stature, which was crowned a month later by an official letter of commendation: "His Majesty is well pleased. All aims of your embassy have been achieved and Britain is once again the dominant power in the Eastern Mediterranean."[22]

The message bore the signature of a new foreign secretary: Lord Hawkesbury. Before retiring that night, Elgin sat down and wrote a lengthy response, titling it, "Memorial to the King,"[23] in which he recorded a complete account of his career to date, listing his many successes, and more importantly, the enormous personal expenses he had incurred in order to finance the Egyptian campaign. He closed with a straightforward request for a mark of royal favor, a knighthood perhaps, or a United Kingdom peerage, which would save him the trouble of being elected to the House of Lords as a Scottish peer.

It was denied.

Throughout these long diplomatic maneuvers, Lady Elgin became nostalgic for Scotland. She had grown tired of embassy life, its stiff demands, the endless receptions, being nice to those whom she detested, acknowledging foolish Turkish gossip, feeding an army of people day after day. It seemed that she no longer had time for herself, what with little Bruce, then Mary Christopher, and now a third child already forming in her womb. There was no respite. She couldn't bear to look in the mirror and see this other Mary Nisbet, tired and spent, consumed by the unrelenting pull of time in her veins. One night, she tried to express these feelings to her husband, but Elgin was mired in his own world. Furthermore, they would not see Scotland until his real work at Athens was completed, and "thus he remained at his desk writing letters, always writing letters . . . this one to Lusieri, commanding him to press the artists into even more diligent efforts."[24]

When Carlyle finally returned to Constantinople from Syria, he requested permission to leave the embassy and go back to England. He had in his possession several dozen manuscripts that he borrowed from the monastery of Saint Saba near Jerusalem, and almost an equal number from the library of the Jerusalem patriarch. In addition to these, he purchased out of his own funds several hundred Arabic manuscripts from private sources and from open bazaars in various parts of Egypt and Palestine. He was a bitterly disappointed man. His only reason for joining the Elgin embassy at Constantinople was to work with these manuscripts, but his wish had never been realized, and further, he had utterly ruined his health. Far worse, he had not received any payment promised by Elgin in his contract. But Carlyle was not one to make trouble. On the day of his departure, he asked Elgin for firmans and letters of introduction, which would at least authorize him to visit more monasteries in Greece before leaving for England. With his jovial nature and spirited recitations of his poetry, he had lent an air of cheerfulness to the embassy, and Lady Elgin in particular was sorry to have him leave.

They were all mired in gloom for days, and although Dr. Scott tried his best to cheer everyone up, he was a poor substitute for Carlyle. In the darkest moment of their dejection, good news at last came from Lusieri:

My dear Lord:

From the day of our arrival in Athens, we have been under the continuous protection of Mr. Logothetis, the British Consul here, with whose assistance we daily pay our respects, along with the usual gifts, to the Turkish authorities.

As your Lordship requested, it will be of interest to know that Athens remains a shabby and miserable town. It is inhabited by a mixed population from every part of the world, and its dwellings are confined to the northeast slopes of the Acropolis Hill. At least half of the residents here are Greeks, a quarter Turks, and the rest Albanians, Jews, and Negroes. Mr. Logothetis tells us that there are no more than thirteen hundred dwellings in all. Around the city stands a wall ten feet high, which was built about ten years ago for two reasons: to keep roving bands of pirates away, and to make the taxes of the enclosed inhabitants easier to collect. Not one of the houses is well-built or commodious, and the streets are narrow and irregular.

We have found the Turkish inhabitants of Athens of a more amiable disposition than those of Constantinople. No doubt they feel the happy influence of a more acceptable climate, which causes them to lose their ferocity. Of the Greeks, I give a far less favorable report. Their character does not rank high amongst the rest of their countrymen in the mainland; nor in the Isles of the Aegean. In fact, a proverb circulates daily around the city: As bad as the Turks of Negroponte, the Jews of Salonica, and the Greeks of Athens!

As your Lordship requested, I now submit a report on the government of Athens. Since the middle of the 17th century, the most powerful man here has been the chief officer of the Sultan's black eunuchs, the Voivode. His top military aide is the Disdar, who commands from his citadel on top of the Acropolis Hill, along with his garrison of soldiers. He alone has the authority to regulate the access of strangers to the Acropolis. Despite Mr. Logothetis' unceasing efforts, we have each been forced to pay the Disdar the monstrous sum of five guineas per day. In addition to this, we are subjected to constant insult, interruption, and extortion from his soldiers, and even from his young son. Through the intervention of Mr. Logothetis, however, the Voivode was summoned, and the Consul demanded that all Englishmen be allowed to visit the Acropolis Hill at anytime without interference. Mr. Logothetis then substantiated our complaints to the Voivode, who turned to the Disdar's son and ordered him at once to be sent into exile. He had compassion for the old Disdar, since the man is ill and at the point of death. Here Rev. Hunt interceded and obtained a pardon for the Disdar's son, but only on the condition that if another complaint occurred, the young Turk would be sent immediately to the galleys as a slave.

The meeting ended with promises from the Voivode that the Acropolis Hill would be open to all Englishmen from sunrise to dusk, and that your Lordship's artists should have access to all facilities without payment of any fee or bribe. Rev. Hunt then presented the Voivode with brilliant cut-glass lustres and firearms, after which he asked the Voivode for an official firman, whose complete context I now submit to your Lordship:

FIRMAN

It is hereby signified to you that our sincere friend, his Excellency Lord Elgin, Ambassador Extraordinary from the Court of England to the Porte of Happiness, has represented to us that he is anxious to read and investigate the books, sculptures, and other works of ancient Greek science and philosophy, and has therefore engaged five painters, now dwelling in Athens, to examine, view, and also to copy the above works remaining here; also to freely go in and out of the citadel of the said city and fix scaffolding around the ancient Temple of the Idols, to model the said ornaments and visible figures in plaster or gypsum, to measure the remains of other ruined buildings, and to excavate where necessary in order to discover inscriptions which may have been hidden in the ruins. Under penalty of death, no interruption shall be given them; nor obstacles put in their way by the Disdar or any other person.

Signed with a signet,
Seged Abdullah Kaimmakam[25]

It was a stroke of luck to have Hunt present at this time. He had accompanied Carlyle on a tour of the monasteries at Mount Athos, and was now in Athens. Normally Elgin would have dispatched one of his secretaries to assist Carlyle in his search for ancient manuscripts, but Morier had returned to England, and Hamilton was a very busy young man in Egypt, acting as Elgin's representative with the Expeditionary Forces there. Hamilton had gained remarkable distinction, first, by his role in the negotiations for the capitulation of Alexandria, and more importantly, for the British acquisition of the Rosetta Stone. Hamilton rowed out with a small escort to recover the stone from a fever-stricken French ship, where it was concealed for shipment to France and Napoleon's Louvre Museum. In this daring endeavor, Hamilton was accompanied by the author and traveler Edward Daniel Clarke and his pupil John Marten Cripps. Hidden with the Rosetta Stone in the hold of the ship, and covered with the rags of the sick people aboard, was also a large sarcophagus that Clarke mistakenly identified as the tomb of Alexander the Great. It turned out to be the sarcophagus of Nectanebes II, the last king of the Thirtieth Dynasty.

Hunt was in Athens for yet another reason. From the day of Egypt's capitulation, the massive French fleet was a constant reminder of Napoleon's intention to invade Greece. Consequently, on advice of his government, Elgin was instructed to send someone into Greece for the purpose "of visiting all the Pashas in the country and impressing upon them the mistake of entering into any negotiations with the French."[26]

To protect the project in Athens from further Turkish intrigue, Hunt had thoughtfully armed himself with a sufficient number of documents from the Porte. Along with these, he also brought a full supply of gifts for the voivode and his staff of officers: chandeliers, firearms, telescopes, jewelry, and endless rolls of fine silk and damask. Elgin grudgingly paid for all these items, confident that Hunt would succeed in his endeavors.

Hunt did not remain long in Athens. It was urgent that he continue on his diplomatic tour of the country in the hope of strengthening British ties with the local pashas. At Ioannina in northern Greece, he carved a strong friendship with Ali Pasha and got the Turk's promise to send Elgin whatever antiquities he found in all the provinces under his jurisdiction. Ali Pasha had observed certain statues that "only seemed to want breath to make them real."[27] At Thebes, Hunt paid an exorbitant price to a peasant for an exceptional cameo of a female centaur suckling her infant. Writing from Olympia, he recommended that Elgin should think seriously about embarking upon a definite program of excavations, and even suggested the removal of the Lion Gate from Mycenae. He rescinded after realizing that Mycenae presented transportation problems, since it was too far from the sea.

During Hunt's absence from Athens, Elgin made arrangements with one of the survivors of General Koehler's mission, Captain Thomas Lacy of the Royal Engineers, to act as supervisor of the Acropolis project. Lacy was not enthusiastic over this appointment, yet he was anxious to free himself from Egypt and the three frustrating years he had served under Koehler. Two days before embarking for Athens, he wrote a sour letter to Hunt: "Congratulate me, for I have at length found means to escape from Koehler's Mission and shall now be at leisure to devote myself to my friends. I embark for Athens: to plunder temples and commit sacrilege. A proper finish to my diplomatic career!"[28]

Throughout his brief stay in Athens, Lacy quarreled continually with Lusieri and eventually severed himself from the scene. For the moment, Elgin was happy to hear of this; nevertheless, someone was still needed to supervise the artists. Deep down, Elgin distrusted Lusieri and suspected that he was consorting with the French agent in Athens, Louis François-Sebastien Fauvel, who was by profession a painter, and as such, had accompanied the young French nobleman Comte de Choiseul-Gouffier on a tour of Greece in 1780.

Although Fauvel had been a political prisoner when Elgin's artists first arrived at Athens, his influence remained sharply present and within days one of the artists, the Calmuck, was accused of concealing drawings and measurements so that he could sell them to Fauvel. Fearing that Fauvel could very well undermine the whole project, Elgin quickly arranged to have him transferred to Constantinople, but even in Fauvel's absence, his accomplices managed to slow down the work of the artists: a French doctor cut off the water supply to Lusieri's work-shop and thus prevented the washing of the antiquities. This same doctor "made every effort to stop all acquisitions by sowing foolish ideas in the weak minds of the Turks."[29]

These obstructions, however, did not deter Elgin from his zeal, and he was now more determined than ever to preserve his great moment in Athens. After a long and dreary winter, during which his rheumatism flared up once again, he received even more encouraging news from Hunt. The firman that was issued by the kaimmakam pasha was now extended to cover a limitless endeavor:

> Under the penalty of death, no interruption shall be given His Excellency, Lord Elgin, nor to his painters who are engaged in fixing scaffolds around the ancient Temple of the Idols. And in modelling the said ornaments, or in measuring the ruins of fallen temples, no obstacle shall be thrown in their way by the Voivode, or any other officer of the Turkish army. No one shall meddle with the scaffolding or implements, and if the said painters wish to take away any pieces of stone with old inscriptions, or sculptures therein, no opposition shall be made.
>
> In the above-mentioned manner, see that ye demean and comport yourselves.
>
> Signed with a signet,
> Seged Abdullah Kaimmakam[30]

Throughout the Ottoman subjugation of Greece, the Acropolis, and especially the Parthenon, was regarded as exceptional by the Turks. Although it suffered its share of accidental damage and the Turks made no positive efforts to preserve it, they did attempt, though in the most feeble way, to prevent the damage from becoming worse. First of all, no one was ever given official permission to remove sculptures still on the building. This was absolute and not even the most unscrupulous voivode or disdar dared break it. Even the permission given to Lord Elgin now was an extremely doubtful exception.

Elgin's spirits were immediately lifted, and at the break of spring he decided to pay a visit to Athens and personally supervise his new plans. Even though she was pregnant for the third time and the thought of another sea voyage resurrected bitter memories, Lady Elgin overrode her husband's objections and insisted she make the trip. Before embarking, she wrote a jubilant letter to her mother in Scotland. "Travelling through this country (Greece) while Elgin's ambassadorial titles and pomp remain, is certainly a very great advantage and we mean to take a number of servants to cut a dash. Lord Bruce and our little daughter, Mary Christopher, shall come with us and will be looked after by Masterman and Calitza, the Greek Nurse. Doctor Scott goes along with us also."[31]

They left Constantinople in the middle of March, their ship a small brig bound for the isle of Malta. Even while drifting through the calm waters of the Dardanelles, Lady Elgin was overcome with nausea. At Chios, they encountered stormy winds and had to remain there for almost two weeks. With the first sign of good weather, they continued on a swift course as far as Patmos isle, but here too another turbulence erupted, sweeping two sailors overboard. There was much flooding below, and Lady Elgin's bed, with all her belongings, was immersed in two feet of water. Only after the brig sailed into sight of Mykonos isle were the crewmen successful in bailing out the cabins.

There was yet another delay on Mykonos, and while they waited for the storm to abate, Lady Elgin again wrote to her mother: "Hunt is in raptures, for the firman is now perfection. It allows all our artists to go into the citadel, to copy and model everything in it, to erect scaffolds all around the Temple, to dig and discover all the ancient foundations, and to bring away any marbles that may be deemed curious by their having inscriptions on them, and that they are not to be disturbed by the soldiers etc. under any pretense whatever."[32]

During their stay at Mykonos, Lady Elgin asked to investigate the place, but the captain warned of pirates and unfriendly surroundings. Elgin intervened and persuaded the captain to grant them permission. Their party included two crewmen, Dr. Scott, and Masterman, whose face had blanched at the mention of pirates. The Greek *paramana* remained on board with the two children.

Just before dusk, they found a deep cave high above the edge of the sea, and Masterman hastily prepared their beds. Meanwhile the two crewmen perched themselves atop a commanding rock and kept a sharp watch for pirates. After Dr. Scott lit a fire, Masterman brought out some bread, cheese, and several bottles of wine that Elgin had obtained from Chios. Against the weird patterns of dancing light on the walls of the cave, both Lord and Lady Elgin were amazed by Dr. Scott's knowledge of ancient Greece. He talked at length about the glories of Athens, and especially the construction of the Acropolis — how for one thousand years after it was built every temple therein stood as perfect as from the first day. Romans and Byzantines invaded the city and stripped everything, yet the temples of the Acropolis were left untouched. Even Alaric the Goth showed reverence for the sacred buildings. But then the destruction began, the initial blow being struck when Constantine the Great proclaimed Christianity the official religion of the empire. Overzealous priests destroyed the east end of the Parthenon to make room for an apse; they also knocked holes in the sides for windows. The Erechtheum was next to suffer, its whole interior torn out and converted into a church. To show their contempt for graven images, these same priests defaced almost every metope and sculpture on the Acropolis.

Another thousand years saw an endless line of conquerors: Franks, Catalans, Navarrese, Florentines, Venetians. Despite these invasions, the buildings on the Acropolis miraculously survived, until Greece fell to the Turks in 1453. The Parthenon was immediately converted into a mosque, and the Erechtheum turned into a harem for the military governor. When war broke out with the Venetians, the Turks used the Propylaea as a gunpowder magazine. In 1645, it was struck by lightning and exploded. The magnificent temple of Athena Nike was then deliberately destroyed by the Turks in order to clear the bastion for a key artillery position. On September 26, 1687, the Venetians under General Francesco Morosini laid siege to the Acropolis, and one of their cannons made a direct hit on the Parthenon, blowing off the roof and leaving a gaping hole between the long columns on both sides. The same blast also damaged the Erechtheum.

When Morosini finally evacuated Athens, he left the Acropolis in such shambles that word soon circulated around the world, and travelers came flocking to Athens to pick away at her remains and bring them back home to adorn their estates. Because the Turks realized that even shattered pieces of marble brought high prices, they deliberately began knocking off heads, arms, legs, even noses from the statues and sold them to these traveling gentlemen. Thus the ravaged glory of Greece was carted off to Paris, Berlin, Munich, the Vatican, Karlsruhe. There was no end. "Every traveller coming to Athens added to the general defacement of the statuary. There are now in London pieces broken off even within our day; and the Turks have been continually defacing them. In some instances, they have actually acknowledged that they have pounded down the statues to convert them into mortar."[33]

As Dr. Scott rambled on, Elgin only half listened, and his wife had already fallen into a deep slumber.

Greece

T HEIR FIRST VIEW of the Acropolis Hill was breathtaking. They were dismayed, however, by the sight of Turkish soldiers everywhere, their tents pitched at random in the most sacred places, while tradesmen of all description sifted through the dense crowd, selling coffee and merchandise. Even the lowest soldier had a servant, a groom, a youthful water carrier, a cook, and someone to pitch and strike his tent. At the northernmost corner, steady volleys of practice rounds from young recruits resounded against the peaceful Attic sky. In front of each tent, janissaries hung copper kettles with skimmer and ladle, but not for cooking purposes. Always attended by a guard, these cauldrons were held sacred by the Turks and believed to be their only protection from insidious defeat.

When Elgin and his wife reached the last step of the Propylaea, they came upon Lusieri sketching under an umbrella along the west side of the Parthenon. A high scaffold rested against the wall. On it stood two men; one was a humpback. He seemed very agile on the scaffold and was not afraid to climb to its highest point. The formatori and draftsmen were busy inside the sanctuary.

Lusieri informed Elgin that he and his artists had encountered re-peated difficulties in their work. Even with the kaimmakam's firman in their hands, the disdar that very morning had refused to allow them on the Acropolis Hill, claiming the only reason "the artists had built the scaffolds was to look down into the tents of the Harem and spy upon their women."[1] Luckily, the British consul Logothetis again came to their rescue and promised to issue the disdar another firman. Mean-while the artists were forced to work on other sites in various parts of Athens: the Theseion, the Agora, the Stoa of Attalos, and the ancient cemetery of Kerameikos. But here, too, they confronted problems: there wasn't one piece of lumber to be found in all Athens for more scaffolding, nor ropes to lift their materials. Consequently, Lusieri had to arrange for a caïque to set sail for Hydra Isle and bring back the necessary lumber. As for the ropes, they had Louis François-Sebastien Fauvel to thank.

Fauvel had established himself as Bonaparte's antiquarian agent in Athens when French relationships with Turkey were at their highest. In time, he had the run of the place and somehow managed to get everything he requested: statues from every temple in the city, metopes, friezes, vases, and jewelry. All of these treasures were collected and sent to France to be stored in the Louvre under Bonaparte's personal supervision, but when Fauvel demanded the sculptures of the Parthenon, the Turks staunchly refused. Undaunted, Fauvel offered a large bribe to the old disdar and managed to obtain an excellent frieze, and also a large metope that was buried in ruins near the Parthenon. Later, he got his hands on still another metope that had fallen from the Parthenon during a storm. These, and many more, he shipped to France, then suddenly, for no apparent reason, he lost favor with Napoleon's revolutionaries. Nevertheless, Bonaparte allowed Fauvel to remain in Athens with all his equipment, but when Turkey declared war on France after Bonaparte's invasion of Egypt, Fauvel was one of the first to be taken prisoner. Lusieri heard about Fauvel's excellent equipment and made an offer to the disdar, which the Turk readily accepted, "giving everything to Lusieri, even the large wooden cart that Fauvel used to transport his heavy materials."[2]

The oppressive heat of the day still lingered in the deep bowl of Athens when the Elgins came down from the Acropolis Hill. They walked leisurely through the Agora, before proceeding into a narrow dirt street cluttered with squalid houses and adjoining hen roosts. Small kiosks were everywhere, each raised upon four poles and covered with a thatched roof. Remarkably, mixed among this filth and disorder were superb buildings of granite and marble.

They resided with the British consul Logothetis during their stay in Athens, as did Lusieri and his artists. It was a dramatic moment for everyone when Lusieri and his crew came into the house after a hard day's labor on the Acropolis Hill. But Elgin never joined in with their stories and jokes. Greatly dissatisfied with what he considered their meager efforts, he daily kept urging Lusieri toward new assignments and projects: "I wish to have of the Acropolis examples in the actual size of each architectural ornament, each cornice, frieze, fluted column, metope and statue; also specimens of the decorated ceilings and the various architectural orders. I want you to embark at once upon a program of assiduous excavation. History assures me that there are riches of all description in such abundance that this dig is deserving of any labour that can be made under your supervision."[3]

When Lusieri reminded Elgin of the disdar's continual interference, Lady Elgin, in an obvious attempt to please her husband, instructed Don Tita "to put about a rumor that Elgin had a new set of powerful firmans from the Sultan, which should settle any lingering doubts about the legality of all excavations and removals."[4]

Greece had long been a trouble spot for the Ottoman Empire. Already there were sporadic outbreaks in the Peloponnesus, and there was increased talk of actual revolution. For centuries the Turks had inflicted countless cruelties upon the Greeks: Christian worship in public was forbidden, children were obliged to learn their Greek letters in caves, girls were taken at an early age and put into harems. But after four hundred years of subjugation, the Greeks had fortified themselves, particularly in the Peloponnesus, and the time at last seemed ripe for the expulsion of all Turks from Greek soil.

This was the chief topic of conversation at the British consul's house every evening during dinner. Occasionally the Calmuck, one of the artists, would interrupt with boisterous jabs at Lusieri, chiding him for being such a slow painter and, half-joking, claiming he often had to rub out part of a view because in the interim the growth of trees and alterations to buildings made the drawing out of date and inaccurate.

Lusieri retaliated by saying the only way he could get the Calmuck to work was by a constant administration of wine. Nevertheless, the Calmuck possessed great talent and, like Lusieri, was dedicated to detail, which particularly pleased Elgin, since "it was an easy task to draw sculptures in a state of decay, but the Calmuck had the gift of restoring them to their original beauty with one stroke of his brush."[5]

Meanwhile, Hunt was still on his extended tour of Greece and kept sending a steady flow of information to Elgin:

I must relate to your Lordship the various excursions I have taken to the ancient cities of the Peloponnesus. But my pen is poor and cannot convey the true picture of Mycenae's glory: her massive walls, the two colossal lions in bas-relief over the main gate, the tomb of Agamemnon etc. etc. I found the door wide open and it grieves me to report that storms of rain have brought in piles of soil and debris, making the entrance so difficult, it was impossible to ascertain the true dimensions of the building.

Continuing my inspection of the Morea, I came at last to Patras. There is much beauty in Arcadia and Elia [Elis]; also at Olympia. The real purpose of my trip, however, was not entirely consumed by artistic motives, since your Lordship instructed me to make note of all military positions in Greece. Conditions in the Peloponnesus are deplorable. Turkish troops are five years in arrears with their pay, and there is a general lack of artillerymen, also of competent instructors. At Nauplia, the troops revolted upon more than one occasion because of poor quarters and foul food.[6]

Elgin went daily to the Acropolis Hill to keep an eye on the artists. His wife usually accompanied him. Lusieri presented a comical picture under his constant umbrella, and forever complained about the laziness of the artists, even though Elgin repeatedly assured him that "his presence in Athens now promised a success beyond his most ardent dreams, and even ventured to add that his endeavours would one day reach the same elevation as those of Pheidias and Pericles."[7]

Elgin was enthralled by his young wife's keen interest in ancient Greek art and culture. It inspired him to flood her mind even further as he stood in front of one frieze after another and brought it to life before her eyes: Theseus freshly victorious over a centaur, while hordes of Lapithae and centaurs were embroiled in battle at the nuptials of Pirithous. At one stage, the Lapithae seemed victorious; at another, the centaurs.

He also remarked upon the magnificent finish of the marble in the inner chamber of the Parthenon. One of the metopes portrayed a solemn procession during a festival. Some of the figures were on horseback; others, just about to mount. A herd of oxen led the procession, followed first by priests, magistrates, and warriors, then by a line of nymphs carrying sacred offerings in baskets and vases. Another metope inside the main entrance of the temple related the history of Athena's birth from the brain of Zeus as he sat on a throne surrounded by the gods of Olympus. In loose-flowing robes, the virgin goddess held the horses of the chariot that introduced her to the gods, but unlike other statues, she was here represented with the captivating beauty of Venus and the invincible armor of the Spartans. On a third metope, a contest was portrayed between Athena and Poseidon, a fierce struggle from which a name for the city would result. Athena gained the victory by proving that her gift of a peaceful olive branch was more worthy than the warlike offering of the god of oceans: a wild-looking horse whose eyes seemed to reflect every cruel deed inflicted upon mankind.

It was impossible to conceive how the marbles were wrought to such depth. Each column was so united, without the aid of mortar, as to make the shafts look like single blocks, even to the most scrutinizing eye. The hair of each figure was braided in a different manner, and their robes looked so delicate they appeared to move with the breeze. Yet Elgin was quick to tell his wife that this was only a small portion of what the Acropolis once contained when Plutarch first beheld it in the first century A.D.: "All the public buildings and temples raised in Rome from the founding of the city, to the age of the Caesars, cannot be put in competition with the edifices erected on the Acropolis Hill during the brief administration of Pericles."[8]

Heliodorus's description of each structure on the Acropolis Hill was so minute it took up fifteen books, and even after the plunders of Lysander, Sulla, and Nero, there were more than three thousand works of sculpture still remaining. All this gave Elgin added reason to persist with his plans "to measure each temple, make elevations and views with the utmost accuracy, mould every block of marble, statue, ornament and inscription."[9] It was an enormous task, and although the amount of work seemed pitifully small, he was determined to carry it through to the end.

Just when the artists had again begun to move forward with a noticeable degree of speed and accomplishment, work was halted once more by the disdar, who brazenly ignored the kaimmakam's warning and demanded five guineas a day from each artist, otherwise no one would be allowed to set foot on the Acropolis Hill. When informed of this, Elgin became incensed and instantly dispatched a message to the sultan in Constantinople. As he waited for a reply, he assigned the artists to periodic visits into the city below, where they made sketches and drawings of ancient but less important sites. Weeks went by without a word from the sultan, at which point Consul Logothetis succeeded in convincing Elgin that they should all take a holiday and visit Delphi and Thermopylae. On their return to Athens two weeks later, Elgin expressed a further desire to visit Epidaurus and Tripoli, but Logothetis advised against it, since there was a constant threat of revolt in that part of the country. However, Elgin decided the risk was worth the potential reward, and the consul yielded and agreed to go with them.

They sailed from Piraeus on a warm morning in April, taking passage on an old Greek brig. Throughout the first day, the sea remained unruffled, and they coasted leisurely around the jagged eastern cliffs of the Peloponnesus. The whole area looked volcanic, its wild mountain peaks still crowned with snow, but along the massive slopes olive trees were already changing color, and fields of poppies had started to bloom. Approaching the Gulf of Argus, they were quickly surrounded by a rich growth of trees and vineyards; in the western horizon, the summits of Maenalus were plainly visible.

Within an hour, the brig skirted the slender promontory and dropped anchor inside the small port of Nauplia. Lady Elgin found a striking change in the style of dress and manner of speech among the inhabitants; still the Nauplians were conspicuously Greek in the way they walked, the passionate sweep of their arms in conversation, the majestic look in their eyes as they sipped coffee in the outdoor tavernas.

After a light meal, Logothetis led them to an old gray fortress on the summit of a high hill overlooking the city. He explained there were "many such Venetian fortifications in the Peloponnesus, and particularly in Maina, the southernmost peninsular of that area, which the Turks now used for garrison posts. Any movement by land or sea could be easily detected from these advantageous positions."[10]

On a sparkling white beach, just a short distance from the fortress, lay the ruins of a Byzantine church. Logothetis, claiming it was an easy matter to transfer religious veneration from goddess to saint in Greece, revealed that the church stood on the identical site of an oracular temple to Demeter, where a strange festival was annually celebrated: "a mingling of ancient Greek rite with Christian ceremony."[11] A steer was taken from the fields and brought into the town, where it was adorned with garlands of flowers and a wreath of laurel. From there, it was led through the streets to the church. Hymns of Apollo were sung, and finally the sacrifice was made, the death blow being delivered by the Greek Orthodox priest of the town. Hymns to the Virgin Mary were then chanted, after which the inhabitants made a fervent dash to the altar and soaked their handkerchiefs in the blood, believing it to possess miraculous power.

When they returned to the brig, Elgin suggested they move deeper into the Morea, but the captain grimly reported that a full-scale revolt had just broken out in Tripoli, and for once the Greeks had agreed upon a leader, Theodoros Kolokotrones, who was to become the great hero in the Greek War of Independence.

With the first breath of May, Athens took on a new countenance. Houses were whitened, birds sang, the olive leaves glistened as the church bells announced the long-awaited Resurrection of Christ. In the early hours of the morning, the Elgins, together with Logothetis and his family, climbed to the Byzantine chapel on the summit of Mount Lycabettus, where they joined the noisy procession of priests and worshipers, circling around the church thrice and carrying lit tapers as the bishops chanted: "He is Risen! Christ is truly Risen!" Almost at the same time, the celebration of cannon fire was heard from the distant hills. Now cocks began to crow; dogs howled; and soon the sun's fingers began grasping at the eastern horizon.

Later that afternoon, they all gathered in the parlor of the consul's house, where they were served red eggs and wine for the Easter celebration. In the ensuing egg-cracking contest, Lady Elgin was proclaimed champion of Athens by an exuberant Logothetis, after which they all joined in the singing of the Resurrection hymn the Greek *paramana* had so painstakingly taught them in Constantinople:

Christ is Risen from the Dead,
With His death, He has defeated Death,
And to those in the tombs,
He has given everlasting Life.

A huge roasted lamb was then triumphantly placed on the table, after which Logothetis raised his glass of red wine and solemnly offered a toast.

The festivities at the consul's house continued far into the night, and Lady Elgin was late in arising the next morning. A breakfast was prepared by the servants of the consul, and while they ate, Madame Logothetis made gossipy inquiries about Lady Elgin's social life in Constantinople: the parties she attended, the receptions, teas, the costumes of the Turkish women, their jewelry and mode of hair.

It was almost noon when Lady Elgin finally arrived on the Acropolis Hill. Scores of new scaffolds had been propped up against the east pediment of the Parthenon, and dozens of workers labored with ropes and pulleys, while many others struggled with windlasses and long wooden beams. On the scaffolds, more men were pounding chisels into a large metope that ran between the triglyphs. Within moments, the metope was pulled free and hoisted into the air, but suddenly the magnificent cornice that adorned it was weakened, and the metope fell to the ground in pieces, leaving a gaping hole between the columns. An eyewitness to the destruction on the Parthenon was Edward Daniel Clarke.

Some workmen, employed under Lusieri's direction, were engaged in making preparation, by means of ropes and pulleys, for taking down the metopes, where the sculptures remained the most perfect. The Disdar himself came to view the work, but with evident marks of dissatisfaction; and Lusieri told us that it was with great difficulty he could accomplish this part of his undertaking from the attachment the Turks entertained towards a building which they had been accustomed to regard with religious veneration and had converted into a mosque. We confessed that we [shared] the Muhammaden feeling in this instance and would gladly see an order enforced to preserve rather than destroy such a glorious edifice.

After a short time spent in examining the several parts of the temple, one of the workmen came to inform Lusieri that they were going to lower one of the metopes. We saw this fine piece of sculpture raised from its station between the triglyphs; but as the workmen endeavoured to give it a position adapted to the projected line of descent, a part of the adjoining masonry was loosened by the machinery, and down came the fine masses of Pentelican marble, scattering their white fragments with thunderous noise among the ruins. The Disdar, seeing this, could no longer restrain his emotions and actually took his pipe from his mouth, then letting fall a tear, said in a most emphatic tone of voice: Telos! (Enough! The end!), positively declaring that nothing should induce him to consent to any further dilapidations of the building. Looking up, we saw with regret the gap that had been made, which all the ambassadors of the earth, with all the sovereigns they represent, aided by every resource that wealth and talent can now bestow, will never again repair.[12]

Another witness was the traveler Edward Dodwell:

During my first tour to Greece, I had the inexpressible mortification of being present when the Parthenon was despoiled of its finest sculptures; and when some of its architectural members were thrown to the ground, I saw several metopae at the south-east extremity of the temple taken down. They were fixed in between the triglyphs as in a groove; and in order to lift them up, it was necessary to throw to the ground the cornice by which they were covered. The southeast angle of the pediment shared the same fate; and instead of the picturesque beauty and high preservation in which I first saw it, it is now comparatively reduced to a state of shattered desolation.[13]

The kaimmakam's original firman was ambiguous and certainly did not intend for Elgin to remove the sculptures and friezes from the Parthenon, but Hunt, with some manipulation, managed to give it another interpretation. After a brief rest from his long diplomatic tour of Greece, he called upon the voivode, requesting permission to take down the best metopes from the Parthenon. The British consul Logothetis was present at the meeting and voiced a timid objection, both as a Greek and an archon of Athens. Hunt curtly reminded him that a consul should not oppose the wishes of an ambassador, then, turning once again to the voivode, insisted that the original firman gave the right to remove sculptures and friezes from the building of the Acropolis Hill. Hunt strengthened his case with a "judicious mixture of threats and bribes,"[14] and the voivode formally granted his permission.

When Elgin was in Constantinople, Edward Daniel Clarke visited him. Clarke had just completed a tour of Egypt, where he claimed to have found the sarcophagus containing the tomb of Alexander the Great. His judgment, however, proved to be false, as it was with several other "discoveries," including that of a small marble relief that he found at the foot of the Acropolis Hill. He decreed that it was the certain work of Pheidias, but it turned out to be "a coarsely-carved piece of an old gravestone."[15]

A few months later, at Eleusis, Clarke achieved genuine success: the discovery of an enormous and battered statue weighing two tons and representing a woman with a basket on her head. A traveler who had visited Eleusis in 1765 reported that "this was the site of a shrine to Demeter, the goddess of corn and fertility."[16] He found the inhabitants mired in superstition, fearing that the fertility of their land depended so much on this statue they even lit tapers and votive lamps before it on certain Christian feast days. At the time of Clarke's arrival, travelers were warned that "the arm of any person would fall off if he touched the statue with violence."[17] But Clarke had already made up his mind to take it. However, he had to move swiftly and secretly in order to gain the victory over his French competitor, Comte de Choiseul-Gouffier. "I found the goddess in a dunghill buried to her ears. The Eleusinian peasants, at the very mention of moving it, regarded me as one who would bring the moon from her orbit. 'What would become of their corn,' they cried, 'if the old lady with her basket was removed?' I went to Athens and made application to the Pasha, aiding my request by letting an English telescope glide between his fingers. The business was done."[18]

Clarke was soon confronted with more obstacles: ropes and pulleys had to be obtained, and the jetty at Eleusis needed repairs. On the night before the statue was to be removed, an ox broke loose from its yoke and began butting the statue violently with its horns. A bad omen! It then ran amuck over the plain of Eleusis, bellowing into the night. At daybreak, the peasants accosted the Turkish officer who had proclaimed the firman, and a riot resulted. Calm was subsequently restored, and the peasants reluctantly agreed to obey the voivode's command. The village priest then put on his vestments and began clearing away the rubbish from around the statue. At this point, Clarke stepped brazenly forward and placed both hands on the old lady. Contrary to the ancient fears of the Eleusinians, his arms did not fall off, and after hours of tedious work, a crew of 150 boys at last managed to haul the huge statue out of the village, all the way to the shore, where it was loaded into a ship that Clarke had chartered for England.*

Elgin found no fault with this. "The Greeks of today," he remarked, "do not deserve such wonderful works of antiquity. Moreover, they consider them worthless. Indeed, it is my divine calling to preserve these treasures unto all ages!"

Later that week, Elgin set off for Delphi with some of his staff, but before leaving, he instructed his wife to go to the Piraeus docks and persuade Captain Hoste of HMS *Mutine* to take on board all the marbles that were lying on the docks. It was a huge shipment, and Captain Hoste had already informed Elgin that it would be impossible to take them all. Lady Elgin, however, used her charms and convinced Captain Hoste.

> I began by saying as the Captain was going straight to Malta, and there being no Enemies to encounter, I ventured to propose his taking them. It would be doing me a very great favor, as you were extremely anxious to get them off. Female eloquence as usual succeeded. The Captain sent me a very polite answer and by peep of Day, I sent down the three cases.[19]

Lady Elgin went to the Pireaus docks again the following morning and was able to persuade Captain Hoste to take, in addition to the three cases, the entire shipment of marbles that were on the docks.

---

*This statue, which no doubt had been worshiped longer than any other in Greece, now stands in a corner of the Fitzwilliam Museum at Cambridge.

This remarkable feat was accomplished through her further allurement and with gifts of money for all the crewmen.

> In hopes that I shall be the first to tell you what I have done, know that besides the three cases I have already told you of, I have prevailed on Capt. Hoste to take three more, two are already on board and the third will be taken when he returns from Corinth. How I have fagged to get all this done! Do you love me better for it, Elgin? And how I have pushed Lusieri to get cases made for these large shipments. I beg you shew delight. Lay aside the Diplomatic Character to Capt. Hoste for taking so much on board. I am now satisfied of what I always thought: which is how much more Women can do if they set about it than Men. I will lay any bet had you been here you would not have got half so much on board as I have. As for getting things you wished down from the Acropolis, it is quite impossible before you return. Lusieri says, upon his first coming here, he was against the things being taken down, but now he is keener than anybody, and absolutely wishes you to have the whole Temple of the Carisomething,* where the Statues of the Women are.[20]

During the strenuous weeks that followed, Elgin pulled down every important sculpture and frieze from the Parthenon. As soon as the marbles were crated for shipment to England, he kept lashing out at Lusieri, demanding that he spare no effort or money toward even further acquisitions from other ancient sites in and around Athens. Hunt joined in and suggested that the entire Erechtheum could be removed and rebuilt later in England. "If a large Man of War would come here, that beautiful little model of ancient art might be transported wholly to England."[21]

Elgin became obsessed with Hunt's idea and wrote immediately to his friend Lord Keith, the commander in chief of naval forces in the Mediterranean. "I have been at a monstrous expense at Athens, where I at this moment possess advantages beyond belief. Now if you would

---

*The Erectheum and its columns of caryatids.

allow a ship of war of size to convoy the Commissary's ship and stop a couple of days at Athens to get away a most valuable piece of architecture at my disposal there, you could confer upon me the greatest obligation I could receive, and do a very essential service to the Arts in England. Bonaparte has not got such a thing from all his thefts in Italy. Pray kindly attend to this, my Lord."[22]

With aroused passion, Elgin now decided to extend his hand far beyond Athens. Taking his wife and a crew of workmen with him, he traveled to Mycenae, leaving Lusieri behind to launch a search through every monastery in and around Athens with the Calmuck and Ittar the humpback. Elgin further commanded that all artists who could be spared from the Acropolis Hill be sent immediately to the Peloponnesus, chiefly Olympia.

Mycenae's ruins so impressed Elgin he ordered his crew to begin excavations at once; the results surpassed all expectations. Their visit to Tripoli was unforgettable. "Having received the most pressing and repeated invitations from the Pasha of the Morea, we set off toward Tripoli in the company of a very numerous Turkish escort, as well as an Albanian guard in the dress of the ancient Macedonians."[23]

That evening, they stayed at Aklatho-Cambo, a small village whose houses were humble mud huts scattered along the slope of an almost perpendicular mountain. At the bottom of the high peaks, and directly through the heart of the village, ran a narrow rivulet that had dried up. One of the village elders told Elgin that the winter rains came down the slopes in such wild streams, they inundated the valleys below. Elgin noticed "several uncommonly beautiful lassies in this village."[24]

The next morning, the inhabitants of Aklatho-Combo, preceded by their priest and elders, came and entreated Elgin to persuade the pasha of the Morea to repair their little church, which was now too ruinous for the performance of divine worship. Although Elgin promised to comply with their request, he never did.

Before setting out for Tripoli they were joined by Tartars and other officers of the pasha. Because she was in late pregnancy, Lady Elgin was placed inside a covered litter that was carried between two mules and guided by six men. The struggle she had trying to get into the litter, or *tarta-van* as it was fondly called by the Turks, evoked much laughter. After many failed attempts, a man was summoned, whom the Turks called the Step. He prostrated himself on the ground, and Lady Elgin stepped on his back to get into the conveyance. As they approached Tripoli, the Tartars hinted that it would be more appropriate for Lady Elgin to make her entrance on horseback.

A parade horse was quickly brought to her, and she mounted it. They were eventually met by all the officers of the pasha's court, on chargers richly caparisoned, and accompanied by pages and guards who played at *dgerit*, a game with a straight white stick and a sport not entirely without risk, since a blow on the temple could prove fatal. Elgin was told that the pasha once cut off the head of an officer who had hit him on the shoulder during the game.

Soon thereafter, the Elgins were treated to more equestrian feats. Many of the Turkish soldiers who had flung the *dgerit* now rode back and picked it up without getting off their horses; others had long poles with hooks at the end by which they pulled up their *dgerits* in the quickest manner. Their dexterity was incredible, and the performance evoked a lusty cheer from Lord Elgin.

At last they came into the city. Lady Elgin did not imagine that Tripoli would ever see another procession like this.

First the Pasha, his officers, the pages and guards, the lead horses with the most brilliant colours, the Lieutenant-Governor and the First Chamberlain riding in front of the Tartars, and a train of at least seven hundred Turkish soldiers on horseback. Elgin was disappointed when he saw no Greek inhabitants on the streets; not one Greek face greeted us from a window or a door. Meanwhile, great cannons from every fort around the walls of the city kept firing away as the First Chamberlain, from out of an embroidered box, started flinging coins into the street.[25]

After the procession had passed through the center of the city, Lady Elgin looked back and saw that scores of bedraggled Greek children had dashed into the dust-filled street and were clawing for the coins. It was a sad sight, one that remained with her even after they had stopped at the house of the dragoman (an official interpreter of high rank) for an immense supper "dressed in the Turkish style."[26]

During their long absence from Athens, Consul Logothetis was assigned the unpleasant task of keeping a vigil on Lusieri and his artists. A French conspiracy was still feared by Elgin, especially while more Parthenon marbles awaited shipment and were in plain sight on the Piraeus docks.

Upon their return to Athens, it was decided that they should leave immediately for Constantinople. Elgin burdened Lusieri with still more instructions, and in the middle of June 1802, they departed from Piraeus on HMS *Narcissus*.

Sailing into the Aegean, the *Narcissus* called at many islands, and here, too, Elgin seized any antiquity he could find. After stopping on the promontory of Sounion and visiting the Temple of Poseidon, Elgin compared it to the Temple of Theseus in Athens, and since the walls had fallen down, shafts of light poured through the few remaining columns. Several bas-reliefs and ornaments of the frieze had also fallen and were so defaced Hunt could not identify them.

Later, on the *Narcissus*, they viewed the isle of Eleni, a barren stretch of rock that seemed to strive desperately to give nourishment to a small herd of goats grazing by the shore. That afternoon they anchored in the harbor of Kea. Mounting donkeys, they later rode into the town over a precipitous road that wound around an almost impassable mountain range. At times, there seemed hardly enough space on the treacherous path for the donkeys to walk.

The town of Kea, whose inhabitants were mostly of Venetian origin, was situated on the summit of a high hill. Its houses were so flat the roofs served as courtyards. That night, the Elgins were honored with dinner, music, and dancing. Their host was Signor Pangali, the Neopolitan Consul. His nine daughters provided marvelous entertainment with their lively renditions of Greek, Italian, and French songs. They also danced minuets and Greek folk dances. Lady Elgin was fascinated by the dress of the women. Their petticoats reached only to the knee, and their stockings were stuffed with cotton so as to make the leg appear more than twice its natural size.

Three days later, the *Narcissus* came into sight of Marathon, and even from the ship Lord Elgin could plainly see the huge mound of Marathon's heroes. Early the next morning, they went ashore and pitched a tent on the plain of Marathon. An ancient setting was provided for them when the sailors of the *Narcissus* surrounded the tent with pillars found scattered on the ground. After dinner, they visited the mound and discovered it partly open as a result of Fauvel's excavations. Elgin ordered the ship's crew to dig at another site nearby, and they unearthed many pieces of pottery, along with numerous articles of silver.

Elgin examined the plain with great care and agreed with Hunt as to the site of the marshes where the Persians perished in their retreat. Not far from the mound rested the remains of a square building, which Hunt identified as the tomb of Miltiades. Elgin instructed the crewmen to dig here too, and they found more antiquities, as well as human bones. Near the marshes, Hunt came upon the Temple of Nemesis, where the Athenians had placed her statue after seizing it from the fleeing Persians who overconfidently had brought it with them to erect as a memorial of their conquest over the Athenians.

On the first day of July, the party landed on Tenos, one of the most flourishing islands of the archipelago. Because of contrary winds, they had to remain here almost one week, residing in the house of the English consul Signor Antonio Vitali. One evening, the Russian consul on the isle, Signor Vicenzo, honored them with a ball and even made a transparency on translucent parchment of Lady Elgin's monogram.

The stormy winds persisted, making it impossible to sail in an open boat, and they had to be transported to Mykonos in a *martigan*, commanded by a French officer who had abandoned his fleet at Toulon. They arrived at Mykonos on a sad day. The vice consul's seventeen-year-old daughter had just died, and the Elgins were immediately thrown into the curious ceremonies of a Mykonos death. Three or four times during the mourning period, the relatives brought in a number of priests, but prior to this a strange composition was created to resemble the dead girl. Prayers were read over it, and then it was set on fire, while the priests and relatives formed a circle around the flames, wailing over the charred object as though it were the actual body of the girl. Professional wailers were also brought in from a distant village to provoke those who had difficulty in shedding tears. Finally the ashes were collected and carried into the church in a solemn ritual.

The Elgins were happy to depart from this "melancholy abode and most barren and wretched island,"[27] setting off in the *Narcissus* as soon as the wind obliged them. At first sight of Delos Isle, they spotted a Latine sailboat giving chase to a large English ship. The *Narcissus* fired on the intruder, and she ran off after putting out twenty-two oars. Captain Donnelly of the *Narcissus* gave chase and got as near to the pirate ship as the heavy seas would allow, tacking and retacking, then firing more than three hundred shots at her. The pirates answered with volleys of musketry, which struck the frigate's deck but did not kill or wound any of the crew. By this time, the pirate ship was so severely damaged, she finally sank. Captain Donnelly, assisted by a boat filled with soldiers from Mykonos, dispatched a party of marines onshore to round up the escaping pirates, and they scoured the island in all directions, taking prisoner the captain of the pirates, Zachary by name, along with twenty-three of his crew. Zachary was a young man of twenty-six, of an open countenance, and very bold, but by no means impudent. They confessed to being natives of Morea, a remote province in the southern Peloponnesus, but insisted that their only object was the prize and that they had never wantonly killed or even wounded anyone.

This incident did not deter Elgin from a thorough search of ancient Delos, and also the opposite isle of Rhenea. He found most of the temples demolished and pieces flung everywhere; however, the base of Apollo's statue and part of his body still remained. The theater was in ruins, but the small pond used for sham naval battles was remarkably preserved. Rhenea possessed many beautiful marble altars, one of which Elgin confiscated and brought on board. It was perfectly round and ornamented with festoons of fruit and flowers.

From there, they sailed to Paros Isle, where they stopped to afford Lady Elgin some relief from the tossing sea. She was captivated by the orange groves, the fountains, and cascades of the island. All of the famous marble quarries were in full operation, and their glistening walls were cluttered with crude sculptures "of nymphs and Bacchanalians dancing."[28]

The marble of Paros, however, disappointed Elgin. It was not as white as the Pentelic in Athens. Most of the temples at Paros had been destroyed to construct the Venetian fort at Parechia, the isle's capital. There was a harvest of onions during this time, and Captain Donnelly bought a two-ton weight at three shillings a hundred. The whole deck of the *Narcissus* was soon covered with this cargo of onions, incarcerating passengers and crew with its repugnant odor all the way to Asia Minor, where it was finally taken off and sold at a handsome profit.

After calling at Smyrna, the *Narcissus* sailed on, reaching the Dardanelles in mid-August.[29] Lady Elgin clung tenaciously to her mal de mer throughout the rest of the voyage, but her recovery was instantaneous the moment she spotted the sun-splattered domes and minarets of Constantinople.

Constantinople

My very dear Mother:

I open my heart to you and say that Matilda [the Elgins' third child] was today innoculated* and took the vaccine without the slightest complaint.[1]

*I*T WAS FORTUNATE that fresh vaccine had been sent from Vienna, which Dr. Scott had previously tried with much success and was now using on scores of people in Constantinople and Belgrade. The plague posed no obstacle to Elgin, however, and he persisted in his strong desire to possess every valuable antiquity in Greece. The Parthenon had now been almost entirely stripped, and not one inch of ground on the Acropolis Hill was spared from excavations. The removals took place daily. Thus far six slabs of the Parthenon frieze had been pulled down, along with all the remaining metopes. Still another slab of the frieze had been unearthed in excavation. Four slabs from the Temple of Athena Nike, which were built into the fortification of the Acropolis Hill, had been dug out and removed, as well as some splendid examples of the architectural details from the capitals, bases, cornices, parts of the pillar at the Erechtheum, the Propylaea, and the Temple of Athena Nike. One section of the Parthenon column had to be sawed in two before the friezes and metopes could be removed.

Largely because of Elgin's tour throughout Greece, not one day passed without a new windfall of treasures. On the morning of their departure from Athens, he gave a horse and green cape to the voivode,

---

*A severe plague was raging through Asia at this time.

who responded immediately with his own gift: the colossal headless statue of Dionysus that stood for centuries above the monument of Thrasyllos on the south side of the Acropolis Hill. Even before they boarded the *Narcissus*, Lusieri suggested "that he might be able to remove the Monument of Lysicrates in its entirety if he offered enough money to the Capuchin Abbot, and Elgin urged him to try."[2]

This whole venture had already cost Elgin thousands of pounds, and still there appeared to be no end in sight, nor any promise from the British government that he would ever be reimbursed. Soon after their arrival in Constantinople, he learned that all the crates that held these new acquisitions were piled up on the quay at Piraeus, awaiting shipment. Lord Nelson had refused to dispatch any of his warships for Elgin's benefit because he wanted to keep his fleet on the alert in case war broke out again with the French. Thus Elgin was obliged to send the marbles piece by piece, with any ship he could find. The frigate *La Diane* took a great number of cases, as did HMS *Mutine*, but the treasures were piling up so rapidly Elgin worried about their safety, and in a last desperate measure, he decided to take out loans from his bankers so he could purchase his own ship, a good-sized brig named *Mentor.*

The ship was fitted with a crew of sailors from Smyrna. Lusieri was told to put absolutely everything on board, and if necessary to charter other vessels in order to get all the marbles and statues off for England. Along with scores of Greek laborers and Turkish soldiers, Lusieri and his crew of artists worked unceasingly, hauling the latest acquisition of marbles to the Piraeus docks and loading them into the *Mentor.* These included fourteen more pieces of the Parthenon frieze, four sections of the frieze from the Temple of Athena Nike, and many other sculptures too numerous to mention. "The largest pieces, which contained the figures from the pediments, had to be left behind, since the captain refused to enlarge the hatches of the ship to get them in."[3]

Under William Richard Hamilton's supervision, "the *Mentor* at last sailed for England with both Hamilton and Lusieri on board, but within two days she ran into a violent storm and struck rocks at the entrance to the harbor of Cerigo, now called Kíthira, a small island off the southernmost coast of the Peloponnesus."[4] Because of her excessive weight, she sank immediately in twelve fathoms of water, and only by good fortune were Hamilton and Lusieri able to scramble ashore. The exact spot of the sinking was carefully marked, and Lusieri posted guards on shore to keep vigil. Realizing that the *Mentor* was now beyond salvage, he hired sponge divers from a neighboring island, and fortunately every case of marble was saved. Lusieri then instructed the workers to bury all the cases in the sandy beach and cover them with seaweed and large stones so as to conceal them from French eyes.

A second ship, HMS *La Victorieuse*, was sent from Constantinople in November, with special instructions to pick up everything at Cerigo. This was done within a few weeks, and finally the entire shipment was on its way to England. Hamilton went with it, while Lusieri returned to Athens, armed with Elgin's instructions to continue with more acquisitions and excavations.

In Constantinople, Elgin was beside himself with joy; for the first time, he felt that the real purpose of his mission was at last being achieved. Although fifty cases of marble sculptures were now on the high seas, heading for England, at least fifty more were still at Athens, including the large and heavy sculptures of both the east and west pediments of the Parthenon, seventeen cases of the frieze, and numerous metopes.

Elgin daily boasted to his wife that he had successfully overcome the indifference of the Greeks, the treachery of the Turks, and the envious intrigues of Bonaparte. On Christmas Day, he promised her that if all went well, he hoped to close down the embassy before the end of January. She tearfully exclaimed that she could not wait to set foot once again on Scottish soil, to catch that first glimpse of the sun on Aberlady Bay, on the firth, and on Archerfield.

She was amazed at the children's rapid growth. She had all she could do to restrain Bruce from escaping the clutches of the Greek *paramana*. Little Mary, of course, yearned to imitate him, but failed nobly. Fortunately, the babe Matilda was too busy eating to pay either of them any heed.

Elgin's appearance had now deteriorated beyond all help. His nose was completely eaten away, and he had grown shockingly gaunt of body. He ate sparingly and slept hardly at all. Many nights Lady Elgin was awakened by his nightmarish commands to Lusieri, his curses upon Bonaparte, and his violent rage at the British government. In addition to all this, she was concerned about the health of her children. "The plague still continues," she wrote to her mother, "and by way of hiding it, the Turkish authorities carry away the dead bodies during the night, which so far is lucky for us, since we have the less chance of meeting them . . . pray for us, dearest mother!"[5]

January brought unceasing rains to Constantinople, making the days so unusually mild, the Turks took it as a bad omen. A woman who resided in a house alongside the embassy palace died suddenly after complaining of swollen glands and high fever, and before nightfall of that same day, a dozen similar cases were reported in that quarter of the city. Constantinople was instantly gripped by panic. Stricken houses were marked with black strokes of paint, over which were scribbled the words *Allah, have mercy!* Dr. Scott hesitated before diagnosing it as the bubonic plague, but Lady Elgin had seen its dreadful hand in Edinburgh when she was twelve: the vomiting, giddiness, intolerance to light, numbing pain of limb, sleeplessness, apathy, delirium, and finally death. Although she feared for her children, she was even more concerned about Elgin, whose weakened state made him more susceptible to the contagion. Already there were traces of redness in his eyes, and he was suffering painfully from constipation. To make matters worse, his speech had become thick and, upon more than one occasion, she saw him staggering across the floor in a daze.

Dr. Scott submitted the entire household to daily examinations, particularly Elgin, and was thoroughly convinced they were in no danger. He was disturbed, however, to learn that Elgin was severely troubled by a disturbance in his bowels, and to cure the problem, Scott prescribed a strong cathartic. He concluded that the redness of Elgin's eyes resulted from lack of sleep, and as for the occasional thick speech and uncertainty of gait, Scott hoped to effect the cure by a daily application of six leeches to each temple for a period of one week.

After dinner each evening, Scott took it upon himself to lecture the household, cautioning everyone that common sense was needed and that panic had to be avoided. He had already formulated a theory concerning the plague, based on extensive scientific studies while he was in Glasgow. He stated that "for hundreds of years the plague had been victorious over mankind because the medical profession had focused its attention upon only the symptoms, not the cause."[6] Up to this time, most medical observers were disposed to lay the full blame for the propagation and spread of the plague to the rat. Yet Scott said it was incontestable that a great mortality among rats was reported during epidemics of plague. Further, a comparison made by him between rat-infested and rat-free districts in Glasgow showed a much higher incidence of plague in the latter. Plague rats were rarely found in ships sailing from infected ports, and although millions of rats had been transported from quay to quay between the great ports of the world, they somehow never brought the disease ashore.

Scott therefore concluded that the contagion was not caused by rats, but by rat fleas. In twenty-one experiments out of thirty-eight, he noticed that more than half the percentage of healthy rats living in flea-proof cages had contracted the disease after receiving fleas collected from rats that were either dead or dying from septicemic plague. This same experiment also proved that close and continuous contact of plague-infested animals with healthy ones did not infect the latter if fleas were not present. Rats could even become infected through the feces of a flea that had fed on plague-infested rats. Consequently, Scott warned everyone to be especially careful about clothing and linens, since these were prime conveyors of the disease. Furthermore, he established a complete smoking system* in the household. Anyone returning from business outside had to be thoroughly smoked from head to toe before entering the house. Lastly, he admonished Lady Elgin for the daily strolls she was in the habit of taking through the Gardens of Pera. These, he said, had to cease immediately.

One evening, Captain Maling called on Elgin "to dispel the rumor that eighteen men on his frigate *La Diane* had succumbed to the

---

*Fumigation, for the purpose of disinfection, was common practice at this time. The best protection was afforded by exposing the body to the fumes of ammonia, sulfur, or mercury. Fumigation by the injection of tobacco smoke into the large bowel was also a recognized medical procedure.

plague."[7] He did admit, however, that the disease was most violent on board several Russian ships that had recently arrived from Egypt.

One of Elgin's lingering concerns was also resolved at this time. He finally completed all arrangements with the sultan to gain the release of the Maltese slaves who had long been held in bondage by the Turks. "For centuries, the Knights of St. John had employed the Maltese as crewmen for their ships in crusades against the Turks. The Ottoman Empire never forgave the Maltese; and those unfortunate enough to have fallen into Turkish hands were either kept in chains at Bagnio Prison or used as slaves in the dockyards at Tophana."[8]

Elgin impressed upon the sultan that Malta was now a British possession, which made the Maltese British subjects, and accordingly he demanded their release. To his surprise, his demand was granted swiftly and unconditionally, and the following day Elgin arranged to have all the newly freed slaves present for the laying of the foundation stone at the new British palace. At first the sultan refused to participate, but he finally relented to Elgin's strong persuasion that he do so as a compliment to the queen of England upon the occasion of her birthday.

Elgin attired himself in full-dress uniform for the ceremonies, and before leaving the house, he and all the others in his staff were cautioned by Dr. Scott to cover their noses and mouths with cloth protectors. Since it was raining hard when they stepped outside, Elgin requested chairs, and the entire party was transported to the new palace. As soon as they came inside the gate, they saw the Maltese slaves standing in two long lines. That same moment Elgin and his party were greeted with three lusty cheers. "The joy these slaves showed surpassed all expectations. They cried, laughed, and embraced one another, and said that as long as they lived, they would pray for the Elgins."[9]

The ceremonies were brief. Even though tents had been pitched and a large dinner prepared, gusty winds and rain drove them inside, where speeches were delivered and gifts handed out. Each of the slaves received new clothes and forty-eight piastres from the sultan, and during the long reception that followed, many dignitaries from foreign countries came forward to praise Elgin for his benevolent action.

* * *

On the sixteenth of January 1803, Elgin left the British palace at daybreak to make his final visit to the Porte. He and his staff had worked
for several weeks to clean out the rooms of the embassy house and put
all records on board the frigate *La Diane*, together with trunks of
clothing, books, gifts, and furniture. Everything was ready for his successor to take charge. Although the entire embassy staff was anxious to
return to England, Elgin was more impatient than any of them. He
had accomplished the objectives of his mission, and now he was faced
with the difficult task of putting his huge collection of marbles in order. After this, he planned to promote his political career.

Returning from the seraglio, he went from room to room, making
certain that nothing was left behind, and just before it was time to
leave, he dispatched a hurried message to Lusieri in Athens: "If I had
still three years and all the resources needed, I would employ them all
at Athens. The slightest object from the Acropolis is a jewel!"[10]

The carriage ride to the docks was a happy one. The tile rooftops
of Constantinople fused brilliantly against the clear winter sun, and the
populace, aware of Elgin's departure, overflowed the street along both
sides of the carriage and shouted, "Elkin! Elkin!" Even the most phleg-
matic Turks waved and bowed, while their women nodded through
veiled eyes.

There was a final reception on board *La Diane*. Gifts were exchanged with the sultan, music was played, guns were sounded. Moving out of the busy harbor at last, *La Diane* was escorted by Selim III,
while on both sides of the shore, crowds cheered and waved miniature
English flags. Elgin seemed pleased, yet it irritated him to know that
the Turks had waited until he was leaving their country before according him proper respect.

An English brig sailed alongside *La Diane* as a precaution against
pirates, and behind them trailed a Ragusan vessel, carrying the several
hundred Maltese slaves back to their island home. *La Diane* was a large
enough ship to carry the full embassy, including Dr. Scott; Masterman;
the courier Duff; the Reverend Hunt; Elgin's two secretaries, Hamilton and Stratton; and the stout Greek *paramana*, Calitza, who had
emotionally announced that she was to dedicate the rest of her life to
the care of the Elgin children.

After a slow passage through the Dardanelles, they dropped anchor off the isle of Tenedos, and though the sea was calm, Lady Elgin insisted they spend the night on shore. A fire was lit and Duff pitched a tent. They awoke early the next morning amidst a fierce storm and had to fight their way through the churning waves to get back to the ship. Lady Elgin went below and huddled the children into their beds, then decided to go on deck with Masterman and the jug of vinegar.

The storm persisted for four days. However, Captain Maling's seamanship brought them successfully into the bay of Mantria, where the entire party went ashore. Hunt was sent to procure horses and asses from a neighboring village, and after giving it much thought, Elgin decided that Captain Maling should continue to Piraeus without them. Everyone on board, with the exception of the captain, had been severely stricken by the sea throughout the storm, and Elgin reasoned that it would be best if they proceeded the rest of the way by land. Athens was not too distant from Mantria and could be reached within two days.

Just before noon, they all mounted their beasts and set off. At first, the Greek *paramana* preferred to walk, but after battling the invincible hills for an hour, she gave in and was assigned to the sturdiest ass. In time, they arrived at a small village, where much bickering and bargaining ensued before Elgin could secure appropriate lodging in a *han*, a humble shepherd's hut of mud and thatched roof. A small fireplace hugged the wall near the door, and while Masterman attended to the beds, Hunt arranged for food to be brought in. They supped, then fell into their beds exhausted. "Almost immediately we were assailed by fleas and the children had to be danced out of their beds every two minutes. But to no avail. The enemy greatly outnumbered us."[11]

In the morning, after a breakfast of goat's milk and cheese, they resumed their journey. Duff contrived a way to carry the children by slinging a large straw basket on each ass and then strapping the conveyance securely around its middle. Both Bruce and Mary were so delighted with this that they, too, had to be strapped down for fear of falling out of the basket. As for little Matilda, she snuggled warmly in the *paramana*'s embrace and fell asleep. Before departing, they were told by the owner of the *han* that Athens was nine hours distant.

At noon, they came upon a sparkling white village perched high on one side of a mountain. At first the inhabitants glared at them with great suspicion, but they soon proved to be remarkably hospitable and offered whatever food they had. They were particularly taken by the children, addressing Bruce as the "Blond Angel" and insisting that Mary and Matilda, with their raven hair and brown eyes, were Greek waifs whom the Elgins had adopted.

The party took a brief nap, then resumed its trek, skirting the towering mountain and trudging wearily across a bleak valley of limestone and sand. The place was utterly devoid of life. At dusk, a heavy rain began to fall. The children were hastily bundled up and told to remain quiet until Duff pitched the tent. But it turned out to be only a squall, and when the rain stopped, Elgin commanded everyone to move on.

Athens

I T WAS SOLIDLY DARK when they entered Athens. Consul Logothetis was overjoyed to see them, and despite the late hour, he
ordered his servants to bring in food and wine. As soon as the
children finished eating, all three were carried by the giant Calmuck to
their bedchambers on the second floor. Elgin meanwhile, after pep-
pering Lusieri with incessant questions concerning the artists' activities in Athens, learned that all remaining cases of the Parthenon
marbles were now on their way to England, thanks to the voluntary assistance of Captain J. S. Clarke of HMS *Braakel*. Not long after the
Mentor had sunk, Captain Clarke was called upon by both Hamilton
and Lusieri for his help in transporting additional cases of marble out
of Piraeus, which he gave willingly. The marbles were loaded into his
ship with great care, "but as the *Braakel* churned out of the Piraeus
harbor, she ran aground and was in danger of sinking for lack of hands
to unload her and pull her free."[1]

Hunt was in Athens at this time, and in the early hours of the next
morning, he paid a hurried visit to the voivode and asked him to send
one hundred men to Piraeus at once. At first, the voivode was re-
luctant, but Hunt's persistence won out. It turned out to be a day of
wild excitement, during which almost everyone in Athens flocked to
Piraeus "to watch the spectacle, and fortunately, the *Braakel* was
saved."[2]

Hearing of this near disaster, Elgin gave vent to his anger and
asked Hunt: "How was the weather?" The chaplain replied: "My Lord,
a Naval person can hardly believe that the *Braakel* ran smack on a bold-
ish shore with a wind off the land, in a clear night and fine weather. Indeed, it was attributed to a terrible obstinacy on the part of the Master,
who had the Midnight watch when it happened."[3]

Nevertheless, without Captain Clarke's* help, Elgin's prized possessions would never have left Piraeus. The operation lasted five full weeks, and no fewer than forty-four cases of the Parthenon marbles were embarked, by far the largest and most important shipment to date. Many others were to follow, since Lusieri apprised Elgin of his additional acquisitions. He had unearthed an area not far from the Parthenon and found colossal sections of that same pediment that was thrown down by the Morosini explosion of 1687. Among these were the torso of Zeus, the Nike, the Hermes, and numerous others. Lusieri also began excavations on the southern side of the Acropolis Hill, uncovering a thesaurus of fallen metopes and parts of a long frieze, but the marble was so heavy and cumbersome, he had to send out for saws to cut off the sections on which the sculptures were carved, and only thus were they able to transport them to the Piraeus docks.

Elgin was horrified to hear that the marbles still lay on the docks in plain sight of Bonaparte's agents, but Lusieri assured him they were well guarded day and night. At this point, Logothetis rose to his feet, glass of brandy in hand, and announced they were all invited to the wedding of his daughter on the coming Sunday. Elgin submitted his regrets, reminding Logothetis that Captain Maling and *La Diane* awaited them at the Piraeus docks, but Madame Logothetis entreated them, declaring it would be a great honor if the Elgins attended. When Elgin finally agreed, more toasts were offered, and waiting until all the others had retired to their bedchambers, Elgin informed Lusieri that he was to remain under his employ until further notice. Since the other artists had no other commitments in Athens, Elgin also instructed Lusieri to give releases to all of them and inform them that they were now free to return to their countries.

Lady Elgin enjoyed a sound sleep that night, her first in nearly a fortnight. The next morning Elgin did not take breakfast, leaving immediately with Lusieri to inspect the cases of marbles on the Piraeus

---

*Captain J. C. Clarke was the brother of Elgin's adversary, Edward Daniel Clarke, which is the crowning point of this bizarre affair.

docks. Madame Logothetis invited Lady Elgin to join her daughter
and herself on a visit to the seamstress, but she graciously declined,
complaining of fatigue. Throughout the rest of the morning she read
to Bruce from Aesop's fables, while the *paramana* looked after Mary
and Matilda.

After the noon meal she took a brief nap, then put on a white linen
dress and black lace hat. Before stepping outside, she left orders with
Masterman and the *paramana* to feed the children promptly at five o'-
clock. In the dusty street, Greek and Turkish faces flitted past her.
Noisy children played in messy and torn clothes, while beggars squat-
ted everywhere with their upturned hands. But her eyes were riveted
on the Acropolis. Suddenly a wave of sadness overwhelmed her. She
couldn't explain it. Her whole body began trembling; tears invaded her
eyes. The feeling continued even after the sun began to drop behind
the massive shoulders of Mount Lycabettus.

It was almost dusk when she turned to leave. On her right hand
the sun had already sunk behind Eleusis, leaving its purple wake on the
gravestones of Kerameikos. At the base of the Propylaea steps, she
stopped, and for one haunting moment, looked up once again toward
the wounded Parthenon before hurrying toward the consul's house.

On the morning of the wedding, Elgin attired himself in full uniform,
and Lady Elgin attended the bride inside the tiny Byzantine Church of
Saint George on the summit of Mount Lycabettus. The ceremony was
unbearably long, and the guests almost suffocated under the dense
clouds of incense. At the reception at the consul's house, the Elgins
seated themselves in one corner of the spacious parlor as guests and
dignitaries greeted the wedding party. For some strange reason, the
Reverend Hunt chose this occasion to tell Elgin about a letter he had
just received from one Ioannes Benizelos, who was master of a school
at Athens maintained by wealthy Venetians.

I am sure if you saw Athens today, you would be very unhappy. One
thing especially would make you sad, as it does all those who have some
understanding of these things: the last deplorable stripping of the
Temple of Athena on the Acropolis and of the other relics of antiquity!

The Temple is now like a noble and wealthy lady who was ravaged and has lost all her diamonds and jewelry. Oh, how we Athenians must take this event to heart, and how we must praise and admire those ancient heroes of Rome (Pompey and Hadrian) when we look on these things![4]

This was the first Greek objection to Lord Elgin's pillage. A short time later, Lord Byron's friend and companion John Cam Hobhouse would add his voice.

I have said nothing of the possibility of the ruins of Athens being (in the event of a revolution in favour of the Greeks) restored and put into a condition capable of resisting the ravages of decay; for an event of that nature cannot, it strikes me, have ever entered into the head of anyone who has seen Athens, and the modern Athenians. Yet I cannot forbear mentioning a singular speech of a learned Greek from Ioannina, who said to me: "You English are carrying off the works of the Greeks, our forefathers. Preserve them well, because we will someday come and redeem them!"[5]

Hunt's reference to the letter from Benizelos did not disturb Elgin, particularly since he had always felt that the modern Greeks bore no resemblance to their ancient heroes. "In fact, they have nothing whatsoever in common with them, and for centuries permitted the Turks to enslave them. Far worse, these same modern Greeks have looked upon the superb works of Pheidias with ingratitude and indifference. They do not deserve them!"[6]

These expressions of indignation had marked effects on Lusieri, who was seen shivering one day at his post on the Acropolis Hill, but not because of ill health. "As he (Lusieri) observed to us, he is lately thus attacked whenever an English or a French frigate anchors in the Piraeus. The young midshipmen are then set loose upon the venerable monuments of Athens, and are seldom deterred from indulging in the most wanton devastation of statues, cornices and capitals, from which they carry off mementoes of their Athenian travels."[7]

Protests of this nature became more frequent by the day, yet no one lifted a hand to stop the pillage. As the English traveler Peter Edmund Laurent remarked, "The last time I visited the citadel, I was much displeased at seeing an English officer of the Navy standing upon the base of one of the Caryatids, clinging with his left arm round the column, while his right hand, provided with a hard and heavy stone, was endeavouring to knock off the only remaining nose of those six beautifully sculptured statues. I exerted my eloquence in vain to preserve this monument of art."[8]

H. W. Williams, still another eyewitness, observed that "when Elgin's agents removed the Caryatid from the Erechtheum, Athena wept over her lost virginity. But there were louder lamentations from the remaining Caryatids as they looked upon their ravished sister. And later, as Elgin's labourers were hauling the last of the marbles to the Piraeus, they had to stop suddenly and drop them to the ground; nor could they be prevailed upon to carry them further, protesting that they could hear the doleful moans of Athena deep within each vein of marble!"[9]

Elgin, of course, regarded all this as foolish talk, the superstitious babble of weak and deluded minds.

La Diane called at Cerigo Isle six days later. Elgin and Hunt went ashore to inspect the remains of the Mentor, while Lady Elgin and the children watched from the deck of the frigate. When at last they returned, Elgin reported there was no hope of ever raising the Mentor, the winter storms having dashed the vessel to pieces. For the rest of that day, he remained by himself, steeped in melancholy. That evening at dinner, he began to rant about the enormous weight of his expenses: the salvage operations had cost him over six thousand pounds, not to mention the loss of the Mentor itself.

A powerful wind grasped hold of La Diane's sails and sent them to Candia (Crete) sooner than expected. Anchoring off the harbor of Canea, they went ashore in the captain's barge and found the climate unusually mild for mid-February. As they walked along the sandy beach, they encountered a sizable colony of lepers, many of whom sat near the shore, staring out to sea. No one dared go near them except Elgin. He was sternly chided by his wife, and they walked onward for another kilometer before pitching the tents. Several of the crewmen went inland to gather some wood, and soon a good fire was lit.

Masterman attended to the cooking: a soup of black-eyed beans, chunks of goat cheese, some olives, and dark bread. After this, the children were quickly bundled up and put into makeshift beds on the sand.

In the morning, they were awakened by harsh voices and scuffling feet. Several hundred men, attired in long pantaloons and wearing black leather bands round their foreheads, had encircled the two tents. Their obese middle-aged leader stepped slowly forward and introduced himself as Nouri Bey, governor of Crete. Then glancing at Elgin, he drew back in horror. Dr. Scott quickly assured him there was no cause for alarm and that Elgin's features had not been scarred by leprosy. Nouri Bey, however, was unconvinced, as were his men, and throughout the strained reception the Cretans kept a safe distance from Elgin.

His discomfort still evident, Nouri Bey then called for chairs, and the party was transported to the governor's palace, a large mansion of white stone, guarded in front by seven Doric columns that Nouri Bey proudly boasted had once belonged to the Temple of Aphrodite at Canea. At this moment, as Lady Elgin wrote to her mother, Nouri Bey's harem made its appearance.

> They were carried across the courtyard in covered boxes, two of which were slung across a mule—like Gypsy panniers. Over their heads were curtains of scarlet cloth to protect them from the eyes of the throng that had already converged around the palace. The women of the harem seemed amused by my manners and dress. One of them came forward and presented me with a gift of rose water, while the others brazenly touched my hair, my jewels, my arms. Throughout the long inspection Masterman stood at my side in nervous despair.[10]

They returned to *La Diane* early the next morning and sailed under the lee of Crete on a straight course toward Malta, arriving there on February 23, 1803. "Because of the raging plague, the authorities on the island ordered them to perform twenty days quarantine."[11] They were permitted, however, to land and stay at Boghi Palace, which was once Malta's finest building until it was damaged severely by French cannons. After being informed that a large segment of the British fleet lay at anchor in Malta, Elgin went immediately to Pratique House with Captain Maling for a talk with the commanders, during which he managed to have the quarantine lifted. Elegant quarters were subsequently provided for the whole party in a large villa owned by a wealthy Italian shipowner.

They remained on Malta two days, long enough to see the Maltese slaves safely home. Elgin was accorded the island's highest honor in a long ceremony on the deck of *La Diane*, but whereas in Constantinople he had been deeply moved by the respect and gratitude of the slaves, he now seemed impatient with the whole business and was anxious to take leave of the place.

At sea, Lady Elgin was determined that her husband's conduct would not intrude upon her own state of bliss, and to combat any negative feelings, she immersed herself in her books. *La Diane* was out of Malta three full days before she realized that the sea had not affected her; but now the very recollection of this thought ignited the problem, even though she tried desperately to put her mind elsewhere: on Lusieri's comical appearance on the Acropolis Hill, the breathtaking view of the Bosporus, the last shipment of marbles safely aboard the British frigate that Lord Nelson had reluctantly dispatched to Piraeus just before they had departed from Athens.

That evening, Elgin made his appearance at the captain's table, but he partook more of the wine than the meal. Hunt began narrating some of his experiences in Epirus, but Elgin was not listening. He refused tea and pastries, and without bothering to excuse himself, got up from the table and retired to his cabin. Lady Elgin remained with Hunt for a brief period, then decided to walk on deck. The wind was bitter cold, and although the sea churned mightily under her feet, she felt no discomfort, other than a resurging heartache for Scotland.

They did not put into Sicily, but instead continued on a direct course for Naples, docking there three days later. The Italian authorities had been holding a packet of letters for Elgin. One was from Lusieri with the news of still more excavations at Delphi and another large bounty of acquisitions; a second letter came from his mother, the dowager countess of Elgin:

Please be advised that the *Braakel* docked recently at Portsmouth and unloaded fifty cases of marbles, which I arranged to have stored (along with the previous shipments) at the house of the Duchess of Portland in Westminster. After a fortnight, she became irritated because they were cluttering her grounds and she begged me to move them elsewhere. Fortunately the Duke of Richmond transported them to his estate, but soon he too shewed his vexation about having so many cases totalling one hundred and twenty tons of marble scattered about his grounds, and thus I was obliged to rent a large house at the corner of Piccadilly and Park Lane which has a spacious garden.

In rapid time, a sizeable shed was built, and after the workmen unpacked all the marbles, we arranged them in the best manner possible, considering their gigantic weight. It was impossible to lay out the collection in a systematic way. This shall have to await your arrival. Therefore, I report to you that the sculptures, inscriptions, metopes, friezes and architectural fragments are now housed inside this shed. In the center stands the Caryatid, the other figures having been placed around her according to size and shape. The torso of Hermes is perched atop an inscribed column and is splendidly balanced at the other side of the room by the horse's head from the East pediment of the Parthenon.

There are additional cases of marbles at the docks. Shipments keep arriving at steady intervals and I have employed agents to be at the London Customs House to look after each piece. As you well know, many of these antiquities have battered noses, broken arms and legs, missing heads. We have a man here whose name is John Flaxman and is called 'The English Pheidias.' Although he says the restored parts would be inferior to the original, which might bring about a constant source of dispute, nevertheless he is of the opinion that the restoration should be done, since it would increase the financial worth of the collection. He estimates the cost to be in the vicinity of twenty thousand pounds.[12]

Sending Hunt to summon a carriage, Elgin angrily sat down and wrote a quick reply to his mother, warning her not to spend another farthing on the marbles. "Twenty thousand pounds for an English Pheidias!"

It was decided by Dr. Scott that the children should not leave the ship. Naples was an unclean city, and there was mounting concern over the plague, which had already seized most of the surrounding towns. Scott consequently suggested that the Elgins continue overland through Italy and into France, leaving the children on board *La Diane* under the care of the Greek *paramana*. With the ship's arrival in England, the children would be entrusted to Elgin's mother.

It was a bitter decision for Lady Elgin to accept, but she had to agree that Scott was right. There were tearful embraces and sad farewells, after which instructions were given to both Hamilton and Stratton concerning the many cases of marbles that still awaited clearance and duty payments at the London customhouse.

As *La Diane* pulled slowly out of Naples harbor, Lady Elgin was again on the verge of tears until her husband reassured her that they had decided wisely, especially since war could break out again. Elgin had learned from the Italian authorities at Naples that Comte Sébastiani had been sent to the Levant by Bonaparte, which made it clear that if war did break out again, Bonaparte would surely invade Egypt.

The Elgins had acquainted themselves with Sébastiani during their stay in Constantinople. Lady Elgin had been particularly impressed. "There is a smart French Beau just arrived from Paris to sign a Treaty of Peace with the Turks. He arrived two days too late. He has called upon us and was excessively civil; there is another young man come with him; they are both equipped parfaitment a la mode and are both handsome. I wish you could see the fuss everybody makes of them."[13]

Since Bonaparte had recently made the brash claim "that only six thousand men would be needed to reconquer Egypt,"[14] Sébastiani's presence in the Levant was looked upon with much apprehension and suspicion by the British government. As marshall of France, Sébastiani's mission certainly implied the intention to inquire into the current state of the Egyptian and Turkish armies.

During the long carriage ride to Rome, Elgin seemed relieved to be free of the children, and he talked enthusiastically about visiting the many galleries there and in Florence. Hunt and Masterman accompanied them on this overland journey. In Rome, Hunt immediately wanted to go on a tour of the city, but Lady Elgin complained of fatigue and insisted they first find suitable lodgings. Within a few hours, they located a house not far from the Colosseum, and the wife of the owner cooked them a meat dish thick with tomato sauce. Even after they had dined, Hunt persisted with his desire to tour the city, but Elgin stiffly decided against it.

Hunt was disappointed again the following morning. Reasoning that Florence was at least a three-day journey, Elgin suggested they leave Rome at once. After breakfast, he arranged for the hire of a post chaise drawn by two horses, and they set off. Meanwhile Hunt, sullen over their hasty departure from Rome, requested that they should at least follow a course along the street of Saint Gregory and thus perhaps catch a few glimpses of "the ancient sites near the Palatine Hill."[15] Elgin, however, thought this unwise and instructed the driver to head northward, along via del Corso.

The tight confinement of the post chaise had an oppressing effect on Lady Elgin, and the road beyond Rome was rough and gutted with holes. Nevertheless, they made good time and by midafternoon arrived at Spoleto-on-the-Tiber, where they ate and rested. Elgin had miscalculated the distance to Florence, and he now was convinced that if they continued at a rapid pace, they might reach the city in only two days. Hunt disagreed.

A new team of horses was hitched to the post chaise, and they moved on, reaching Perugia shortly before dusk. With the help of the village priest, Hunt found lodgings in a small inn, but there were only two available rooms. Masterman and Hunt were given separate bedding on the floor, which Masterman regarded as highly improper, and, as a result, Elgin had to persuade the innkeeper to place a small partition between the beddings.

The next morning, Lady Elgin felt tired, but she braced herself and managed to eat most of her breakfast. Fortunately, the road out of Perugia was well paved, and they passed swiftly through many little towns following the Tiber all the way into Arezzo. After another exchange of horses, they set off once more. Lady Elgin's malaise was worse, but she was determined not to complain. By this time, Hunt had overcome the depression that had preyed upon him since leaving Rome and, with an animated voice, embarked on a long narration of his tour of Greece, particularly Mycenae, Olympia, and the Morea. At this point, Masterman surprised everyone by singing softly:

A highland lad my love was born,
The Lawland laws he held in scorn;

But he still was faithful to his clan.
My gallant braw, John Highlandman.

She was joined in the chorus by all the others, even Elgin:

Sing, hey my braw, John Highlandman!
Sing, ho my braw, John Highlandman!
There's not a lad in a' the lan'
Was match for my John Highlandman![16]

It had just stopped raining as they entered Florence. Behind the low, fast-moving clouds, streaking patterns of gray and white clashed against the streets and buildings of the city. They had no difficulty finding lodgings, and immediately after dinner Hunt again showed his eagerness to launch out on a tour, but once more Elgin dampened his hopes, advising that it would be best to wait until morning.

Hunt was first to arise. Everyone dressed warmly because the air was raw. The streets were already swarming with people; church bells pealed; priests and nuns swept past them. At the Duomo, the ancient Cathedral of Santa Maria del Fiore, which was also the largest and most important church in Florence, matins had just ended, and a throng of worshipers was pouring down the front steps. They waited for the church to clear, then walked inside and examined each work of art on the walls, the windows, and the altar.

Although construction of Santa Maria del Fiore had begun in the late thirteenth century, its marble facade was still unfinished. Wars, internal bickering, strife, floods, and earthquakes had delayed its completion. Alongside it stood the magnificent bell tower of Giotto. Elgin was much impressed by its numerous bas-reliefs, and even climbed its many steps to the terrace, from which there was a commanding view of Florence.

Across the cobblestone street loomed the Baptistery. Lady Elgin admired the scenes depicted on the Ghiberti panels that recalled ten events of the Old Testament: from the creation of Adam and Eve to the reception of King Solomon by the queen of Sheba.

They walked directly to the Uffizi Gallery, and went first to the paintings of Raphael. From there, they examined the works of Andrea del Sarto, Perugino, Ghirlandaio, and Botticelli. Each painting was arranged in strict chronological order. Elgin's favorite was Michelangelo's *Holy Family,* while Lady Elgin preferred a canvas of Botticelli's: *The Adoration of the Magi,* in which were depicted lifelike portraits of important members of the Medici family.

They dined in a small inn just off the Piazza San Firenze, then spent the rest of the afternoon at the Pitti Palace, the residence of the duke of Florence.

It was dark when they returned to their lodgings. Masterman had a hot meal waiting, and shortly before the hour of sleep, the maid prepared a hot bath for Lady Elgin.

Part 2

Paris

THEY TRAVELED FROM Leghorn to Marseilles by ship. It was a calm crossing, and the French coast in the bright afternoon enchanted Lady Elgin. From Marseilles, they continued by barge up the Rhone and into Lyons, where Elgin arranged for the hire of a carriage. The following day they set off for Paris, but they were on the road less than two hours, when they were apprehended by a detachment of soldiers under the command of a stern young lieutenant. Elgin was totally unaware that war between France and England had broken out once again, or that First Consul Bonaparte had issued the following decree:

> All English enrolled in the Militia from the age of eighteen to sixty, and holding a commission from his Britannic Majesty, who are at present in France, shall be made Prisoners of War, to answer for the Citizens of the Republic who have been arrested by the vessels or subjects of his Britannic Majesty before the declaration of war. The Ministers, each as far as concerns him, are charged with the execution of the present decree.*[1]

In their zeal to carry out Bonaparte's instructions, the ministers reasoned that all British male subjects had an obligation to serve their

---

*The decree produced a good bag of prisoners, although not as many as had been hoped. After ten years of war, the English upper and middle classes could hardly wait to make a trip to the Continent. In the few months of peace, it is estimated that no less than two-thirds of the then House of Lords visited Paris, including five dukes, three marquises, and thirty-seven earls. No wonder the French called the visitors milords. The decree netted about five hundred, of whom about half were aristocracy and gentry, and the remainder professional men and merchants. Nearly all these *détenus* were rich, and quite apart from their value as hostages, they contributed significantly to France's invisible exports. (William St. Clair, *Lord Elgin and the Marbles*, p. 123.)

country and theoretically might become officers. Thus they felt that every male British subject should be considered a prisoner of war. Consequently, Elgin and his party were to be detained at the Hotel de Richelieu in Paris until further notice. Lady Elgin was heartbroken.

> We intended remaining a week or ten days at most in Paris. I must have made some sad mistakes in writing you if you did not understand that. We were most positively assured by all the French Generals and Commanders and Ministers between Leghorn and here, that even should war be declared, we might go through France in the utmost security. We only learned that war was declared when it was too late to turn back. How could one imagine that an ambassador would be detained this way. Never since the world began was such a thing done before. The night we arrived here, Elgin — finding Lord Whitworth [the British ambassador in Paris] gone — immediately wrote to M. de Talleyrand to ask whether he had better set off for London instantaneously or whether we might remain a few days to rest after our long journey. M. de Talleyrand's answer was that we might remain as long as we pleased and that we should have our passports whenever we pleased. The very next day, Elgin was declared a prisoner of war on parole. Who could expect this?[2]

Charles Maurice de Talleyrand-Perigord (1754–1838) was foreign minister under Napoleon from the first days of the Revolution. Before accepting the post, Talleyrand weighed the matter very carefully, because he had to be certain about the aims and ideals of the French Republic. His greatness was attributed to his parents, both of whom were descended from the most noble and powerful families of France. They were in constant attendance at the court of Louis XV and, as was the case with most aristocrats, neglected their son by entrusting him to the care of a nurse in Paris. At the age of four, Talleyrand fell from a high chair and so injured his foot it crippled him for life. In his adolescent years, he was sent to a seminary to prepare for the priesthood.

As a subdeacon, Talleyrand witnessed the coronation of Louis XVI at Rheims. He was ordained a priest four years later, and while in Paris, found every opportunity "to mix in the circle of philosophers who frequented the salon of Madame de Genlis."[3] At this time, the first rumblings of the Revolution were being heard throughout France.

Elgin was shocked to hear that "almost overnight, the Treaty of Amiens had been tossed to the wind, and Bonaparte now demanded that England abandon not only Malta, but Egypt and Gibraltar as well."[4]

Incensed over his detainment, Elgin emphasized to the guards that he was a diplomat and not a soldier. Moreover, it was a firm conviction of all wars that only soldiers participate, and even during the eighteenth-century wars, the Dover-to-Calais packet continued to run uninterrupted, its gentlemen on the Grand Tour suffering only minor inconveniences. But his objections fell on deaf ears.

Their carriage was escorted into Paris by four soldiers on horseback. Through its open windows, Lady Elgin fastened her eyes on them. They did not look like soldiers: faces unshaved, layers of mud caked over their boots and breeches, uncouth peasants. The whole episode seemed unreal to her, and when at last they entered into the capital, she saw scores of men — young and old—crowded along both sides of the boulevard, staring at the horsemen and carriage. The few French women on the streets appeared to be unconcerned by the passing carriage. Parasols in hand, they continued their stroll, heads erect, long dresses flowing in the wind.

The Hotel de Richelieu was a red granite structure, with flower boxes running along its entire front. Two tall cypresses guarded a colossal metal door, while directly above their heads, an iron balcony jutted over the street. A uniformed attendant came to escort them inside, but he was gruffly pushed away by one of the soldiers. Meanwhile, his companions removed the baggage from the carriage and carried it inside.

The lobby of the hotel had thick red carpeting that continued up a circular staircase. The Elgins followed the soldiers to the top of the stairs, turned sharply to the right, then walked down a dimly lit corridor until they reached the last door. Before entering, they were issued a stern warning: "They were free to move about in the hotel and also in the gardens, but, upon arising each morning and before retiring at night, they had to register their names with the soldier posted outside their door. Under no condition were they permitted to leave the hotel without written authority."[5]

Everyone was crestfallen when the soldier finally closed the door. Hunt feebly tried to assure them that their detainment would be of a short duration, but no one believed him.

While Masterman began rearranging some of the old furniture and complaining about the dust everywhere, Elgin sat at the mahogany desk near the window and wrote an angry letter to Talleyrand, objecting to the arrest and demanding their immediate release. He handed the letter to the soldier outside the door, then went to his bedchamber to take a nap. Seizing this opportunity, Masterman quietly confided to Lady Elgin that she was most anxious to return to Scotland because her father had given assent to her marriage in a promise that could not be broken. Lady Elgin assured her that when the time was right, the matter would be given proper attention.

After dinner, Hunt reported to the guard in the corridor and requested permission to take a short walk through the gardens of the hotel. He came back moments later to say that the place was crawling with English *détenus*. Elgin, who now looked more refreshed after his nap, made no comment, but Lady Elgin was quick to express a sincere desire that "surely there must be at least one good whist player in the lot!"[6]

Early the next morning they all registered their names with the soldier on guard and walked into the gardens. It was a mild day in May: birds frolicked in the magnolia trees, the scent of jasmine filled the air. They were soon joined by several other *détenus*: an aged widow named Mrs. Fitzgerald, Mr. and Mrs. Cockburn, Colonel Joseph Craufurd, and Mr. Richard Sterling — all British to the core. The Cockburns were a devoted couple and held hands throughout the conversation. Mrs. Fitzgerald was pleasant and quite sociable. Colonel Craufurd walked with a pronounced limp and vehemently castigated Lord Whitworth for deserting the embassy on the very day war was declared. Sterling was a thin middle-aged man, quiet and of delicate nature.

Before leaving the gardens, Mrs. Cockburn extended an invitation to all for dinner at her suite that evening, adding that she had also invited a young scientist named Robert Fergusson, a Scot and a bachelor. With a glint in his eyes, Colonel Craufurd boasted to Lady Elgin that he himself never had experienced the need for a wife, and went on to say in a jocular voice that "in every relationship between a man and woman only one point should be borne in mind: the brief encounter. To expect or demand more than this was absurd, since a woman's virtue lay neither in beauty nor charm, but in novelty."[7]

His remarks mortified Mrs. Cockburn, but Lady Elgin found them quite amusing. Waiting until the old colonel had hobbled up the stairs, Mrs. Cockburn felt obliged to explain that he was approaching senility. Elgin, however, doubted this and inquired as to the cause of his limp, upon which Mrs. Cockburn tartly replied that Colonel Craufurd claimed it was from an old wound, but those close to him suspected he had the gout.

As Elgin and Hunt dressed for dinner, Lady Elgin told Masterman to step into the corridor and ask the guard for her imperial, the large valise. The soldier brought it in himself and stood alongside as Lady Elgin opened it. She deliberated a moment before deciding to wear her pink lace gown. She looked for the matching pearls but couldn't find them nor the rest of her jewelry. Everything of value was missing!

After registering their names with the guard, they went directly to Mrs. Cockburn's suite. With the exception of Colonel Craufurd, who sat in a white wicker chair, the other guests had formed a semicircle in front of the wide bay window and were sipping sherry from their glasses. A young maid from the hotel was serving. In the center of the parlor a long table was laid out, and the place settings were meticulously arranged. Just as dinner was about to be served, a tall young man with a thick crop of blond hair and mustache was received at the door by Mrs. Cockburn. A black cloak was recklessly thrown over his broad shoulders. He conversed for a moment with Mrs. Cockburn before being introduced to the Elgins. Surprisingly, Elgin remembered him as a young lad, and Fergusson responded by recalling frequent visits to Broomhall with his family.

Elgin inquired about the elder Fergusson's health, and Robert

Fergusson smilingly replied that for a man of seventy his father was in excellent physical condition and daily supervised the workers on his estate at Raith.

Fergusson himself was twenty-six, but even at that young age as a geologist he had already made notable contributions to science and was a fellow of the Royal Society. France was to be the last stop of an extended tour through the Continent, upon which he had embarked almost a year before his detainment. While tea was being served, Fergusson talked at length with Elgin about Bonaparte, and at the height of the conversation, the young bachelor looked up and noticed that Lady Elgin was staring at him.

Talleyrand's reply to Elgin's letter came in three days. "The Foreign Minister regrets the inconvenience of your detainment in Paris, but since the order has been issued directly by Bonaparte, there is little that I can do, except offer my sincere hope that your detention will be of short duration."[8]

Elgin was despondent and refused to take his morning stroll through the gardens with the others. For almost two weeks he ate very sparingly and shunned conversation, even with his wife. One afternoon, shortly after Lady Elgin had taken her nap, she came down into the gardens and learned from Colonel Craufurd that Count Sébastiani was in Paris. Confident that, as the new marshall of the French army, Sébastiani would certainly be influential with Bonaparte, Lady Elgin quickly extended a written invitation to him, and on July 12, 1803, Sébastiani made his appearance at the Hotel de Richelieu. Prior to his arrival, Masterman tidied up the suite, placing fresh flowers in clean vases, and then prepared a dessert.

His hopes newly revived, Elgin sat at the desk "and wrote a lengthy dispatch to Lusieri in Athens, alerting him to keep a constant watch on the large collection of Parthenon marbles that still lay on the Piraeus docks at the full mercy of the French."[*9]

---

*At this point, Elgin's credit was considered too risky by most European bankers. His only hope lay in Malta, where he hoped to borrow the necessary money for this latest shipment.

Sébastiani was escorted to their suite precisely at noon. To Lady Elgin, he appeared to be even more handsome than at the time of their first meeting in Constantinople. He was attired in a red and blue uniform weighted down with medals and decorations. From the outset, he was genuinely pleased to see them and tried to make jest of their plight by saying he couldn't understand "why Elgin was turning the world upside down to get out of such a beautiful country as France. After all, they had been accorded the deepest courtesy."[10]

Elgin did not find this amusing and again demanded their immediate release. Sébastiani smilingly reminded him that their countries were at war and that England had detained hundreds of French civilians. Until they were released, all British subjects in France had to be detained as well. But aside from this, Sébastiani stressed that Bonaparte's animosity toward Elgin could never be appeased because Elgin had successfully stolen the Parthenon marbles that Bonaparte had wanted for the Louvre.

It was an easy matter for Lady Elgin to overwhelm Count Sébastiani with praise and flattery, and like a true French gentleman, he proved receptive. Putting on his hat and gloves, he kissed her hand, then promised he would call upon Bonaparte and discuss with him the possibility of their release. But despite his repeated assurances, Elgin nourished a strong suspicion that Sébastiani was not to be trusted.

Several days later Sébastiani paid another visit to them, but with the sad news that Bonaparte had refused to consider their release at this time. Furthermore, "a decree was about to be issued for the expulsion of all English *détenus* from Paris, after which they were to be transferred elsewhere in the country and put to work on farms."[11]

Through Sébastiani's persuasion, Bonaparte took heed of Elgin's health and agreed to assign them to Barèges, a summer resort high in the Pyrénées, whose hot baths were a mecca for tourists.

Barèges

ISCONSOLATE ABOUT THEIR PLIGHT, Lady Elgin once again sought refuge in a long letter to her mother:

> Barèges is the most dreary place I ever saw; immense high hills without a tree. There is a ride which one can call practicable, and it continues going down a hill for an hour and a half. There are many beautiful spots at an hour or two's distance from this, but Barèges itself is most miserable. However I firmly believe it has saved Elgin's life. He feels better every day; gets up at six or seven o'clock in the morning, and goes out a shooting for four or five hours with the Duke of Newcastle who is also detained here, then about one o'clock he goes out riding with me. He has now begun to take baths twice a day — when he returns from shooting, and at eleven o'clock at night. He remains almost an hour each time.[1]

The baths at Barèges held no interest for Lady Elgin because they were frequented primarily by gossipy ladies who had nothing better to do than pry into other people's lives, whereas she preferred to devote her time to her primary pleasure, the companionship of her books. As for her evenings, they "were spent at dinner parties, concerts and whist. Social life at the spa was different from that at home or at Constantinople."[2]

Toward the end of August 1803, one of the foremost collectors of antiquities in Europe came to visit the Elgins. Lady Elgin wrote to her mother:

> Le Comte de Choiseul-Gouffier is here. He is very pleasant. Poor man, he had been most unfortunate. After having lost almost all he possessed, he had just enough money to maintain a Villa near Paris and set his heart upon placing the marbles etc. that he had collected at Athens.

However he has just received information that the Frigate, on board which his Antiquities were placed, has been taken by the English. The tears were really in his eyes when he told us. He said, after having lost his fortune and very nearly all the Antiquities he had with so much trouble and expense collected, and having hid these for so many years, he is now completely overcome by their loss.[3]

Because of his allegiance to the king of France, Choiseul-Gouffier had been treated unkindly by Bonaparte, but after Choiseul-Gouffier returned from exile in 1802 Bonaparte forgave his disloyalty and even granted him the small villa near Paris. His entire collection of antiquities, however, was confiscated by Bonaparte and placed in the Louvre. Choiseul-Gouffier was able to withstand these misfortunes, "but the loss of one piece particularly distressed him: a section of marble from the Parthenon frieze that his agent had successfully hauled to the Piraeus docks and brought on board the French frigate *L'Arabe.*"[4] The ship was only one day out of port when war broke out. She was captured and taken as prize by the English warship *Maidstone*, and since it was the law that all enemy property taken be divided equally among the crew, *L'Arabe* and all her contents were sold at auction in Malta, "with the exception of the Parthenon frieze, which was confiscated by Lord Nelson and ordered to be sent to England."[5]

Elgin was surprised to learn that this frieze was "still being held at the London Customs House."[6] He was even more at a loss for words when Choiseul-Gouffier appealed to him for assistance, confident that two gentlemen of noble tradition should have no bitterness toward each other. The Frenchman was willing to pay transportation charges for the return of the frieze, but Elgin assured him this was not necessary and gave his solemn word that he would dispatch an immediate message to Lord Nelson, requesting that the frieze be sent at once to Choiseul-Gouffier's villa in Paris.

The next day's post brought a short letter from Captain Maling: "He had delivered the children in perfect health to the Nisbet family at Archerfield."[7] Nothing else. Not a word about the marbles at Park Lane, nor even Choiseul-Gouffier's frieze, which was now open prey at the London customhouse. Surely if Captain Maling had been alert, he would have spotted it.

For the first time in their marriage, Lady Elgin expressed anger over Elgin's obsession with the marbles and his lack of concern for his children. From the day the Parthenon marbles were taken down and shipped to England, the entire household had not known a moment of peace. Far worse, she now found it difficult to endure the aching loss of her children. In despair, her only relief came from hourly thoughts of Archerfield, of her father's house looming over the firth, and in the soft hush of silence, the voices of Bruce, Mary, and Matilda running toward her and shouting "Mitera*!"[8]

In September Count Sébastiani paid them a visit and reported that Bonaparte had agreed to Masterman's safe passage back to England but that the Elgins and Hunt were to be detained in France as prisoners of war. Sébastiani tried to assuage Elgin's wrath by offering the weak excuse that Bonaparte wanted Elgin to remain in France, because he considered him the unofficial ambassador since Lord Whitworth had abandoned the post. Abruptly, and rather curtly, Sébastiani then spoke about the wave of rumors circulating throughout France and the Continent, accusing Elgin of deliberate ill-treatment of French prisoners in Constantinople. "Ah, c'est ce Milord Elgin qui a si maltraité nos compatriotes à Constantinople!"[9]

One story was most troubling to Elgin. It emphasized that he had caused "a French diplomat named Beauchamp to be put to death, whereas Elgin had successfully intervened with the Porte to relieve the sufferings not only of all the French prisoners confined in the Seven Towers, but in addition had rescued Beauchamp from the hands of Sir Sydney Smith, who wanted him beheaded as a spy. Elgin furthermore gave the French diplomat money and a passage to return to his country."[10]

Another rumor claimed that Elgin had attempted to deceive the French at El Arish, even though he was one of the few to come out of the muddle with honor. Finally, and perhaps most insultingly, a warning was initiated by Bonaparte that no one in France should dare come near Elgin for fear of contamination from syphilis.

---

*The modern Greek word for *mother*.

Two days after Sébastiani's visit, a contingent of French soldiers stormed into their cottage at Barèges and seized Elgin. They commanded him to dress, then took him under heavy guard to the fortress at Lourdes, a few miles to the south. The order for his arrest was issued by Alexandre Berthier, prince of Neuchâtel, vice constable of France, and minister of war. Berthier was also Bonaparte's chief of staff and constant companion, dining with him and traveling in the same carriage. He previously had served with Lafayette in the American Revolutionary War.

When the soldiers took Elgin away, his wife was not present in the cottage. They permitted him, however, to leave her a brief note of explanation:

> I am to go to Lourdes; it is fortunate that we know (and particularly you) the Commandant so well. The officer who is come has been remarkably polite. And now, my Angel, I may speak of my feelings: God knows the wretchedness I have had from this; I dare not think of you. At first, the stupefaction of the blow stunned me. When I think of all you have suffered from Constantinople: my ill health, and this detention, I am unable to bear myself. Our marriage has been a continued scene of suffering to you and I can't make it up. God in Heaven bless my Dearest Angel.[11]

Lady Elgin was shocked by her husband's imprisonment. "Elgin is to be confined at the Castle of Lourdes, the most dreadful place you ever saw. The Castle is situated on a high rock close to the Pyrenean Mountains, and is so remarkably unhealthy and cold, the soldiers at Barèges say how much they pitied the poor English who were to be confined there."[12]

Now that Masterman had been granted permission to leave the country, Lady Elgin felt obligated to escort her maid as far as Paris. This decision had further aims: in Paris, she would seek a personal audience with Talleyrand to plead her husband's case, and she also hoped to call upon several of her acquaintances from the Hotel de Richelieu.

Hunt accompanied her and Masterman on the long journey to Paris. They got as far as Rabastens the first day and after an overnight stop there resumed their trip. Despite the poor roads and a steady down-pour, they made excellent time into Cahors. When they awoke the next morning, the storm clouds had disappeared and the sun was shin-ing brightly. The French countryside was suddenly transformed: houses and trees glistened under the penetrating rays of the sun, birds sang, children frolicked in the green pastures. Toward midafternoon, they pulled into Limoges.

Hunt secured lodgings in that town's only hotel, an ancient struc-ture of two stories, badly maintained and reeking with stale cooking odors. Lady Elgin's bed was so abominably uncomfortable she aban-doned it and reclined instead on a lumpy sofa.

Not a soul was at the desk when they prepared to leave the next morning. Hunt argued that they should not be required to pay for such gross inconvenience, but Lady Elgin restrained him, and Hunt be-grudgingly left twelve francs on the desk.

At this time, Lady Elgin was almost eight months pregnant with her fourth child. Nevertheless her energy was remarkable, and both Hunt and Masterman found it difficult to keep up with her. At midday, they were inside the village of Ambazac, where they stopped for toast and tea. Hunt also arranged for a new team of horses, which brought them into Orléans before nightfall. Lady Elgin implored him to be more sagacious in his choice of sleeping quarters, and he came back an hour later with the cheerful news that he had procured the residence of the mayor, who had been called to Paris on urgent business. The mayor's wife was "an overbearing creature, who eventually calmed her-self after she was offered Masterman's service in the preparation of supper."[13]

The sprightly horses pulled the carriage into Chartres at noon the next day. Hunt located a small café above the left bank of the Eure, high atop a hill "crowned by Chartres's ancient cathedral."[14] While they ate, Hunt talked about the cathedral: how it had been founded in the eleventh century on the very site of an earlier church that was de-stroyed by fire, and how another conflagration had laid waste the new structure even before it was completed, but clergy and congregation had set themselves to work and finished its final construction in the year 1240.

Below them were spread out the farmlands of Beauce, commonly called the granaries of France. The Eure divided into three branches here, and travelers usually crossed into the plains by several bridges, ancient and fringed with the remains of many old fortifications. It seemed to Lady Elgin that the chief attraction of Chartres, in addition to its cathedral, lay in the sharp contrast between the steep and narrow streets of the ancient town and the modern tree-lined boulevards, whose width could contain at least ten carriages riding abreast of each other.

Before retiring that night, she entertained the notion of bribing Talleyrand, but Hunt vehemently cautioned against it, then breaking out with one of his rare smiles, he reminded her that she already possessed the best weapon in the world, one that Talleyrand could not ignore: *motherhood*.

Lady Elgin was not permitted to see Talleyrand until the third day after her arrival in Paris. "His rooms were inside the old Luxembourg Palace, which had been constructed to resemble the Pitti Palace in Florence."[15] A spacious garden, abundant with trees and flower beds, stretched out from the south facade. There was frenzied activity inside the palace: men scurrying from room to room, officers conversing loudly in the corridors, soldiers snappily attired standing guard in front of doors. After a brief wait, she was escorted into an inner office off the hall, where a thin-shouldered man sat hunched over an enormous desk of oak. He was not aware that she had entered the room, and the adjutant had to touch him softly on the arm.

It seemed to Lady Elgin that "Talleyrand's fragile body was held together only by his tight-fitting clothes."[16] He listened carefully to her request and promised to do his utmost about obtaining Elgin's release from the prison at Lourdes. It was a cordial and friendly meeting, at the close of which, Lady Elgin captivated the foreign minister "by protesting her helplessness."[17] Before taking leave of him, she asked for Masterman's passport, and Talleyrand assured her that it would be delivered the following morning to the Hotel de Richelieu where she was again staying.

After dinner that night, she exuberantly wrote to her husband:

I have this moment dined and drank my beloved Elgin's health from the bottom of my heart. How does my Elgin do? This morning I was awaked by the firing of an amazing number of guns. I hear the First Consul [Napoleon] returned last night to St. Cloud, and the report is that the expedition is landed in Ireland — 50,000 men. At this moment, I am in a fever with indecision. I am very very unhappy at being separated from you. I am told that the opinion of the world about you is much changed. People know the mistakes they have made about things at Constantinople. One man in particular, who was most violent, now owns his mistake and says so publickly. But still you have enemies. I want you sadly; you have no idea how deserted I feel, tho' I must say everybody pays me as much attention as possible. The weather is dreadfully bad, very rainy and blowy.[18]

Masterman's passport arrived at noon the next day. The maid already had her luggage packed and waiting in the corridor, and when the moment for her departure was at hand, she fell to her knees before Lady Elgin, weeping and exclaiming that it was wrong to leave at such a time, what with Lord Elgin in prison and Lady Elgin's fourth child expected in less than two months. But Lady Elgin insisted that she go. It was too late and too dangerous to alter Talleyrand's decision.

Lady Elgin was too overcome to walk downstairs with Masterman. Instead, she waved from the window, then sadly watched the carriage pull away. For the rest of that day she felt miserable and prayed to be delivered from a gnawing loneliness. "I am in sad distress today, for I have parted with M. I never thought I could have felt so furlorn [sic] but she is a great favourite and I am sure much attached to me. The parting, as you may imagine, was sad. What a loss she is to poor me!"[19]

Hunt left the suite and returned later in the afternoon to announce that he had scoured the whole capital before procuring a new maid, a capable young lady of twenty-one, who carried the best recommendations, having been employed for six years in the household of the American ambassador. Her name was Félicité: a demure little thing with dancing brown eyes and raven hair that was cut scandalously short, like that of a young lad.

It was decided that they should leave for Barèges early the next morning. Lady Elgin joined the other *détenus* in the hotel that evening and was disappointed to hear that Robert Fergusson had left the capital for a fortnight's visit to Le Havre. Before retiring, she sent out streams of letters to all her acquaintances, English and French, who might help in effecting her husband's release from prison. She also wrote a long plaintive letter to the British foreign secretary, and one to her father, asking him to "stir up political support."[20]

She dreaded the long return journey to Barèges, and as soon as she stepped into the waiting carriage, her thoughts rushed to Elgin. It seemed that only yesterday he had been feted by kings and sultans, while whole armies stood at rigid attention, and now he was shivering inside a damp and unhealthy prison, away from everything — his family, his devoted staff, his grandiose plans.

Toward the end of the month, Lord Hawkesbury's long-delayed response to Lady Elgin's request concerning Elgin's possible exchange for General Boyer finally arrived.

Downing Street

Madam

I have received the honour of your Ladyship's letter, which I lost no time in laying before His Majesty. It would have given His Majesty the most sincere satisfaction to have contributed to the release of Lord Elgin by allowing his Exchange for General Boyer — but a sense of duty renders it impossible for Him in any way to admit or sanction the principle of exchanging Persons made prisoners according to the Laws of war, against any of His own Subjects who have been detained in France in violation of the Law of Nations and of the pledged Faith of the French Government.

The Account of the imprisonment of General Boyer was wholly without foundation. That Officer has never been in Confinement, but has been considered merely as a Prisoner of war on Parole, and is at present residing at Chesterfield in the enjoyment of as much liberty as is ever accorded to Persons in similar Situations.

I can assure your Ladyship that it is with very deep regret that I find myself unable to render you the Assistance you desire. I should have felt the greatest pleasure in contributing by any practicable means to Lord

Elgin's release and to the deliverance of your Ladyship and Him from the very unpleasant Situation in which you have been placed by arbitrary Proceedings of the French Government.

I have the honour to be,
Hawkesbury[21]

During his confinement at Lourdes, Elgin managed to write a long memorandum to King George III, explaining in great detail the incidents of his arrest and imprisonment.

I was being detained in Barèges at the same time that Pichegru, Moreau, and Georges* were in prison at Paris, when an aide de camp of the general commanding the division arrested me under an order that I was to be sent into close confinement in the Prison of Lourdes situated in the Pyrenees, in retaliation for severities said to have been exercised in England against the French General Boyer, who had been taken prisoner in the West Indies.[22]

Just before his arrest, Elgin had received intelligence by post from Paris about a French officer arriving from England who entirely explained away the odium that had been thrown on the British government by exaggerated misrepresentations on the occasion of General Boyer's transference (for misconduct) from Mansfield to Norman Cross in England.[23] Elgin was subsequently placed in the custody of gendarmes and brought to the town of Pau, where he made his report to the prefect of the department, Comte de Castelane, a gentleman no less in sentiments and manners than by birth. After hearing of Elgin's arrest, the count exclaimed: "J'aurais volontiers donné cinquante mille ecus de ma poche que ceci ne fut pas arrivé chez moi!"[24] (I would willingly have given fifty thousand crowns that this matter had not come to pass under my jurisdiction.)

Encouraged by the count's example, the receiver general of the department then gave Elgin a public breakfast on his passage to Lourdes through Pau, "which was the means of so deranging the measures that had been regulated for transporting him to prison, that the

---

*Three generals implicated in a plot against Napoleon.

first escort was forgotten and they proceeded so wholly unattended, they reached the village of Lourdes without being perceived by a strong detachment of Gens d'Armes who had been posted to relieve those who were expected to have brought them on their way."[25]

Elgin was left at the inn that night under heavy guard. The Pyrenees at this time were completely under snow, and the weather very severe. Most of the windows at the inn were broken, and the walls had no plaster, "nor was there a bed or a single article of furniture provided."[26] While at the inn, Elgin was handed a Paris newspaper, and it was a no less striking coincidence that the paper, edited by a native of that district named Barriere, contained the gross declaration that Elgin had been guilty of the greatest atrocities toward French prisoners in Constantinople.

The commandant of the prison at Lourdes was regarded as a close friend, with whom Elgin had spent the preceding summer at Barèges in great intimacy and fellowship. It was only natural that Elgin expected to get the same treatment at Lourdes, but instead of his former good manners, the commandant proved to be a stern and austere jailor.

I was not removed to the Prison at Lourdes till it was dark. The procession was conducted with a very marked ostentation of rigour and a studied endeavour to heighten the gloom and impressiveness of the scene. I was led up by many windings along the side of the rock on which the Prison stands, and through a number of old Gates which were opened with much solemnity and guarded by numerous Detachments of Soldiery. At length I was lodged in a dreary and intensely cold room.

In point of fact, from the moment of being arrested, I had abandoned all expectation of being released from this imprisonment. I had even destroyed all my papers and made my Will. I professed my conviction that the sentence of death was virtually pronounced against me and asked for nothing but that when the blow was to be struck, the Commandant would give me the satisfaction of being befriended by these honorouble feelings of an Officer of the ancien regime which I knew him naturally to possess. They left me at a very late hour with evident reluctance.[27]

He was in the prison only a few days when a sergeant of the guard came mysteriously to his cell and drew from under his coat a letter from a person styling himself "a fellow Prisoner who intimated that though confined au secret and unable to come to me, nevertheless he would receive me and assist me through my vexations whenever I was disposed to go and converse with him at the window. I immediately tore the letter to pieces; gave the Sergeant a Louis d'or as an expression of my thanks to him, but warned that if he or any of his comrades brought me any further communications, verbal or in writing, I should instantly deliver it to the Commanding Officer in their presence."[28]

Fortunately Elgin, through his long experience with spies and foreign intrigue, was able to crush any further overtures from this fellow prisoner. Throughout most of Elgin's unbearable imprisonment at Lourdes, the commandant called upon him, but always under much reserve. On one of these visits, the commandant spoke incidentally of the above-mentioned prisoner and added that a consultation of medical men had been called with a view to afford Elgin the benefit of exercise, since his health was obviously impaired. The next day, to Elgin's surprise, this same prisoner was walking along a terrace near Elgin's window, "evincing every disposition to enter into a conversation,"[29] which Elgin successfully resisted.

His confinement at the prison of Lourdes continued for a number of weeks under many severities, until early one morning the commandant came to him with a messenger bearing his official discharge. No explanation was given concerning the reason for his arrest, and quite remarkably, "no sooner was the messenger dismissed than the Commandant resumed all his former gaiety and freedom of intercourse."[30]

There had been a deep underlying reason for Elgin's arrest. Bonaparte's animosity toward him had become even more inflamed when the French general Boyer was captured and thrown into prison in England. Stories of his ill-treatment so enraged Bonaparte, he issued an order that an English officer of Boyer's rank should be arrested "in retaliation." Unfortunately, Elgin was the one selected.

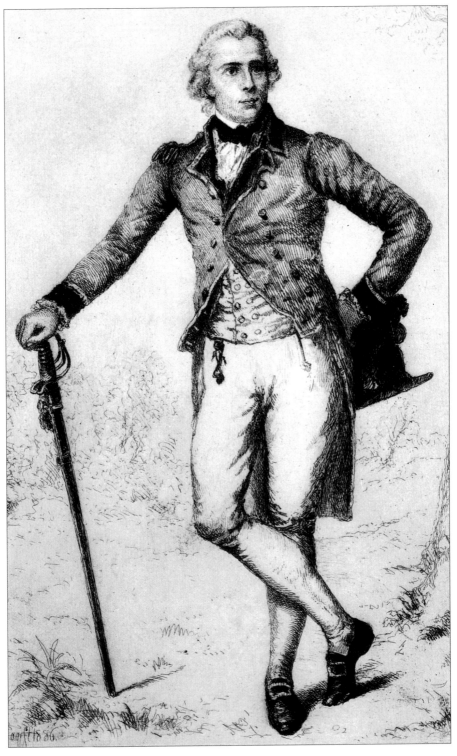

Lord Elgin, from a drawing by C. P. Harding.
BRITISH MUSEUM

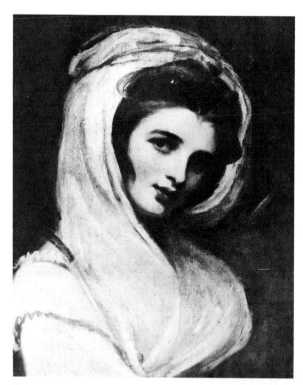

**Lady Hamilton,
by George Romney.**
NATIONAL PORTRAIT GALLERY,
LONDON

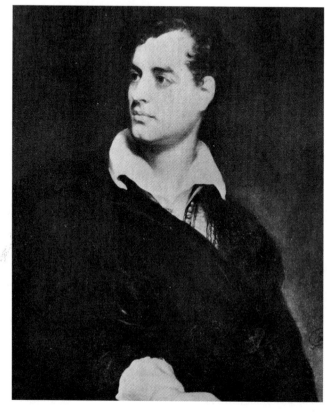

**Lord Byron at the
age of twenty-six.
Portrait by
Thomas Phillips.**
NEWSTEAD ABBEY,
NOTTINGHAM PUBLIC
LIBRARY

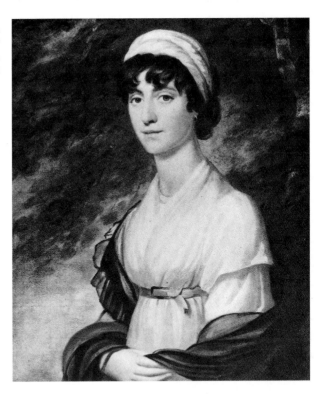

Lady Elgin, from a
painting by
John Hoppner.
BRITISH MUSEUM

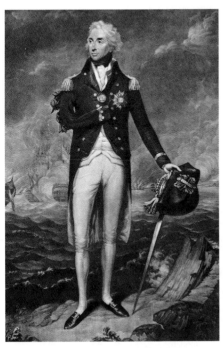

Lord Nelson, engraved by W. Barnard,
from a painting by F. L. Abbott
and formerly in the possession of
Lady Hamilton. BRITISH MUSEUM

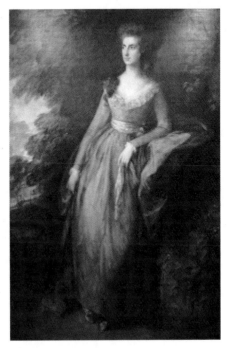

Mrs. William Nisbet, mother
of Lady Elgin. Portrait by
Thomas Gainsborough.
NATIONAL GALLERY OF SCOTLAND

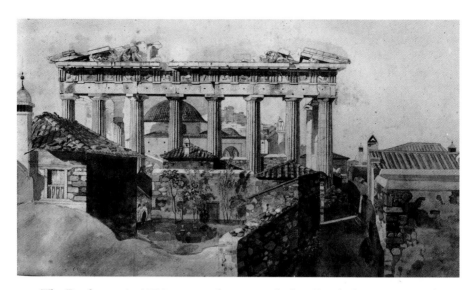

The Parthenon in 1776, twenty-three years before Lord Elgin was named ambassador to the Ottoman Empire. Note the small mosque in the ruins. Watercolor by William Pars. BRITISH MUSEUM

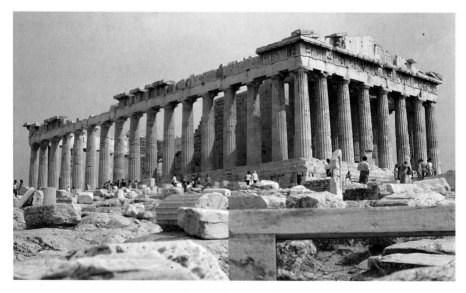

The Parthenon today.
VAS VRETTOS

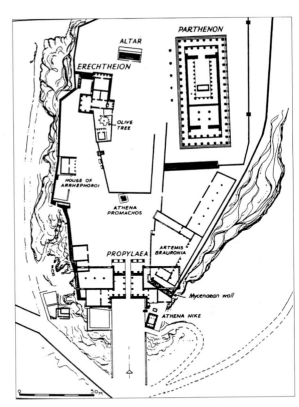

Plan of the Acropolis, circa 400 B.C.

UNIVERSITY OF
TEXAS PRESS

ALTAR

PARTHENON

ERECHTHEION

OLIVE
TREE

HOUSE OF
ARRHEPHOROI

ATHENA
PROMACHOS

PROPYLAEA

ARTEMIS
BRAURONIA

Mycenaean wall

ATHENA NIKE

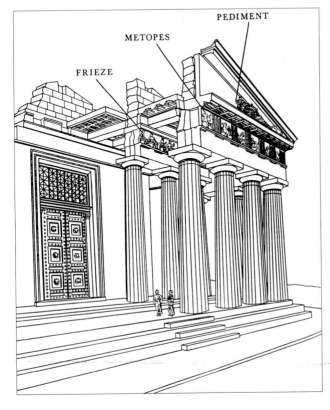

PEDIMENT

METOPES

FRIEZE

Sectional diagram of
the Parthenon,
showing the position
of the sculptures.

UNIVERSITY OF TEXAS PRESS

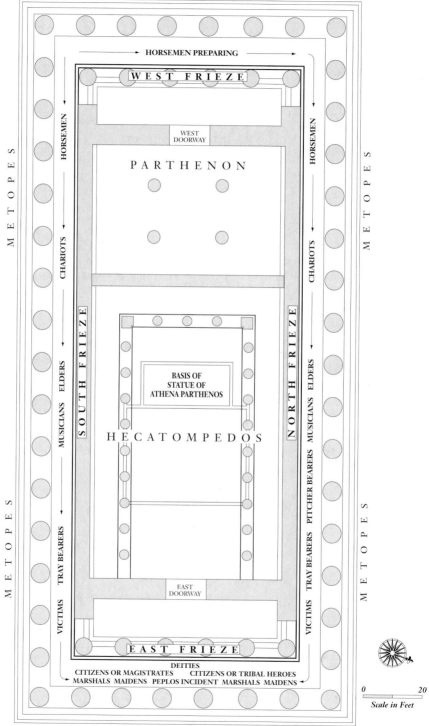

METOPES
WEST PEDIMENT

← HORSEMEN PREPARING →

WEST FRIEZE

HORSEMEN

HORSEMEN

WEST
DOORWAY

PARTHENON

CHARIOTS

CHARIOTS

METOPES

METOPES

METOPES

METOPES

SOUTH FRIEZE

NORTH FRIEZE

MUSICIANS   ELDERS

MUSICIANS   ELDERS

BASIS OF
STATUE OF
ATHENA PARTHENOS

HECATOMPEDOS

TRAY BEARERS

PITCHER BEARERS   TRAY BEARERS

VICTIMS

VICTIMS

EAST
DOORWAY

EAST FRIEZE

DEITIES
CITIZENS OR MAGISTRATES   CITIZENS OR TRIBAL HEROES
← MARSHALS MAIDENS PEPLOS INCIDENT MARSHALS MAIDENS →

EAST PEDIMENT
METOPES

0   20
Scale in Feet

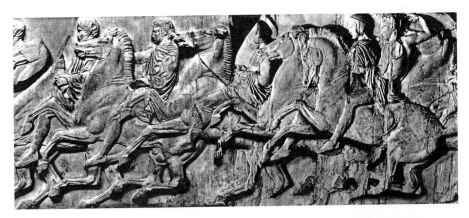

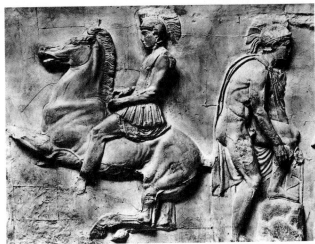

ABOVE: **Group on horseback.** From the Panathenaic Procession. Ionic frieze of the Parthenon.
BRITISH MUSEUM.
RIGHT: **Horsemen.** North frieze, Parthenon.
BRITISH MUSEUM.
BELOW: **Horsemen.** West frieze, Parthenon.
BRITISH MUSEUM.

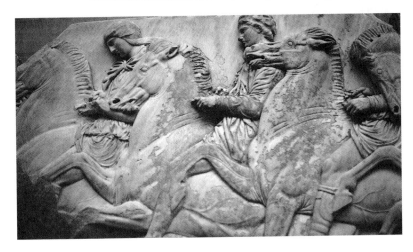

FACING PAGE: **Plan of the Parthenon, showing the disposition** of the Panathenaic Procession.

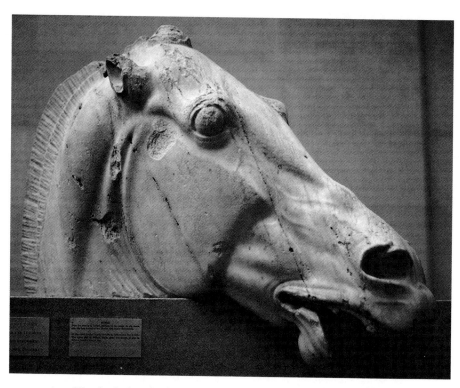

Head of a horse, from the east pediment of the Parthenon.
BRITISH MUSEUM

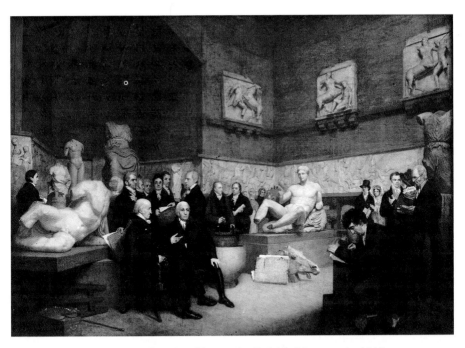

ABOVE: The Elgin Marbles at the British Museum in 1819.
From a painting by A. Archer. BRITISH MUSEUM.
BELOW: The Ilissos or Cephisus River. West pediment, Parthenon. BRITISH MUSEUM

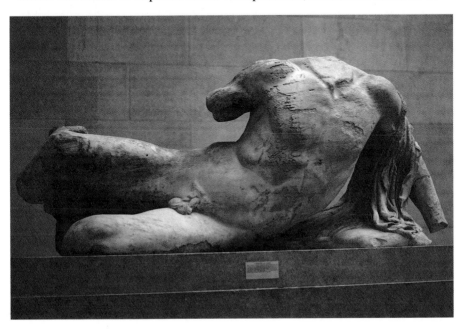

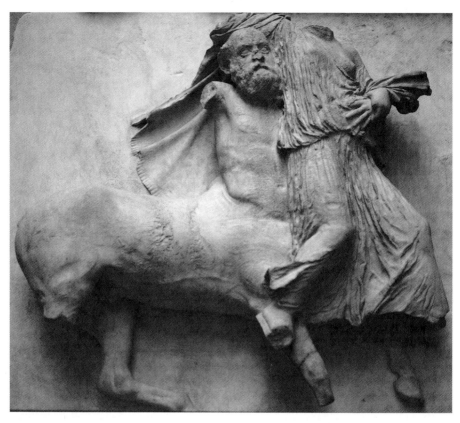

Centaur carrying off maiden. Metope, Parthenon.

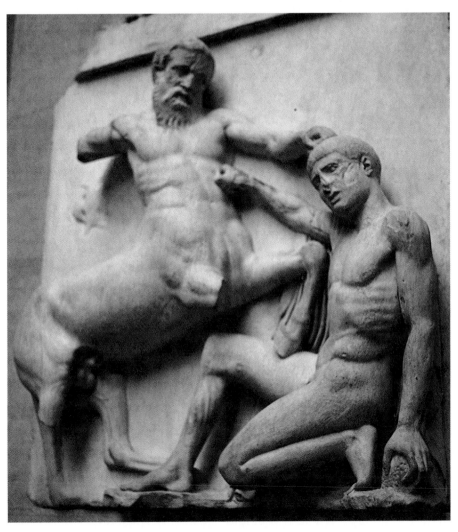

Combat of the Centaurs and Lapithae. Doric frieze, Parthenon.

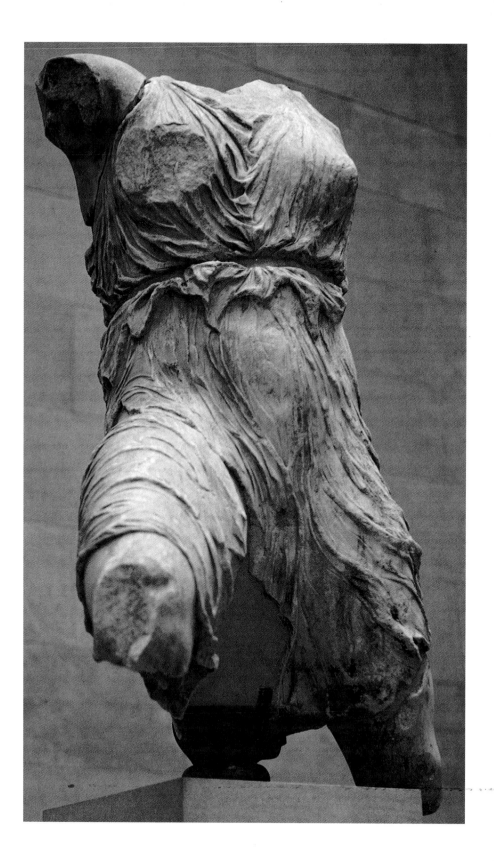

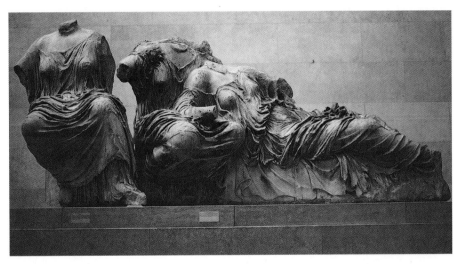

Hestia, Dione, and Aphrodite. East pediment, Parthenon. <small>BRITISH MUSEUM</small>

<small>FACING PAGE:</small> **The goddess Iris. West pediment, Parthenon.** <small>BRITISH MUSEUM</small>

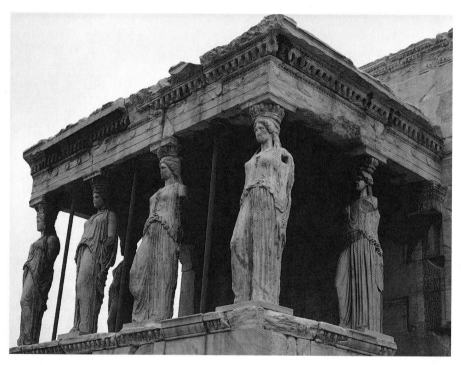

The Erechtheum. Acropolis, Athens.
VAS VRETTOS

Caryatid from the Erechtheum on the Acropolis.
BRITISH MUSEUM

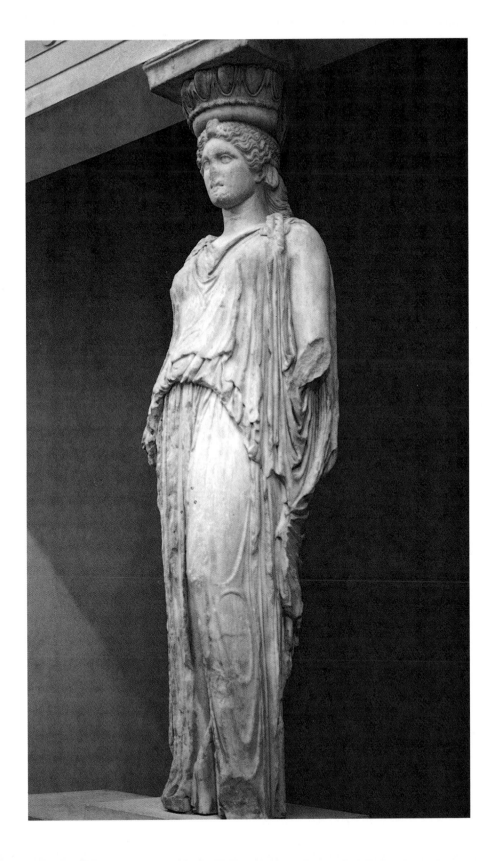

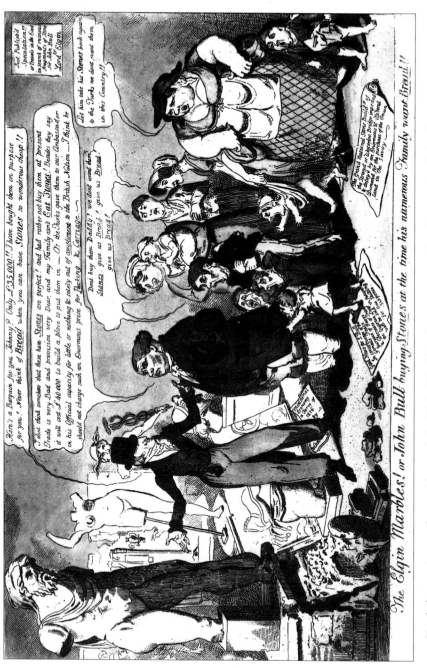

The Elgin Marbles! or John Bull buying Stones at the time his numerous Family want Bread!!

English reaction to the purchase of the Elgin Marbles, from a cartoon by George Cruikshank. BRITISH MUSEUM

Pau

THROUGH THE SMALL WINDOW of her bedchamber, Lady Elgin
had a clear view of the snow-covered Pyrenees. October had
already spent itself, yet there was much warmth in the air.
Leaves still clung to trees, and a powerful scent of grapes in harvest
permeated the atmosphere. True to his word, Talleyrand not only negotiated Elgin's release from his wretched confinement at Lourdes, but
he also arranged the Elgins' transfer from Barèges to this fine winter
house in Pau.

Lady Elgin was frightfully upset when she saw her husband for
the first time after his imprisonment. He arrived in Pau early one
morning, thin and gaunt of body, his face pale, except for the raw
blotch of skin that was once his nose. He expressed no interest concerning the presence of the new maid, and at dinner, he became mo-
rose and kept staring at the floor.

Although she had held off all this time, Lady Elgin now decided
to inform her husband that Talleyrand was willing to grant them a safe
return to Scotland on the condition that Elgin cede the entire
Parthenon collection to Bonaparte and the Louvre. Elgin's response
was silence.

On March 4, 1804, the Elgins' fourth child, William, was born at
Pau, and a short time after this, Lady Elgin gave herself entirely to the
festive life of the town.

The situation here is most delightful such a variety of beautiful rides
and drives, you would be quite enchanted. We are allowed to remain
perfectly quiet and only go to town to present ourselves occasionally to
the Authorities. I have not seen a soul; almost all the other families are
in the country. In winter, Pau is the greatest of places: balls, great din-
ners and suppers, and plenty of card playing, tho' unfortunately only for

sous. Elgin, with all his luck, says of a long evening that he could never contrive to lose more than half a crown.[1]

On the last week of March, their acquaintances from the Hotel de Richelieu were assigned to Pau: the Cockburns, Colonel Craufurd, and Mr. Sterling. Mrs. Fitzgerald had passed away during the summer. Lady Elgin casually inquired about Robert Fergusson and learned that he was back again in Paris.

During their long detainment in Pau, Elgin was dismayed to learn that a furor had been touched off in the English press concerning the presence of the Parthenon marbles at Park Lane. The people of London had voiced strong opposition to Elgin's taking them away from Athens and transporting them to England. In response to this harsh criticism of the press, Hunt sent a letter to Lady Elgin's mother (who, along with her husband, William Nisbet, had just returned to England after a previous visit with the Elgins in Constantinople) in which he included a detailed description, written by Lady Elgin, of the marbles and sculptures obtained by her husband. Hunt hoped that Mrs. Nisbet, who carried considerable influence at court, might arrange to have their daughter's accurate appraisal of the situation published, both in London and Edinburgh, and thus affect Elgin's bad press.

Hunt included Lady Elgin's letter in its entirety, since it disclosed the magnitude of Elgin's acquisitions, together with the accurate history and description of each confiscated treasure. In the preface of his letter to Mrs. Nisbet, Hunt writes,

I cannot forbear availing myself of the opportunity it affords of sending you a sketch of what was done by Lord Elgin's Artists at Athens and the other parts of Greece, after you left us. The enthusiasm you felt on the spot, and which I so often witnessed in our walks on the Areopagus, the Pnyx, and the Acropolis, convinces me that none of the details contained herein will appear trifling or minute that relate to monuments you studied with so much attention, whose respective merits you appreciated with so correct a taste, and with which Lord Elgin's name is now so intimately connected. The project that has been suggested to his Lordship of forming his collection of original marbles, as well as the models, casts, drawings, and plans, into a public exhibition at London, has made us endeavour to recollect the principal objects it contains. The names of Cimon, Pericles, Pheidias, etc., to whom we owe the chefs d'oeuvre of architecture and sculpture at Athens, have so strongly interested your daughter, Lady Elgin, that, not satisfied with the light and amusing descriptions in the *Travels of Anacharsis* in the Athenian Letters or in the *Thousand and One Voyages en Grece*, she also studied the works of Plato and Aristotle, Herodotus, Plutarch, and other original Greek authors, with an eagerness I have seldom witnessed; and I am sure you will read with interest the extracts and observations she has made on every passage that throws light on the scenes she saw with so much delight, and which she now recollects to you with increased fondness:

The first ancient monument procured by my husband, Lord Elgin, was the famous Boustrophedon Inscription from the promontory of Sigaeum in the Troad, which almost every Ambassador from Christendom to the Porte, and even Louis XIV in the zenith of his power, had ineffectually endeavoured to obtain. It is the most ancient and curious specimen extant of Greek writing — at an epoch when the alphabet was very imperfect, and when the lines went alternately from right to left, and from left to right, like the furrows made by oxen in ploughing,* to which the word Boustrophedon [turning like oxen in plowing] alludes. This marble alone, so long a desire in Europe, is surely sufficient to place Elgin's name in a conspicuous rank with the Arundels, the Sandwiches, and Wortleys, to whom Greek literature is so much indebted. From the ruins of the Temple of Minerva at Sigaeum, Elgin also procured some most beautiful Alto-relievos in Parian marble, containing a procession of Trojan matrons presenting and dedicating an infant to Minerva, with the accustomed offerings. General Koehler had also obtained for Elgin a statue and a bas-relief from the ruins of the Temple of Apollo Thymbrius in the Troad, neither of which I have seen, but if the Sculptures [sic] be in a style resembling that of the Sigaean procession, they are valuable indeed.

At a subsequent visit I paid to the Troad with Mr. Carlyle, he procured some interesting inscriptions and I afterwards had the good

---

*Solon's Laws were also written this way.

fortune to discover and obtain a Statue of Minerva Iliensis near Thymbria, the drapery of which is exquisite.

The initial acquisition we made at Athens was the most perfect of the Metopes from the ruins of the Parthenon, on which I recollect my father and yourself rivetting your eyes with so much admiration. This was the first of them that had been so successfully lowered. Choiseul-Gouffier's attempt to secure one had merely been connived at; and for want of time, cordage, and windlasses, it fell from a considerable height and was broken into fragments. I do not recollect to have ever felt my heart throb with greater violence than when I saw this treasure detached from the entablature of the Parthenon and depending only on the strength of Ragusan cordage; nor did my anxiety cease till I had got it on board an English frigate at Alexandria, to be forwarded to England. The subject of the sculpture appears to be Theseus or his friend Pirithous victorious over a Centaur.

The first Metope we obtained from the Temple of Minerva on the Citadel of Athens has been followed by the acquisition of eight or ten others representing a continuation of the Battle between the Centaurs and Lapithae at the nuptials of Pirithous. Each Metope contains two figures grouped in various attitudes: sometimes the Lapithae victorious, sometimes the Centaur. The relaxed muscles of one of the Lapithae, who is lying dead and trampled on by a Centaur, is amongst the finest productions of art, as well as the group adjoining it of Hippodamia, the bride, carried off by a Centaur, and struggling to throw herself from the Monster's back, while he is grasping her with brutal violence, with one hand twisted into her dishevelled tresses. The furious style of his galloping, and his shrinking from the spear that has been hurled after him, are expressed with prodigious animation. How great a misfortune it is that many of these should be so much mutilated! But even in that condition, they are much superior to anything that modern restoration could effect, were the attempts made even by the hand of Canova [the most famous sculptor in Europe and an apostle of neoclassicism]. They are all in such high relief as to be absolutely groups of statues, and they are in general finished with as much attention behind as in front, in order that they might strike the eye of the spectator with effect, in whatever direction he approached the Acropolis from the plain of Athens.

They originally ran all round the entablature of the Parthenon and formed ninety-two groups. The zeal of the early Christians, the barbarism of the Turks, the explosions when the Temple was used as a gun-powder magazine, have demolished a very large portion of them, so that except those snatched from impending ruins by Elgin, and secured to the arts, it is in general difficult to trace even the outline of the original subject.

The frieze which runs round the top of the walls of the Cell is full of sculpture in bas-relief, designed to occupy the attention of those who were waiting in the vestibule and ambulatory of the Temple till the sacred rites commenced. This frieze, being unbroken by triglyphs, presents much more unity of the subject than the detached and insulated groups on the metopes of the peristyle. It represents the whole of the solemn procession during the Pan-Athenaic festival: many of the figures are on horseback; others are just about to mount; some are in chariots; others on foot, as oxen and other victims are being led to sacrifice. The nymphs called Canophorae, Skiaphorae, etc., are carrying the sacred offerings in baskets and vases. Priests, Magistrates, and Warriors form a series of most interesting figures, in all the variety of costume, armour, and attitudes. Some antiquaries who have examined this frieze with minute attention say it contains portraits of the leading characters at Athens during the Peloponnesian War, particularly of Pericles, Pheidias, Socrates, and the young Alcibiades.

This frieze was originally near six hundred feet in length, and by being protected from the effects of weather and other injuries by the shelter and projection of the Colonnade, those parts that had escaped the explosions of gunpowder are still in high preservation, literally lacking nothing but the gilded bronze ornaments, which one may see were once fixed to them, such as reins and bits for the horses, and other minute objects that could be more easily executed in metal. The whole frieze is of Pentelic marble, superior to Parian for bas-reliefs. Many large blocks are in Elgin's possession, some taken from the wall itself, and others recovered by excavating under the ruins.

The tympana of the two frontispieces of the Parthenon were also adorned with groups in Alto-relievo, which, over the entrance of the Temple, contained the mythological history of Minerva's birth from the brain of Jove. In the centre of the group was seated Jupiter, in all the majesty the sculptor could give to the King of Gods and Men. On his left were the principal Divinities of Olympus, among whom Vulcan came prominently forward with the axe in his hand, which had cleft a passage for the Goddess. On the right was Victory in loose floating robes, holding the horses of the chariot which introduced the New Divinity to Olympus. Unlike all other statues of Minerva, she was here represented with the captivating graces of Venus, whereas the ferocious Spartans gave the Queen of Love a helmet and a spear.

The elegant and amiable people of Athens delighted to see the warlike Pallas with the cestus of Venus. When Athens lost her freedom, she shewed her adulation to the Roman Power by adding the Statues of Hadrian and Sabina to this group.

One of the bombs fired by Morosini [the doge of Venice who took Athens in 1687] from the opposite hill of the Museum injured the roof and many of the figures, and the attempt of General Königsmark to take down the sculpture of Minerva ruined the whole.

By purchasing the house of one of the Turkish Janissaries that was built immediately under it, and then demolishing it in order to excavate, Elgin has had the satisfaction of recovering the greatest part of the Statue of Victory, in a drapery which reveals all the fine form beneath, with as much delicacy and taste as the Flora Farnese. In addition, we found there the Torso of Jupiter, part of Vulcan and other fragments; along with these, Elgin also had the Hadrian and Sabina taken down and sent to England.

On the other frontispiece was the contest between Minerva and Neptune about giving a name to the city. The Goddess of Wisdom gained the victory by proving how much greater a benefit she should confer by the peaceful and productive olive, than the God of Ocean by his warlike gift of a horse.

In digging beneath this pediment, some beautiful pieces of sculpture have been procured by Elgin, and from the ruin of the Temple itself has been lowered the head of a horse, which far surpasses anything of the kind I have seen in the truth and spirit of the execution. The nostrils are distended, the ears erect, the veins swollen (I had almost said throbbing), his mouth is open, and he seems to neigh with the conscious pride of belonging to the Ruler of the waves. Besides this inimitable head, Elgin has procured from the same pediment some colossal groups, each containing two female figures, probably Sea Deities. They are formed of single massive blocks of Pentelic marble and are reclining in most graceful attitudes. From the same place has also been procured the Statue of a Sea or River God attendant on Neptune (Ilissos), which is in great preservation. He is in a sitting posture, with one leg extended, the other bent. Their size and weight were such as to force us to construct a car on purpose to convey them all to the Piraeus, and there, Captain Clarke of the *Braakel* Man of War (brother of the Eleusinian Dr. Clarke), had the goodness to make a huge float to take them on board, his launch being unequal to so heavy a freight.

From the Posticum or Opisthodomos of the Parthenon, I procured some valuable inscriptions written in the manner called Kionedon, next in antiquity to the Boustrophedon. The letters of each line are equal in number, without regard to the meaning, even monosyllables being separated into two parts if the line has had its complement; and the next line begins with the end of the broken word. The letters range perpendicularly as well as horizontally, so as to render it impossible to make any interpolation or erasure of the original text. Their subjects are public decrees of the People — accounts of the riches contained in the Athenian Treasury delivered by the Administrators to their successors in office. These include enumerations of the statues, the silver, gold, and precious stones deposited in the Temples, and estimates for public works, etc.

The Parthenon itself, independently of decorative sculpture, is so exquisite a model of Doric architecture, that Elgin has conferred an inappreciable benefit to the Arts of England by securing original specimens of each member of the Edifice. These consist of a capital of a column, and of one of the pilasters of the Antaeassises of the columns themselves, to shew the exact form of the curve used in channelling — a triglyph, a motule from the cornices, and even some of the marble tiles with which the ambulatory was roofed. So that not only the sculptor may be gratified by studying every specimen of his art, from colossal statues down to Bas-reliefs executed in the golden age of Pericles and under the inspection of Pheidias, but the practical architect may examine into every detail of the building, even to the mode of uniting the tambours of the columns without the aid of mortar, so as to make the shafts look like single blocks to the most scrutinizing eye.

In addition, every detail of the Temple has been moulded into what the Italians call Madre Forma, in a hard composition of wax and gypsum so as to enable Elgin to make plaster casts at pleasure of the sculpture and the architectural ornaments, the exact size of the original. The Temple has also been planned, and its elevations and restorations made by Signor Balestra (one of the artists employed by Elgin). You had an opportunity of appreciating his merit during your stay in Athens but Elgin's choice has received a most flattering approbation, in the Pope's having since selected that artist to superintend the works of a similar kind carrying on at Ostia and in the Forum of Rome. Lusieri's magic pencil will now, I trust, have finished the picturesque views of the Parthenon, which we saw commenced with so happy a choice of the various points of view, and the Calmuc Theodore, who had completed his drawings of the sculptures on the metopes, frieze, and pediments, has since made a restored copy of the group on the Western Pediment and on the entablature, in the grand elevation.

The same works have been executed on the Temple of Theseus, but not a morsel of sculpture has been displaced, nor the minutest fragment of any kind taken from the building itself. Where indeed can be found a being imbued with the least feeling or taste, who would think of defacing that exquisite structure, which after an interval of 2,200 years, still retains the beauty and brilliancy of its first days? The metopes in Mezzo-relievo containing a mixture of the labours of Hercules and Theseus have been modelled and drawn, as well as the frieze representing the battle between the Centaurs and Lapithae, some incidents of the Battle of Marathon, and some mythological subjects.

Let me now return to that favourite Hill of Minerva and resume the list of Elgin's labours and acquisitions there. The original approach to it from the plain of Athens was by a long flight of steps, commencing near the foot of the Areopagus and terminating at the Propylaea. Pericles was most proud of this edifice, which cost so prodigious a sum the Athenians hesitated about granting him the supplies he demanded for it: "Let it then be inscribed with my name," replied the haughty Pericles, "and I will advance the money."

Its front was a hexastyle colonnade of two wings surmounted by a pediment. Whether the metopes and tympanums were adorned with sculpture cannot be ascertained, since the pediment and entablature have been destroyed, and the inter-columniations built up with rubbish in order to convert it into a battery of guns. Although the plan of the Propylaea contains some deviations from the pure taste that reigns in the other structures of the Acropolis, yet each member is so perfect in the details of its execution that Elgin was at great pains to obtain a Doric and an Ionic capital from its ruins.

On the right hand of the Propylaea was a Temple dedicated to the Wingless Victory, an epithet to which many explanations have been given. It probably alludes to Theseus reaching Athens himself, before the news of his triumph over the Minotaur, and the abolition of the odious tribute had got there: or perhaps the Athenians wished to flatter themselves with the notion of Victory having taken up so permanent a residence with them as to have no further occasion for wings. It was built from the spoils won in the glorious struggle for freedom at Marathon, Salamis, and Plataea. On its frieze were sculptured many incidents of those memorable battles, in a style that has been thought by no means inferior to the metopes of the Parthenon. The only fragments of it that had escaped the ravages of barbarians were built into the wall of a gunpowder magazine near it, and the finest block was inserted upside downwards. It required the whole of Elgin's influence at the Porte to get leave to remove it, but he at length succeeded.

The metopes on the frieze represent Athenians in close combat with the Persians; and the sculptor has taken care to mark the different dresses and armour of the various forces serving under the great King. The long garments of the Persians had induced former travellers, from the hasty and awkward view they had of them, to suppose the subject was the battle between Theseus and the Amazons who invaded Attica under the command of Antiope, but the Persian tiaras, the Phrygian bonnets, and many other particulars clearly point out the mistake. The contest of some warriors to rescue the body of a dead comrade is expressed with uncommon animation.

These bas-reliefs were put on board the *Mentor*, which was so unfortunately wrecked off Cerigo, but they have all been recovered by expert divers from the islands of Syme and Calymna near Rhodes. I shall be most happy to hear that the Gymnasiarch's throne, which you procured at Athens, and which shared the fate of these sculptures, has like them been hauled up again.

Near the Parthenon are three temples so connected in their structure, and by the rites celebrated in them, that they may be almost considered as a triple temple. They are of small dimensions, and of the Ionic Order. One is dedicated to Neptune and Erechtheus; the second to Minerva Polias, the Protectress of Citadels; and the third to the Nymph Pandrosos. It was on the spot where these temples stand that Minerva and Neptune contended for the honor of naming the city.

Athenian superstition long shewed the mark of Neptune's trident; also the briny fountain that attested to his having opened a passage there for his horse. The original olive tree produced by Minerva was venerated in the Temple of Pandrosos as late as the time of the Antonines.

The Temple of Minerva Polias is of the most delicate and elegant proportions of the Ionic Order. The capitals and bases of the columns are ornamented with consummate taste; and the sculpture of the frieze and cornice is exquisitely rich. One has difficulty to conceive how marble has been wrought to such a depth, and brought to so sharp an edge. The palmetti, onetti, etc., have all the delicacy of works in metal. The Vestibule of the Temple of Neptune is of more masculine proportions, but its Ionic capitals have infinite merit. To examine the roof, one had to climb with much difficulty and then creep through an opening made in the wall, which has since been closed. Future travellers will thus be prevented from seeing the inner door of the Temple, which you so much admired, and which is perhaps the most perfect specimen in existence of Ionic ornament. Both these temples have been measured; and their plans, elevations, and views made with the utmost accuracy. The ornaments have all been moulded; some original blocks of the frieze and cornice have been obtained by Elgin; also a capital and a base.

The little adjoining chapel of Pandrosos (the Erechtheum) is quite a concerto in architecture. Instead of Ionic columns to support the architrave, it has six statues of Carian Women (or Caryatids). The Athenians endeavoured by this device to perpetuate the infamy of the inhabitants of Carias, who were the only Peloponnesians favourable to Xerxes in his invasion of Greece. Their men had been reduced to the deplorable state of slaves, and the women condemned to the most servile labours. And thus they are exhibited here. The drapery of their ancient dresses is fine; the hair of each figure is braided in a different manner, and a diadem they wear on their heads forms the capital. Besides drawing and moulding all these particulars, Elgin has procured one of the marble Caryatids. The Lacedemonians had used a similar vengeance in constructing the Persian Portico, which they had erected at Sparta in honour of their victory over the forces of Mardonius at Plataea, placing statues of Persians in their rich Oriental dresses, instead of columns to sustain the entablature.

Our artists and architects have also made a ground plan of the Acropolis, in which they have not only inserted all the monuments I have mentioned, but have also added those whose position could be ascertained from traces of their foundations. Among these are the temple and cave of Pan, to whom the Athenians felt so much indebted at the Battle of Marathon. It is now nearly obliterated, as well as that of Aglauros,* who devoted herself to death to save her country. In it, the young men of Athens received their first armour, enrolled their names, and took the oath to fight to the last drop of their blood for their country. Near this was the spot where the Persians scaled the walls of the citadel when Themistocles had retired with the main forces of Athens and all her navy, to Salamis.

How small is that portion which can now be ascertained of what the Acropolis once contained! Plutarch tells us that all the public buildings raised in Rome from the foundation of the city to the age of the Caesars could not be put in competition with the edifices erected on the Acropolis during the administration of Pericles alone. Heliodorus' description of these buildings took up fifteen books. Far from having exhausted the subject, Polemon Periegetes added four more volumes. In the time of Pliny — even after the plunder of Lysander, Sylla, and Nero — there were more than three thousand statues remaining in Athens.

The remains of the original walls may still be traced in the midst of the Turkish and Venetian additions, and are distinguishable by three modes of construction at very remarkable epochs: the Pelasgic,† the Cecropia,‡ and that of the age of Cimon and Pericles.

I must now quit the walls of the Acropolis and attempt a concise account of what has been done in Athens, and in other parts of Greece and Asia Minor during Elgin's Embassy at the Porte. The ancient walls of Athens, as they existed in the Peloponnesian War, have been traced by our artists in their whole extent, as well as the long walls that led to Piraeus. The gates, so often mentioned in the Greek classics, have been ascertained, and every public monument that could be recognized has

---

*A sister of Herse and Pandrosos. The latter, faithful to her promise to Athena not to spy on Erichthonius, was the only one of the three who did not have the fatal curiosity to open a basket entrusted to their care. They were daughters of Cecrops, King of Athens.

†The origin of the Pelasgi is lost in antiquity. They founded the theology of the Greeks and were employed by them in constructing the most ancient part of the fortifications of the Acropolis.

‡Cecropia was the original name of Athens, from its founder King Cecrops.

been inserted in a general map, as well as detailed plans given of each. Extensive excavations were necessary for this purpose, particularly at the Great Theatre of Bacchus; and at the Pnyx, where Pericles, Alcibiades, Demosthenes and Aeschines delivered their animated orations, "those thoughts that breathe and words that burn."

The Theatre built by Herodes Atticus to the memory of his wife, Regilla, and the Cumuli of Antiope Euripides, etc., have also been opened, and from these excavations, along with various others in the environs of Athens, we have procured a complete and invaluable collection of Greek vases. The Colonies that were sent from Athens, Corinth, etc., into Magna Graeca, Sicily, and Etruria, carried with them this art of making vases, and since the earliest modern collections of vases were made in those Colonies, they have improperly acquired the name of Etruscan. Those found by Elgin at Athens, Aegina, and Corinth will prove the indubitable claim of the Greeks to this art. None of those in the collection of the King of Naples, or of Sir William Hamilton can be compared to those that Elgin has procured, with respect to the elegance of the forms, the fineness of the materials, the delicacy of the execution, or the beauty of subjects delineated on them.

A Tumulus, into which an excavation was commenced under Elgin's eye during our residence in Athens, has furnished a most valuable treasure. It consists of a large marble vase, enclosing one of bronze five feet in circumference, of beautiful sculpture, and encircled with a wreath of myrtle wrought in gold. Near it was a smaller vase of Alabaster beautifully ribbed. The position of this Tumulus is on the road that leads from Port Piraeus to the Salaminian ferry and the town of Eleusis.

From the Theatre of Bacchus Elgin has obtained the very ancient Sun Dial, which existed there during the time of Aeschylus, Sophocles, and Euripides — also a large statue of Bacchus dedicated by Thrasyllus [Thrasybulus] in gratitude for his having obtained the prize of Tragedy at the Pan-Athenaic Festival. A beautiful little Corinthian temple near it, raised for a similar prize gained by Lysicrates, and commonly called the Lantern of Demosthenes, has in addition been modelled and drawn by our artists with minute attention.

My friendship with the Bishop of Athens gained me permission to examine the interior of all the churches and convents in Athens. This search furnished many valuable bas-reliefs, inscriptions, ancient dials, a Gymnasiarch's chair in marble, on the backs of which are figures of

Harmodius and Aristogiton with daggers in their hand; and the death of Leaena, who bit off her tongue during the torture rather than confess what she knew of the conspiracy against the Pisistradidae.

The fountain in the courtyard of our Consul Logothetis' house was decorated with a bas-relief of Bacchantes, in the style called Graeco-Etruscan, which he presented to Elgin, as well as a Quadriga in bas-relief, with a Victory hovering over the Charioteer, probably an ex-voto for a victory at the Olympic games.

Amongst the tombstones found in different places are some remarkable names, particularly that of Socrates. In the Keramicos [Kerameikos] Cemetery Elgin discovered an inscription in Elegiac verse on the Athenians who fell at Potidaea, and whose eulogy was delivered with such eloquence in the funeral oration of Pericles.

This, Madame, (as nearly as I can recollect,) is a list of the original articles in Pentelic marble that have been procured by Elgin and sent to London thus far. We have the assurance that many more are to follow, since Lusieri is busily at work on further acquisitions from Athens and various other parts of Greece.[2]

During the long detainment in France Elgin was continually assailed for his activities in Greece. The chief protagonist was Lord Byron. The young poet had developed a close correspondence with the British consul in Athens and had recently written to Logothetis to inform him that Byron and his friend John Cam Hobhouse were about to leave Falmouth for a grand tour of the Continent. They expected to reside with Logothetis on their arrival in Athens.

Byron had just received his master of arts, which he considered a nobleman's degree and a farce, and to celebrate the event the two college friends, before embarking on their tour, indulged themselves at Newstead Abbey,* fitting up several apartments to entertain their guests in strange rites with monkish costumes.

* * *

---

*The ancestral home of Lord Byron. Situated "in the enchanted Sherwood Forest, close to Nottingham, it had been a monastery of the Augustinian Order." (André Maurois, *Byron*, p. 3.)

Byron and his companions were delayed in Italy after leaving Geneva, where Byron entered into an aesthetic relationship with the poet Shelley. In Venice, he fell in love with Teresa Guiccioli, the young wife of an elderly count. Before leaving Italy, it was rumored that he also seduced a hundred women of the lower class.

They next traveled to the Dardanelles, and on a warm spring morning, Byron and a British lieutenant named Ekenhead swam across the strait, a treacherous distance of nearly five miles. The water was bitter cold, and the violent current from the melting mountain snows made the feat extremely difficult.

> If, in the month of dark December,
>   Leander, who was nightly wont
> (What maid will not the tale remember?)
>   To cross thy stream, broad Hellespont![3]

Logothetis was looking forward to Byron's arrival with great anticipation. In one of Byron's letters to the consul, several paragraphs were devoted to the young poet's tendency toward obesity; he was able to maintain his weight problem, he wrote, only through a strict diet of biscuits, rice, and vinegar. His promiscuities, however, had already left their scars on his psyche. "I am so changeable, being everything by turns but nothing for a long period of time. I am such a strange mélange of good and evil, it is impossible for anyone to really know me."[4]

When the news of Byron's arrival at Piraeus reached Logothetis, he frantically began stocking his house with food and drink, but when three days had passed without any sign of Byron, Logothetis, deeply offended, ordered two of his servants to launch an immediate search throughout the city. The men did not return until well past midnight, by which time most of the household had retired, with the exception of Logothetis and Lusieri.

For some reason, Byron had chosen to lodge himself, together with Hobhouse and William Fletcher (Byron's valet at Newstead Abbey) inside the monastery of the Capuchin fathers, a mile from Logothetis's house. The consul found this unpardonable and, accompanied by Lusieri, set out at dawn the next day to go after the young poet. Before entering the monastery, they stopped for a moment at the gate. "Hymettus looming before it, the Acropolis Hill behind. A monument of Lysicrates stood at the entrance, while just off the side to the left, lay a peaceful grove of orange trees."[5]

In the quadrangle, they came upon a group of hooded monks, within whose circle two young novices flailed away at each other, their white bodies bare to the waist. Loud cries of approval resounded as each blow was landed, most of the cheering emanating from the eldest of the group, a gray-haired abbot whose hood had fallen in disarray over his frail shoulders. A third man stood between the young fighters. He was of medium height and shockingly thin. When he saw Logothetis, he broke away from the circle and ran to embrace him. The consul

chided Byron for scorning his hospitality, and then inquired about the young fighters who stood ready to resume their positions, arms raised, fists clenched. Byron laughed and exclaimed that the two novices were embroiled in a bitter and ancient battle: a contest between East and West, Patriarch and Pope! For the moment, the Papal representative appeared to be winning, which caused Logothetis to rush toward the Greek novice and demand that he avenge his religion and his race. Although the young man's face was puffed with red welts, the blood trickling from his nose and mouth, he somehow responded to Logothetis' challenge, and with a surge of new strength, threw a desperate blow at his adversary's stomach, causing him to double over in pain. The abbot, with obvious displeasure, moved in and stopped the fight, at which point Byron roared: Hail Byzantium![6]

The monks slowly dispersed to their cells, and within moments the quadrangle reverberated with the loud clang of the chapel bell announcing the noon meal. Byron invited them into the refectory, where bowls of bean soup were being served. The monastery was a sagging structure with low ceilings and cracked walls. The monks stood impatiently behind their benches as the abbot invoked his blessing, and even before he had finished, they plunged into the food, slurping loudly and shoving huge chunks of dark bread into their mouths.

Byron seemed to enjoy all this. He and Hobhouse went to the far-thest corner of the refectory and seated themselves with the monks. Logothetis, noticeably uncomfortable in the presence of monks, stiffly nudged Lusieri toward the table, and they sat alongside Byron and Hobhouse. Between mouthfuls, Byron eagerly began speaking about his travels.

And when we left Falmouth, Hobhouse here took one hundred pens along, together with two gallons of ink and a year's supply of paper. Wretched soul! He fashions himself a writer . . . and I never heard such grumbling in my life until William Fletcher, seated there on your right hand, decided to travel with us. He was my valet at Newstead and wanted desperately to join us, despite the fact that he had been married only a few days prior. Throughout most of the voyage, he wept and wished he were back with his Sally. Meanwhile the ocean was unkind to Hobhouse and even induced him to vomit first his dinner, then his boring impressions of the entire journey. I caught everything flush between the eyes![7]

Byron took a savage bite of bread before continuing his animated recital of their earlier adventures on the way to Greece.

At Lisbon, we had encountered a continent at war. The English had just taken over the city from the French and it was in a deplorable state: dead bodies lay exposed in the churchyards with saucers on their breasts, their burial delayed until enough money was put into the saucers for the priests. Yet elsewhere in Portugal there was enchantment. I loved the orange trees that sprinkled the green valleys with necklaces of gold. I swam the Tagus; rode on an ass; conversed with monks in Latin; swore in Portuguese; suffered with diarrhea and insect bites.

He stopped to look at Logothetis for a moment, then laughed loudly.

Comfort must not be expected by folks that go a pleasuring. We next journeyed from Lisbon to Seville on horseback, across a country where death and love merged into one. The women of Seville were the most lovely in the world. Their black eyes and fine forms obsessed me. We lodged in a house with two such creatures and when it came time to leave, I was embraced by the younger of the two sisters, who cut off a lock of my hair, then presented me with one of her own, which measured three feet in length. Her parting words were: "Adieu, you pretty fellow. You please me much."[8]

Both Hobhouse and Fletcher remained quiet while Byron rattled on. Hobhouse was seventeen, very fair, with intense features; Fletcher was of darker complexion and quite short. In time, the monks finished eating and, after a hasty benediction from the abbot, began filing out of the refectory. Byron meanwhile helped himself to another bowl of soup as he picked up the thread of their journey.

We next boarded the Malta packet from Gibraltar and walked the deck, staring at the sea, breathing in the wondrous poetry of the Gibraltar cliffs. With the lighting of the lamps, I would go forward and sit on a roll of sailcloth, remaining there for hours and watching the moonbeams dance on the waves. No doubt, my fellow passengers mistook my yearning for solitude as cold arrogance and judged me harshly. Far worse, once I had assumed this attitude of detachment, I had to stay with it, because I was still enraptured by the immature thought that it was noble to seek such melancholy pleasure.[9]

At Malta, Byron said he took lessons in Arabic from an old Egyptian monk; he "also had a platonic love affair with the wife of Elgin's arch-enemy, Sir John Spencer Smith."[10] At last they reached Albania, a barbarous land whose mountains reminded Byron of Scotland. The goatherds even wore skirts to the knee. When the pasha of Ioannina heard of their arrival, he invited them immediately to his house, where they dined in elegance, surrounded by Albanians with embroidered tunics, Tartars in tall hats, rows of black eunuchs, and a steady chorus of drums. Meanwhile the muezzin chanted from every minaret in the city: "There is none other God than Allah!"

The pasha in Albania possessed seventy full years and had a thick white beard, was always smiling, and had the manners of an English gentleman. Yet he thought nothing of roasting his enemies at the stake or throwing ten women off a cliff if they annoyed his daughter-in-law. Byron, who strongly believed that holiness and virtue were more prevalent in a band of rogues than under a priest's cassock, found such conduct intriguing. Despite the apparent frailty of his body, he possessed a strength of spirit that seemed to transform him into a titan. Every day the three young Englishmen plodded up the impossible Albanian mountains, and when they finally left the country and boarded a Turkish man-of-war to set sail for Greece, they were beset by a sudden storm.

We were nearly lost in a Turkish warship, owing to the ignorance of the captain and crew. Fletcher yelled after his wife, the Greeks called on all the saints, the Mussulmans on Allah, while the captain burst into tears and ran below deck, beseeching us to call on God. Their invocations, however, fell upon deaf ears, and as the sails were being torn to shreds, Fletcher whimpered: "We shall all find a watery grave!" The storm continued for almost three hours, and when it finally abated, the ship lay stranded on a beach, at which point a wild-looking band of Suliotes [mountain inhabitants of northern Greece] appeared. Captain and crew were afraid we would be harmed, but instead the Suliotes dried our clothes, fed us, entertained us with their klephtic [patriotic] songs, and as we were about to pull away with the rising tide, I offered their chief a few coins. The old Suliote angrily admonished me: "I wish you to love me, not to pay me!"[11]

Before going to the Capuchin monastery, Byron stopped at the house of a widow in Athens, and while there instantly fell in love with her three daughters, all of them under fifteen. And to further complicate matters, he also fell in love with Teresa, their mother.

Maid of Athens, ere we part
Give, oh give me back my heart;
Or since that has left my breast
Keep it now and take the rest.
Hear my vow before I go:
Zoe mou, sas agapo!*[12]

Several days later, the Greek consul and Lusieri paid another visit to the Capuchin monastery. The day was unbearably hot; the air sticky.

---

*"My Zoe, I love you."

When they entered the sweltering quadrangle, they saw Byron stripped to the waist, absorbing punch after punch from a novice monk twice his size. As soon as the monk noticed Consul Logothetis, he dropped his arms and raced toward him, explaining that Byron had asked to be thrashed; that he had burst into the novice's cell at daybreak and commanded him to do it.

In one fleeting moment faces glide past me, faces that once brimmed with life, with joy. But now they are gone. Alas, there is something incomprehensible about death. In all this world I had but two people who cared for me. Really cared. And they are both gone! And you, charming but cynical Matthews, how often did I admonish you: "Matthews, you swim badly. If you persist in keeping your head so high, you will surely drown yourself!" Charon [ferryman who transported the dead across the River Styx], what have you dealt me? My mother and my best friend! But peace be to the dead; let us resume the dull business of life. As to immortality, if people are to live again, then why die? If our carcasses are to rise once more, are they worth rising? And if mine is, I hope it shall have a better pair of legs than these!"[13]

Byron recovered after a glass of brandy, and with the novice monk's assistance, Logothetis and Lusieri carried him into the cool shade of his cell, where Byron's disjointed words eventually came together. Fletcher, it seemed, had left for England to settle the estate of Byron's deceased mother; as for Matthews, he had drowned in the Cam the previous month, swimming alone and poorly, caught in the waterweeds.

At this point, Consul Logothetis again demanded that Byron leave the monastery and come stay at his house, but Byron threw him a helpless gaze. "If you could but look into my soul and see its torment! I am like a tiny vessel in a storm. My life has no meaning, no direction. When Father D'Yvree* gave me permission to inhabit one of the cells here, I kissed his crucifix in tears."[14]

Religion, like everything else, had to be a passionate expression for Byron. In the middle of his lamentations, he suddenly turned on Lusieri and began denouncing Lord Elgin, even threatening to shame

---

*The abbot of the Capuchin monastery in Athens.

him before the world unless he called away his despoilers from the Parthenon. "What right had he to remove the precious stones of a weak nation? What right had he to raise his hand against a building that had stood whole for two thousand years?"[15]

> But who of all the plunderers of yon fame
> On high, where Pallas lingered, loth to flee
> The latest relic of her ancient reign,
> The last, the worst, dull spoiler, who was he?
> Blush, Caledonia! Such thy son could be.
> England! I joy no child he was of thine;
> Thy free-born men should spare what once was free,
> Yet they could violate each saddening shrine
> And bear these altars o'er the long reluctant brine.

> What! Shall it e'er be said by British tongue
> Albion was happy in Athena's tears?
> Though in thy name the slaves her bosom wrung,
> Tell not the deed to blushing Europe's ears;
> The ocean queen, the free Britannia, bears
> The last poor plunder from a bleeding land;
> Yes, she whose generous aid her name endears
> Tore down those remnants with a Harpy's hand,
> Which envious Eld forbore and tyrants left to stand.

> Cold is the heart, fair Greece! that looks on thee,
> Nor feels as lovers o'er the dust they loved;
> Dull is the eye that will not weep to see
> Thy walls defaced, thy mouldering shrines removed
> By British hands which it had best behoved
> To guard those relics ne'er to be restored.
> Cursed be the hour when from their isle they roved
> And snatched thy shrinking gods to northern climes
> abhorr'ed.[16]

Félicité took admirably to her duties, complex and demanding as they were. She was exceptionally competent with little William and spent most of her free moments with him. Lady Elgin continued her busy life at Pau during these long winter weeks. Occasionally, Mr. and Mrs. Cockburn joined the Elgins for whist, but Mr. Cockburn was a poor player, and Lady Elgin doubted whether he would ever grasp the game. Once each week, the *détenus* dined together, but this proved burdensome to Elgin, whose mind was hundreds of miles away. Not only did he continually manifest his anxiety over the Parthenon marbles at the Piraeus docks, but he kept sending a flood of letters to Lusieri, coaxing him toward even more acquisitions and excavations, no matter what the cost. Already in heavy debt with his bankers in London, he arranged a loan with a bank in Malta. In January alone, he wrote three times to his mother, alerting her to spare no expense in confiscating Choiseul-Gouffier's frieze from the Parthenon "which all this time was being held under heavy duty charges at the London Customs House."[17]

On the second day of February 1804, Lady Elgin received word from her mother in Scotland: "Mrs. Nisbet had finally warmed to the Greek Paramana, and even went so far as to admit there were no English nurses to compare with this obese Greek woman who took exactly the same care of the children whether Mrs. Nisbet was present or absent."[18] But the Greek *paramana*'s fondness for garlic and thick sauces was still frowned upon at Archerfield. Lady Elgin was pleased to learn that Bruce was keeping diligently to his study of Greek. Tearfully, she recalled his daily greeting in Constantinople, so soft and brimming with love: "Kali Mera. Mitera. S'agapo! [Good morning, Mother. I love you!]" And Mary and little Matilda tried their best to imitate him, their thin lips moving along each strange syllable, stumbling but never giving up. True Scots!

But here in France, William's health bothered Lady Elgin. Unlike her other children, he was of very delicate constitution, more susceptible to illness, and no doubt for this reason, exceptionally attached to her:

> William has cut his first tooth without the least fever or anything to annoy us. He is really the finest child I ever saw. Such long eye lashes — so firm, so good of skin — and then he has such a merry little intelligent face of his own, as would quite captivate you I am sure. I don't know what we should do without him; he is the life of the whole house.[19]

William had a small appetite, and Lady Elgin fretted over this, believing it was the symptom of some dread disease. Mrs. Cockburn recommended a physician in Pau who was considered an authority on children's ailments, and after a lengthy examination, he pronounced William fit, much to the vexation of Lady Elgin, who was convinced the child was seriously ill. To improve William's appetite, the French physician prescribed a teaspoonful of red wine before each feeding; Lady Elgin was also encouraged to submit the child to regular visits at the baths in Barèges as soon as the summer season began.

They never got to Barèges.

In the first week of April, the French authorities at Pau notified the Elgins that they were now free to return to Paris. One evening they visited their friends and everyone seemed in fine humor, even the usually sour Mr. Sterling. Colonel Craufurd entertained them by narrating hoary tales of military life in Egypt.

Hunt left the house early the next morning and made negotiations for the hire of two carriages. By noon, they were ready to embark. After the drivers attended to the luggage, Félicité stepped into the carriage, carrying William in her arms. Lady Elgin sat beside her in the rear seat, while Hunt and Elgin shared the front seat. All the luggage was put into the second carriage. At the outskirts of Pau, their driver turned toward the Bordeaux road, but Lady Elgin, having already traveled it several times, suggested they go via Toulouse and Lyons. The route mattered little to Elgin; he was simply happy to be leaving Pau. Even little William seemed content and lay snuggled in his blanket, a pink glow on his face.

As the carriages sped across the countryside, hamlets and towns flitted past them. Lady Elgin observed a surging look of joy in her husband's eyes, which surely was brought about by a rekindled hope of imminent freedom and the promise of seeing Scotland at last. Toulouse skipped by almost before they realized it: a few squalid houses of white stucco, a solitary granite church, cows grazing in a quiet meadow. It was an exceedingly long journey, and Hunt wondered if they should have taken the Bordeaux road after all, but Elgin saw no point in turning back now. Besides, he had always yearned to visit Lyons.

Just before dusk, as they entered a small village, Lady Elgin became suddenly concerned about her son. The child's brow felt alarmingly hot, and his body was shivering. Elgin decided to stop here. The name of the village was Burlats, and they took lodgings at a small inn across the street from a church. William was given some warm milk and eventually fell asleep. However, he startled Lady Elgin in the middle of the night, violently ill with vomiting and high fever. Hunt dressed quickly, summoned one of the drivers, and together they hurried into the neighboring village of Brassac, where they succeeded in finding a physician. The aged doctor took one look at the child and immediately subjected him to an application of eight leeches on each temple, followed by an added ordeal of cupping and blood-letting. William was too weak to resist.

By midafternoon, his fever had subsided, and he was able to take a little beef broth, which the innkeeper's wife had graciously prepared. Elgin was anxious to continue their journey, but both Lady Elgin and Hunt prevailed upon him to wait until William was more fit for travel. Elgin sulked momentarily, but at dinner he recovered enough to engage in a heated political discussion with the innkeeper.

They left Burlats the next day at dawn.

Lyons truly astounded them: the baths, tombs, relics of an ancient theater, three aqueducts, and even traces of a subterranean canal that once conveyed the waters of the Rhone into a lake specially constructed for miniature sea battles. From the moment they entered the city, Hunt deluged them with his depth of learning, going as far back as the Gauls and Segusians, explaining how Lyons was once wedged between the Rhône and the Saône, and bordered by fine quays that were joined by twenty-four bridges. Agrippa had made Lyons the starting point of four great roads, and Augustus had given the city a senate, making it the seat of an annual assembly of deputies. Although it was burned to the ground shortly after the birth of Christ, Lyons was successively adorned by Trajan, Hadrian, and Antoninus. Saint Irenaeus met his martyrdom here during the savage persecution of Septimius Severus; and in the thirteenth century, two ecclesiastical councils convened inside the Cathedral of Notre Dame de Fourvière.

As Hunt plowed on, Lady Elgin half listened. William's fever was acting up again, and, pleadingly, she whispered to her husband to look for a physician.

Their son William died in Paris on April 8, 1805. Lady Elgin was distraught and on the verge of delirium.

Pray for me, my dearest Mother, take me in your arms. Your prayers will be heard tho' mine were not listened to. I have lost my William, my angel William. My soul doated on him; I was wrapt up in my child. From the moment of his birth, to the fatal night it pleased God to call him, I have devoted myself to him.

I am resigned to the Will of the Almighty, but my happiness is destroyed forever. My William, my adored William is gone, gone, and left me here.[20]

Lady Elgin refused to have the child buried in France, and while Elgin pleaded their case to Talleyrand in Paris, she arranged to have William embalmed and placed in a bier. Several weeks went by before Talleyrand finally sent word: Bonaparte had relented and agreed to grant her and Hunt permission to return to Scotland so that the child could be buried in Elgin's family vault in Dunfermline, but Elgin was to remain in France on orders from Bonaparte.

Lady Elgin was deeply troubled about abandoning her husband at a time like this, but she couldn't bear another day in France; and to add to her misery, she was now pregnant with her fifth child. Passage was arranged for embarkation in three days on an English brig that was docked at Calais. "Robert Fergusson, she learned later, would also be returning to England on board the same ship."[21]

In October 1805, on the morning of her departure, French soldiers burst into their suite at the Hotel de Richelieu and ordered Elgin out of bed. He was arrested and transported immediately to the prison at Melun.

When I was a prisoner in Paris, I received a mysterious letter from an English traveller which complained of Lusieri's taking down of the frieze of the Parthenon. The next morning a common gens d'arme came and took me out of bed, and sent me into close confinement at the prison of Melun away from my family. Such was the influence exercised by the French at this time.

Lady Elgin hated to leave her husband under such circumstances, but there was nothing she could do about it.

The Channel crossing was perilous. Stormy winds engulfed the brig from the moment they left Calais, forcing Hunt to confine himself to his cabin throughout the voyage, while Lady Elgin chose to remain on deck, bundled up in several blankets and refusing to look back at the unfriendly French coast.

At first sight of Dover, the storm abated, and the brig drifted peacefully around Folkestone, putting herself on a straight course for Portsmouth. A favorable wind soon found her sails, and she continued swiftly past Hastings and Brighton, coming finally into Portsmouth harbor. Before leaving the ship, Lady Elgin dined at the captain's table. Robert Fergusson sat beside her and, noticing her weak physical state, offered to assume full responsibility for the burial of William at Dunfermline.*

When they reached London, Hunt parted with her. His hopes of ever realizing an independent fortune were all but shattered. Elgin had not reimbursed him one farthing up to this point, and Hunt now felt compelled "to transfer his services to the Duke of Bedford."[22]

This revelation was a blow to Lady Elgin, and she begged Hunt to reconsider, but he was too embittered and wanted nothing more to do with Elgin.†

Later that day, Lady Elgin was given a newspaper that carried a story demanding the immediate return of the Parthenon marbles to Greece. The article was spurred by the report that a famous prizefighter named Gregson had been induced to stand naked in Elgin's museum at Park Lane and pose for two hours in various attitudes so that his anatomy might be compared with the statues. "A considerable number of English gentlemen paid as much as a guinea to witness this performance."[23] A month or so later, three actual boxing matches took place inside the museum between the best pugilists of the day.

During her long stay in London, Lady Elgin resided at 60 Baker Street. Her parents owned a palatial winter house at Portman Square nearby, and they entreated her to live there, but she was in dire need of

---

*Fergusson escorted the bier to Scotland and was present at the funeral.
†Hamilton alone, out of all the party that had sailed to Constantinople, was to remain loyal to Elgin until the very end.

peace and rest, and she preferred to remain at Baker Street. Although she was anxious to see her children, she felt she should not leave for Archerfield until her health permitted. Mrs. Nisbet's trusted maid, Mrs. Gosling, was assigned to Lady Elgin at Baker Street, along with two servants.

On January 15, 1806, Lady Elgin gave birth to her fifth child here, a girl named Lucy. A few days after the child was born, she wrote to her husband in France, "I have suffered so much from this event that I shall never subject myself again to that intercourse with you which might be productive of such effects!"[24]

Throughout these months, Robert Fergusson was a frequent visitor at 60 Baker Street, "even after the last guest had left."[25] In the course of her long recuperation, Lady Elgin suffered continuous stabs of conscience about her husband, and to atone for this disposition of mind, she wrote a long letter to King George III, imploring him to intercede in Elgin's behalf. She also wrote to the king of Prussia and to the emperor Alexander of Russia.

Meanwhile the furor over Elgin's removal of the Parthenon marbles continued unabated. During the prolonged debates, *The Times* of London published the following article:

> One of Bonaparte's confidential ministers recently disclosed that any high intercession from kings or emperors relating to Lord Elgin's imprisonment in France might very well prolong his Lordship's captivity since Bonaparte could not deny his pride by rejecting it. However it was observed that if the application came from any learned Society in England on the ground that his Lordship was an enlightened and liberal patron of the arts and had recovered many remains of antiquity at a great personal expense, it is not improbable that the application might succeed.[26]

Lady Elgin had nothing to lose, and since Robert Fergusson was a fellow in the Royal Society, she asked him to submit the formal application:

TO THE FELLOWS OF THE FRENCH INSTITUTE

> The rage of war ought not to interrupt the intercourse of men of science and we rejoice in the progress and success of your labours. Being

always ready on our part to lend assistance to your scientific men who may visit our country, we beg leave to represent the following case for your consideration:

A British Nobleman, an Ambassador imbued with the love of the arts and science, has — at a great personal expense remitted to England a very large collection of ancient Greek art. But these precious remains have neither been published nor exhibited, to the great disappointment of artists and the learned world because, in his absence, it is impossible to form any arrangements for that purpose. These noble fragments of antiquity remain packed in large cases and moulder in obscurity, exposed to the dangers of negligence and accident. Withdrawn from the destructive ignorance of the Turks who have already converted into lime too many similar works of Grecian genius, they have passed now into learned hands without conferring any of the numerous advantages that might otherwise have been expected to arise from their study and inspection.[27]

Before leaving France, Lady Elgin had been instructed by her husband to make a full inventory of the collection at Park Lane before leaving for Scotland. She braced herself for the ordeal, walking slowly to the museum, which was just off a small street behind Piccadilly. She passed through a small garden whose trees and flowers looked sad and neglected, and came finally before a large wooden structure. Its front door was open, and several groups of visitors were huddled around the metopes and statues that were strewn haphazardly on the floor. Nervously, she made a record of each piece, describing its exact position and arrangement. When she stepped before the caryatid, it was as though she had entered a tomb. She walked fitfully across the floor, past the torso of Iris that had been taken from the west pediment of the Parthenon, then on to that of Ilyssos and the magnificent metopes of the centaurs doing battle with the Lapithae. Unable to continue, she cast one last uneasy look at Aphrodite reclining on her mother's lap, the folds of her garment clinging to her skin.

She slept hardly at all that last night at 60 Baker Street. A carriage was waiting for her early the next morning, and only after she stepped into it did she feel a sense of comfort, knowing that at last she was on the way to her beloved Scotland. With her rode Mrs. Gosling, holding the infant Lucy in her arms, while the two other servants and the luggage followed in a cabriolet.

It was raining when the carriages pulled free of London. After they passed Waltham Abbey, the storm became more severe, and they were forced to stop at Cambridge for the night. In the morning, they fought their way through rain and mud and arrived at Wainfleet, where they found accommodations in a small but comfortable inn. They made their best time on the third day. Mrs. Gosling negotiated for a change of horses that afternoon, and they continued on a road that weaved along the banks of the Witham. Lingering at York for tea and biscuits, they then continued as far as Richmond and secured lodgings at a spacious inn in the very center of the town.

Darlington was reached the next day, and as they ate their noon meal at a small inn alongside the river Tees, Lady Elgin was pleased by little Lucy's voracious appetite and tolerance of travel. On the opposite bank lay Stockton, its grimy chimneys pouring thick columns of purple smoke into the cloudy sky. After crossing the old wooden bridge into Stockton, they entered Newcastle just as dusk was descending.

Early the next morning they moved off again. Lady Elgin sat back against the seat and fastened her eyes on the unwinding hills. There was much greenery everywhere. How it moved her heart to see heather once again! Sinking deeper into her seat, she closed her eyes, and when she awoke she discovered it was much later than she had imagined. The sun had already sunk behind the western hills, and a chilling mist was settling over the fields.

The carriages made swift time into Berwick-upon-Tweed, but the town was buried in darkness, and Lady Elgin saw nothing except the lighting of the lamps in the windows. They retired for the night at a small hotel near the outskirts of town, but it was impossible for her to sleep, knowing that Archerfield and her children were now less than thirty miles from her heart.

Scotland

*L*USIERI ASSUMED that the Elgins had reached Scotland after all this time — two years had passed, after all, with no news from them — and his long dispatches kept arriving at Archerfield with monthly regularity. The following letter was written on June 30, 1804:

Athens

My dear Lord:

Immediately after your Lordship's departure from Athens I set forth plans for further removals and excavations as instructed. We soon amassed still another large collection of marbles and succeeded in hauling them to the Piraeus for shipment — but during this time Count Sébastiani persuaded the Turks to break their alliance with Russia in favor of the French, and when the British heard about it, they sent their fleet to the aid of Russia. When their ships, however, passed through the Dardanelles to make a show of force in Constantinople, the Turks fired at them from the forts in the Straits, inflicting heavy losses.

As a result, this had a devastating effect on our shipment of marbles. The Voivode prevented us from putting them on board the waiting warship and I was forced to flee Athens, leaving your Lordship's fine treasures at the mercy of the French. The cases which contained a numerous assortment of vases were broken into and then sent overland to Epirus in northwest Greece, from whence they were forwarded to France and the Louvre Museum. But the real prize, Your Lordship's fine collection of marbles, presented a more difficult problem for the French. Because of their excessive weight, they could not be hauled over the mountains from Ioannina, the capital city of Epirus, and consequently the French Admiralty was called upon for assistance, but it was your Lordship's good fortune that not one French ship could be spared from the war effort.

I set out for Sicily and managed to reach there only after many tribulations. At Palermo, I negotiated with an agent of the Levant Company to act as your Lordship's representative and we arrived at a plan to save the marbles, which involved not only the persuasion of Lord Nelson to dispatch yet another war vessel to the Piraeus, but also the more daring scheme of seizing the French agent Fauvel by force of arms and holding him as ransom until the marbles on the docks were safely embarked. I equipped your Lordship's representative with large sums of money, which I had to borrow from several sources until such time as your Lordship can reimburse them. Much of this money went toward the purchase of silver pistols and English watches, since additional bribery was to be expected from the Turks. Lord Nelson was then warned that any warship sent to the Piraeus should also be accompanied by a strong transport ship, along with horses, tackle, ropes and carts.

Your Lordship's representative from the Levant Company went at once to Constantinople and obtained a firman that allowed me to return to Athens. I presented it to the Voivode, and in taking possession of my house, I found the doors and windows broken. A ladder was attached against the garden wall, enabling anyone to enter at will. Everything of value had been stolen: vases, scaffolding, ropes, and all my equipment. My first concern, however, was the shipment of marbles on the Piraeus docks. To my complete astonishment, they still remained there untouched. Working swiftly, I obtained permission from the Voivode to embark the collection on a chartered vessel from the Isle of Hydra. The marbles were quickly put on board and the ship was about to set sail, when an order arrived from the Porte, demanding that all the marbles be unloaded at once.

Bonaparte and his agents had again thwarted us, and as each case was hauled out of the ship and put on the docks, Fauvel stood there, cane in hand, gloating.

The following day, Nelson's warship and transport vessel arrived at the Piraeus. I called upon the Voivode and showered him with gifts, but he refused to permit us to load the marbles into the ships. Within a fortnight, however, the Turks became thoroughly disenchanted with the French for some reason and once again began veering toward an alliance with Britain.

Your Lordship's representative in Constantinople wrote to me a short time after this and said he had succeeded in obtaining the Sultan's order to the Voivode for the embarkation of the marbles. The firman reached Athens on 2nd June, but by that time Nelson's ships unfortunately had sailed out of the Piraeus. Needless to say, Fauvel found great delight in this. However Lord Nelson once again came to your Lordship's assistance and sent the most available warship to the Piraeus directly from Smyrna. Even in this last hour, the French tried to block our plans through Fauvel's bribery and intrigue, but the Sultan's firman was sovereign, and thus the marbles were hauled on board the warship and she finally set sail for Malta, and thence to England.

I must now report to your Lordship the rebellious scene which took place on the docks as the warship was being loaded. The trouble was instigated by the pen of Lord Byron whose poems have ignited the world against your Lordship's taking of the Parthenon marbles.[1] I include herein a brief section from Byron's *Childe Harold's Pilgrimage*, Canto II, Note 2:

> It is to be lamented that a war more than civil is raging on the subject of Lord Elgin's pursuits in Greece. We can all feel or imagine the regret with which the ruins of cities, once the capitals of empire, are beheld — but never did the smallness of man nor the vanity of his very best virtues of patriotism and of valor to defend his country appear more conspicuous than in the record of what Athens was, and the certainty of what she now is. This theatre of contention between mighty factions — the struggles of orators, the exaltation and deposition of tyrants, the triumph and punishment of generals — is now become a scene of petty intrigue and personal disturbance between the bickering agents of Lord Elgin and Bonaparte. The wild foxes, the owls and serpents in the ruins of Babylon were surely less degrading than such as these. The Turks have the plea of conquest for their tyranny; and the Greeks have suffered the fortune of war incidental to the bravest. But how are the mighty fallen when two lascivious men contest the privilege of plundering the Parthenon, each triumphing in turn according to the tenor of succeeding firmans! Sylla could not punish; Philip subdue; and Xerxes burn. It remained for one paltry Scotch nobleman and his despicable painter to render Athens contemptible as themselves.[2]

Lusieri finished his letter by asking to be released from the bonds of his contract with Elgin. As with his previous messages, he again reminded Elgin that he "had yet to receive any of the salary promised him."[3] Like Hunt, Carlyle, and everyone else on Elgin's staff, Lusieri had not collected one penny for his labors. Even worse, the world now looked upon him with hatred and contempt.

After several months of squalid confinement, Elgin finally obtained his release from the prison at Melun and was allowed to return to London. "His release was brought about in large measure by a direct plea to Bonaparte by Lord Grenville during the brief period of his service as prime minister."[4] Before obtaining his safe passage from France, Lord Elgin was obliged to sign a document in the presence of Talleyrand, promising that he would return to France whenever the French government required it.

Elgin was elated to be back home at last. It was now common knowledge that he had compiled an enormous expense in bringing the Parthenon marbles to London, but he was hopeful of retrieving these losses by immediately putting before Parliament the proposition of purchasing his collection for the British Museum.

His joy of being free, however, was more than offset by the discovery that his wife was having an illicit affair with another man, Robert Fergusson. Through several of his friends, including his secretary at Constantinople, Alexander Stratton, Elgin had in his possession several letters between his wife and Fergusson that were irrefutable. In fact, the exchange of correspondence had begun while they were prisoners in France.

I can boast of loving you with a passion never felt before [the letter from Fergusson began], and I hope the time of our union approaches. Good God! how can you submit to that man's gross conversation? How can such language be addressed to a wife? Your husband's conversation is abhorrent to you, and you must break your fetters.[5]

A second letter from Fergusson to Lady Elgin was even more inflammatory. "You must prove and act upon your disgust; you must exasperate him; you must consider his approach as a violation of your person and force him to a separation!"[6]

In still another letter, there was a powerful declaration of Fergusson's deep love for Lady Elgin. "If ever love reigned in all its purity, it is in our hearts. I shall die with thy image upon my heart, and shall hold up my face to heaven and declare my most faithful love, even when expiring."[7]

Through the connivance of his former secretary at Constantinople, William Richard Hamilton, Elgin had also impounded many of the letters that Lady Elgin wrote to Fergusson, such as:

> Elgin was very much agitated indeed, but he said nothing. After tea, he got up suddenly and went into his room for a couple of hours. He coughed dreadfully, which he always does when he is annoyed. I told him of my wish to go and see where my beloved William is laid, and that I wished to go alone. It is something I cannot account for you, but I feel as if he was our own. Elgin went out early this morning. I have not seen him. I must do him the justice to say he has taken upon himself to keep his promise and allow me to proceed to England without him, but I hardly think it possible he can go on with it. I shudder when I dare think of it and too thoroughly I feel I cannot live without you.[8]

From these identical sources, Elgin had confiscated additional letters, most of them written in the same manner, with detailed instructions about how the illicit affair should be conducted. The case reached such bizarre levels, Elgin's own friends were passing the letters between Fergusson and Lady Elgin.

Elgin's wrathful jealousy demanded instant retaliation, and although he won a quick civil action in London, he was now compelled under English law to undergo a second and very expensive trial in Edinburgh. Divorce was permitted by Scots law, whereas in England it was granted only by a private and even more costly Act of Parliament. Fergusson did not contest the civil action in London and thus the decision went against him by default, but he and Lady Elgin were determined to plead their case in Edinburgh.

The Nisbet household understandably was oppressed by turbulence in the weeks that followed. Elgin's decision to bring shame and disgrace upon his wife bordered on madness, since he would be dragging his own name into the mess. However, the real motive for his action was revealed when the following account appeared in *The Times*:

> Lord Elgin's operations in Athens have left him penniless. Accompanying his proposal to Parliament for the purchase of the Parthenon marbles, his Lordship referred to his huge personal expenditures:

Pay of the Artists at Athens	£9,200
Conveyance of the Artists to and from the East	£1,500
Pay of Workmen at Athens and elsewhere	£15,000
Storage of the Marbles at Malta	£2,500
Cost of the *Mentor*, its salvage, etc.	£5,000
Cost of moving the Marbles to England etc.	£6,000
Total	£39,200[9]

This staggering sum pertained only to the first collection of marbles sent to England. A comparable figure was to be attached to subsequent shipments, making a grand total of seventy-four thousand pounds. Parliament was not willing to pay such a price, and during its long deliberations, two incidents occurred that gravely affected Elgin's case. The first concerned John Tweddell, a young scholar of exceptional ability, who took a grand tour of Switzerland, Germany, Russia, Turkey, Egypt, Palestine, and Greece. He had completed five huge books of journals; also four volumes of Greek inscriptions, seven portfolios of drawings, eight books of etchings and paintings, and numerous other works of artistic and academic value. To imbue his work with professional distinction, he engaged the famous French painter Preaux, who had formerly been employed by both Choiseul-Gouffier and Edward Daniel Clarke. Tweddell was determined to surpass Clarke's massive accomplishments and even purchased many choice drawings from Fauvel, but he died suddenly of a fever in Athens, and Fauvel arranged to have him buried in the Theseum.*[10]

---

*Fauvel's motive did not stem from loyalty. By digging Tweddell's grave, he hoped to unearth the tomb of Theseus.

A large collection of Tweddell's papers had been assigned to Thomas Thornton of the Levant Company for safekeeping in Constantinople, but most of these were destroyed in a fire. The rest were sent by British consul Logothetis at Athens to Sir John Spencer Smith, who was ambassador to the Porte at that time, with the request that they be put in boxes and forwarded to Tweddell's heirs in England.

Lord Elgin had just succeeded Smith when the papers arrived in Constantinople after a hazardous journey in which the ship carrying them was wrecked in the Sea of Marmara. However, most of the boxes were saved, although they were damaged when they reached the British embassy in Constantinople. Elgin had all the papers laid out in the cellar of the British Palace to dry, and he assigned Hunt and Professor Carlyle to sort and catalog them. After this tedious work was done, Elgin ordered the papers to be packed and sent to England at his expense, but somehow a mistake occurred, and the papers were never dispatched. Inexplicably, many of the drawings found their way to the home of William Nisbet in Scotland; and Hunt later admitted "that he had copied some notes from Tweddell's journals, hoping they would be useful on his own journeys through Greece."[11]

These matters were eventually brought to the attention of Sir John Spencer Smith, who wrote to Tweddell's family and laid the blame entirely on Elgin. Tweddell's brother, the Reverend Robert Tweddell, immediately decided to investigate the whole affair. He wrote to Elgin, politely asking him to relate the complete circumstances regarding the loss of his brother's papers, covering up his real purpose by claiming he intended to write a biography of his brother.

Elgin responded with a full account of everything he could remember, upon which the Reverend Tweddell wrote again, requesting that Elgin clear up certain points that had arisen. Elgin once more obliged, supplying the Reverend Tweddell with a steady flow of letters for a period of six months.

The Reverend Tweddell employed the same tactics with Thomas Thornton of the Levant Company; also with Hunt. Since Carlyle had died unexpectedly while Elgin was imprisoned in France, the Reverend Tweddell approached one of the professor's friends and was successful in extracting many valuable recollections, which were then handed over to a lawyer. When Edward Daniel Clarke was informed of all this, he quickly added his opinions to the debate:

> That the literary property of this gentleman, after being in the undisputed possession of the British Ambassador at Constantinople, should absolutely have disappeared in toto and eluded the most diligent inquiries of his family and friends, presents a subject for the deepest regret, and is a circumstance of the most unaccountable nature. Upon this point, however, the author refrains from saying all that he might in the expectation of seeing this strange mystery unfolded by a kindred hand which may justly aspire to the best information.
>
> It is to be feared that if any other part of Mr. J. Tweddell's observations upon Greece ever see the light, it will be in the garbled form of extracts made from his writings of those who ransacked his papers, without any acknowledgment being made of their real author.[12]

All this adverse publicity proved to be destructive during Elgin's negotiations with Parliament, and when the sad matter finally came to an end, his prospects of arriving at a satisfactory sale were severely damaged.

The second unfortunate incident related to the valuable manuscripts that Professor Carlyle had borrowed from the Greek monasteries before departing from the East. They were lent to him by the patriarch of Constantinople on the written condition that Carlyle "promise to return them to the Patriarch when the purposes for which they were borrowed were completed, or whenever the Patriarch should demand them."[13] As a secretary to Elgin's embassy, Philip Hunt affixed his signature alongside Carlyle's, thus making the British government a responsible party in the contract.

These ancient manuscripts ranged in date from the tenth to the fifteenth century and contained priceless texts of the New Testament. Six were taken from the monastery of Saint Saba in Syria; four came from the library of the Jerusalem patriarch at Constantinople; and eighteen were borrowed from various monasteries in the Prinsen Islands near Constantinople. It was Carlyle's hope to have them collated in England so that he might produce a revised version of the New Testament. Until this time, many scholars had attempted to lay their hands on these rare manuscripts, but the Greek monasteries had strictly forbade it, and their monks were bound to an oath administered before taking their vows: to preserve and protect all property of the monastery.

Overcoming these obstacles, but only through the sanction of Elgin's embassy, Carlyle had undeniably obtained the manuscripts by irregular means, and when he finally reached England, he realized that his collection "amounted to near a tenth part of all manuscripts of the New Testament that have yet been examined in Europe."[14] He quickly assembled a group of scholars and theologians to assist him in the gigantic task of collation. To make their work less burdensome, Carlyle printed a memorandum: "Hints and observations which Mr. Carlyle Takes the Liberty of Suggesting to the Consideration of the Gentlemen Who Have Kindly Promised Their Assistance in Collating the Greek Mss. of the New Testament." To make their work easier, the manuscripts from Saint Saba were marked S, the four from Constantinople bore the reference C, and the eighteen from the Prinsen Islands were designated I.

Just as the work was launched and moving toward a sound goal, Carlyle suddenly fell ill and died. His family was heartbroken. Carlyle's trip to the East had cut into their entire fortune, and the manuscripts were the only things of value left in their possession. To escape financial ruin, Carlyle's sister arranged to have published a posthumous edition of Carlyle's poems; she also decided to sell the manuscripts, but before doing so, she wrote to Philip Hunt and asked his advice. Hunt suggested they should be deposited with the archbishop of Canterbury in the library at Lambeth. This had never occurred to Miss Carlyle, and she gratefully replied to Hunt,

> As to the manuscripts, I think that as the survivor, you have an undoubted right to dispose of those brought from Constantinople in any way you please; nor could you have fixed upon any place more agreeable than under the patronage of the Archbishop of Canterbury. It would give me great pain to separate what has cost us so dear to collect together. At the same time, I do not conceive myself authorized to

refuse any compensation for them which the Archbishop, after inspection, may think proper to make me. My brother, the day before he died, said to me that, as his unfortunate journey had been attended with a great pecuniary loss to his family, I must make what I could of his manuscripts.[15]

Elgin was to suffer bitterly from Hunt's blunder. While his proposition for the sale of the Parthenon marbles was being considered and debated in Parliament, a curt letter was sent to the British government from the new English ambassador at Constantinople, stating that the patriarch had now formally requested the return of the borrowed manuscripts. Fearing a scandal, the foreign secretary asked the archbishop to honor the patriarch's request, but the archbishop balked. Several months later, a second letter arrived from the ambassador at Constantinople, angrily declaring "that the National character suffers by this neglect and that the Patriarch looks on the transaction as a breach of confidence!"[16] The message ended with a sharp criticism of Elgin's embassy.

Under such mounting pressure, the archbishop finally acceded, but he sent back only the four manuscripts that Carlyle had marked *C* for Constantinople, whereas the patriarch's request included the six manuscripts from Saint Saba and the eighteen from the Prinsen Islands. This touched off a long and heated argument. Elgin's reputation was now at stake, and he pleaded with the archbishop, but it was hopeless. The archbishop refused to comply.*

In addition, Elgin had to combat the unrelenting assaults of Richard Payne Knight, who kept insisting that Elgin's collections were not the original Parthenon marbles at all but Roman copies. Responding to these charges, Elgin offered one hundred and fifty pounds to Ennio Quirino Visconti, director of the Louvre, to come to London and examine the marbles. Aside from the fee, Visconti was to stay in London for a fortnight at Elgin's expense and then prepare a memorandum of his examination before returning to Paris. "Visconti had been director of the Capitoline Museum at Rome and had followed the

---

*To this day, the manuscripts are at Lambeth Library.

masterpieces of Italy to Paris, and he now presided over the greatest accumulation of works of art that the world is ever likely to see. His reputation as the greatest connoisseur in Europe was well deserved."[17]

Visconti accepted the offer, and his memorandum was a triumph for Elgin:

> Neither Stuart's drawings, nor Choiseul-Gouffier's fragments and casts, had been able to give me the idea of the works of Pheidias, which the sight of the actual objects has done. The frieze, the metopes, the pediments — all showed every perfection and were every bit as excellent as the famous statues of Italy. There can be no doubt that the Parthenon marbles were executed under the supervision of Pheidias himself; and if the classical statues of Italy were an inspiration to the Michelangelos and Raphaels of the sixteenth century, will not the Elgin Marbles inaugurate a new era for the progress of sculpture in England?[18]

Confident at last of defeating Knight, Elgin at once set about ordering a printed edition of Visconti's appraisal to be included in his own *Memorandum on the Subject of the Earl of Elgin's Pursuit in Greece*, and as soon as it was published, he distributed copies to each member of Parliament, with the suggestion that the whole matter be referred to a select committee of the House of Commons, which would then investigate his expenditures and decide what price the government should offer for the marbles. During the hearings of the select committee, Visconti sent a full report of his examination, striking a hard blow to Knight's claim that the sculptures were not done by Pheidias. "In their new situation, in the midst of an enlightened nation particularly disposed to afford encouragement to sculpture, the Elgin Marbles will rouse the talents of the young artist to exertion and will direct him in the road which leads to perfection in his art. We have only to regret that the noble idea which induced Lord Elgin to rescue them from the daily ravages of a barbarous nation was not entertained a century and a half earlier."[19]

The select committee consisted of eighteen members of Parliament, each with different shades of opinion. Only two had any substantial knowledge of Grecian art and sculpture: F. S. N. Douglas and John Nicholas Fazakerly.

Lord Aberdeen, a distinguished scholar with a retentive memory and a wide knowledge of literature and art, was examined by Henry Bankes of the select committee on March 8, 1816.

"Did your Lordship bring home any Marbles from Athens and from any other parts of Greece?"

"Yes."

"In your Lordship's opinion, could any private traveller have had opportunities of accomplishing the removal of these Marbles?"

"I do not think a private individual could have accomplished that which Lord Elgin obtained."

"Has your Lordship any opinion whether these sculptures are the work of Pheidias?"

"From the testimony of ancient authors, there can be no doubt that they were executed under his immediate direction."[20]

That same day, Fazakerly was also examined by Henry Bankes.

"You were at Athens at the time the Aegina Marbles were removed?"

"No, I was there immediately prior to their removal in 1811."

"Do you know whether great difficulty was experienced in removing them out of Greece?"

"Certainly, very great. The Aegina Marbles were deposited in a building almost underground and considered there in some degree in secret. They were not generally shown, and it was understood that the Turkish government had opposed their removal. Mr. Charles Robert Cockerell, a young architectural student, called upon me to consult with the English Consul upon the means of enabling him to remove them from Athens. The Consul told me that he felt great embarrassment on the subject, adding that they could only be removed either in secret or by bribery."

"And where are these Marbles now?"

"In Munich. They were sold for six thousand pounds to the Prince of Bavaria."

Taylor Combe, an authority on ancient coins and medals, was then called before the select committee to assess the coins and medals that Elgin had acquired in Greece, which also were to be included in the collection for the British Museum:

"Are you well acquainted with the Medals collected by my Lord Elgin?"

"I am."

"Of what number do they consist?"

"Eight hundred and eighty: sixty-six gold, five hundred and seventy-seven silver, and two hundred and thirty-seven copper."[21]

When it came time for Elgin himself to be examined, he presented his case to the select committee in a convincing tone of voice, recounting how the idea of improving the British arts was first suggested to him by his architect Thomas Harrison; how he went ahead at his own expense to obtain the services of artists, draftsmen, architects, and formatori; and how his real purpose for rescuing the Parthenon marbles was spurred by the great destruction perpetrated daily on the Acropolis Hill by the Turks, unscrupulous travelers, and the ravages of time and weather.

He reminded the committee that when it came to the subject of the Parthenon marbles he never skimped, producing authentic accounts that showed every penny spent, from the first day of his embassy to the very last. His many gifts to the Turkish authorities at Athens alone amounted to seven thousand pounds. The interest on the large sums of money borrowed from his bankers at Malta came to 18 percent. On top of this, there were the artists, the costs of transporting the marbles to the Piraeus docks, the price of three ships, and the loss of the *Mentor*. A heavy sum was also attributed to the museum at Park Lane and to the staggering duty charges leveled at the London custom house. Repeated questions were put to Elgin on the legal authority for his operations, and particularly the validity of his two firmans from the Porte.

"In point of fact, your Lordship has not in England any copy of those written permissions from the Turkish government?"

"None. I employed three or four hundred people a day at Athens;

and all the local authorities were involved in it, as well as the Turkish government.

In presenting the enormous expense of £74,240 to the select committee, Elgin pleaded,

"I beg once more to repeat, that I do not offer this view of my expenses as a criterion of the intrinsic value of my Collection. I ever have been persuaded that, in justice to the Public, this should be calculated on other grounds. But it is, I trust, sufficient to prove, that in amassing these remains of antiquity for the benefit of my Country, and in rescuing them from the imminent and unavoidable destruction with which they were threatened, had they been left many years longer the prey of mischievous Turks, who mutilated them for wanton amusement, or for the purpose of selling them piecemeal to occasional travellers, I have been actuated by no motives of private emolument, nor deterred from doing what I felt to be a substantial good, by considerations of personal risk, or the fear of calumnious misrepresentations."

But Richard Payne Knight was not one to give up easily. Undaunted by Visconti's appraisal, he now did his utmost to discredit Elgin's endeavors in Greece, exclaiming at one point, "You have lost your labour, my Lord Elgin. Your marbles are overrated. They are not the works of Pheidias. They are Roman, of the time of Hadrian!"[22]

Elgin immediately struck back and brought in the most eminent names in the art world to give testimony to the authenticity of the marbles. Said Joseph Nollekens: "The Elgin Marbles are the finest things that ever came to this country." John Flaxman (the English Pheidias) agreed: "The finest works of art I have ever seen." Sir Thomas Lawrence, the British portraitist, showered his praise on the marbles: "There is in them an union of fine composition and very grand form, with a more true and natural expression of the effect of action upon the human frame than there is in the Apollo Belvedere or in any of the other most celebrated statues."

Benjamin West was too ill to attend the hearings; nevertheless he sent his opinions in writing, strongly supporting Elgin. He agreed that the Elgin Marbles should not have been restored by Flaxman or anyone else, and closed his remarks by saying that the acquisition of the Elgin Marbles would bring a great improvement in the fine arts of Great Britain.

Throughout the long interrogations of the select committee, Benjamin Haydon "stood patiently by, waiting to be called, but the day passed and he was not."[23] Three days later, he wrote a stinging letter that was printed in London's leading newspapers. He titled it: "On the Judgment of Connoisseurs Being Preferred to That of Professional Men," and it was of course an indictment against Richard Payne Knight and the elite group of the Society of Dilettanti, whose opinion, rather than that of professional artists, was given priority by the select committee.

In no other profession is the opinion of the man who has studied it for his amusement preferred to that of him who has devoted his soul to excel in it. No man will trust his limb to a connoisseur in surgery; no minister would ask a connoisseur in war how a campaign is to be conducted; no nobleman would be satisfied with the opinion of a connoisseur in law on disputed property; and why should a connoisseur of an art be preferred to the professional man?

Haydon's article did more good for the artist than for Elgin. "It was widely published and even translated into several European languages."[24] Members of the select committee claimed they were not influenced by it and had already drafted their report when the article appeared; nor were they carried away by Richard Payne Knight's last efforts to sway them from Elgin's supporters. In fact, Knight injured his case when he appeared as a witness before the select committee.

Q. Are you acquainted with the Elgin Collection?
A. Yes, I have looked them over, not only formerly, but I have looked them over on this occasion with reference to their value.
Q. In what class of art do you place the finest works of this collection?

A. I think of things extant, I should put them in the second rank —
some of them. They are very unequal. The finest I should put in
the second rank.

Q. Do you think that none of them rank in the first rank?

A. Not with the Laocoön and the Apollo, and those which have been
placed in the first class of art. At the same time, I must observe
that their state of preservation is such that I cannot form a very
accurate notion; their surface is gone mostly.

Q. Do you consider them to be of a very high antiquity?

A. We know from the authority of Plutarch that those of the
Parthenon, which are the principal, were executed by Callicrates
and Ictinos, with their assistants and scholars; and I think some
were added in the time of Hadrian.

Q. In what class do you rank the fragments of the draped female figures?

A. They are so mutilated, I can hardly tell. But I should think most
of them were added by Hadrian. They are but of little value, except from their local interest, from having been part of the
Temple.[25]

Soon after his testimony, Knight delivered a paper to the select
committee in which a figure was finally put against the main items of
the Elgin collection. The total came to less than twenty-five thousand
pounds, and Knight's last remarks were an open insult to Elgin: "The
amount is far more than twice what these marbles could fetch on the
open market!"[26]

Knight's opinions were damaging to Elgin. After two whole weeks
of examination and study, the committee's report was at last prepared
and made public. It recommended an unyielding price of thirty-five
thousand pounds, which was less than half of what Elgin had personally expended. During the heated negotiations, Elgin was unexpectedly released from one of his debts: Giovanni Battista Lusieri fell
victim to a horrible death in Athens, brought about by the rupture of a
blood vessel. He had borne the full weight of Greek animosity against
Elgin and had to barricade his house every night, in fear of his life. On
the day of his death, the neighborhood was surprised to find him absent from the Acropolis Hill. They went to his house and discovered

him lying on the floor in a pool of blood. A black cat was perched on his chest. Scattered about him were some tattered clothes, his ever-present umbrella, and several drawings, all of them unfinished.*[27]

After a long stay on the Continent, Byron returned to England in late 1811. *Childe Harold's Pilgrimage* had just been published, "and within three days the edition was sold out; another four editions were to go through the press before the end of the year. Almost overnight, the young disreputable Lord Byron had become one of the most famous and most sought-after men in England."[28]

A large part of the second canto of *Childe Harold's Pilgrimage* was a bitter attack on Lord Elgin. Elgin had been forewarned about Byron, by both Lusieri and Logothetis, but he refused to give the poet serious thought, at least not openly. In a letter to Hobhouse, however, written much later, Byron made a startling disclosure:

> Lord Elgin has been teasing to see me these last days. I wrote to him at his own request all I knew about his robberies, and at last have written to say that, as it is my intention to publish in Childe Harold on that topic, I thought proper, since he insisted on seeing me, to give him notice so that he might not have an opportunity of accusing me of double-dealing afterwards.[29]

Elgin may have wanted all this publicity, even though it was unfavorable. In any case, he was decidedly influenced in his attitude toward Byron by his secretary Hamilton, who, after being advised about Byron's criticism of Elgin, remarked, "I do not consider him [Byron] a very formidable enemy in his meditated attack, and I shall be much surprised if his attack on what you have done does not turn out one of the most friendly acts he could have done. It will create an interest in the public, excite curiosity, and the real advantage to this country and the merit of your exertions will become known and felt as they are more known."[30]

---

*Lusieri was buried in the grounds of the Capuchin monastery at Athens. Several English benefactors erected a monument for him that can still be seen alongside the tombstone of John Tweddell on one side of the English church.

Hamilton was badly mistaken. Elgin never dreamed he would be eternally stigmatized in a poem. Only once throughout the entire work does Byron attack any individual, and that person is Lord Elgin. Within a few short months, an unknown dreamer and "scurrilous versifier' had become a great romantic poet, and *Childe Harold* was eagerly read in every drawing room in England."[31]

When the prince regent joined Byron's forces, it gave rise to a wave of personal assaults on Elgin. Edward Daniel Clarke, always present and willing, leaped into the fray, congratulating Byron on the publication of *Childe Harold* and chiding Elgin and his agents for "want of taste and utter barbarism. Removed from their original setting, the Parthenon marbles have lost all their excellence!"[32]

Elgin soon learned that a host of other voices were to speak out against him, most of them travelers who had recently returned from the East, like member of Parliament and traveler F. S. N. Douglas. "It appears to me a very flagrant piece of injustice to deprive a helpless and friendly nation of any possession of value to them. I wonder at the boldness of the hand that could venture to remove what Pheidias had placed under the inspection of Pericles."[33]

A large number of these travelers had no call to fault Elgin because they were despoilers themselves. One of them, Edward Dodwell, chided Elgin for his "insensate barbarism and devastating outrage, which will never cease to be deplored;"[34] the Reverend T. S. Hughes spoke of Elgin's "wanton devastation and avidity for plunder."[35] J. C. Eustace, an author and traveler, had the audacity to condemn Elgin "without ever having been to Athens."[36]

These scathing attacks of condemnation did not come from England alone. The French, too, added their indignation. Chateaubriand affixed his support to the cause against Elgin, "although he too had a piece of the Parthenon in his pocket when he left Athens."[37]

There was no end to the furor. Elgin was constantly subjected to an avalanche of cruel jokes and jibes, "and even the ugly disfigurement of his nose was cruelly attributed to venereal disease."[38]

Another sharp attack came from Byron's poem "The Curse of Minerva." One of Elgin's friends tried to prevent its publication, and for a time it seemed that Byron would oblige. At a later time, the young poet was visited by the American statesman and orator Edward Everett of Massachusetts, and Everett asked him "whether his poem which he speaks of as printed but not published would ever be given to the world." "Oh, no!" Byron replied. "It is a satire upon Lord Elgin which a particular friend has begged me to suppress."[39]

Byron nevertheless printed a few copies and sent them to select friends, including Edward Daniel Clarke. A pirated copy found its way into the *New Monthly Magazine*,[40] and the poem was soon brought to the attention of the world. It begins with the poet sitting disconsolately within the ruined walls of the Parthenon as evening is falling over Athens. Suddenly Minerva (Athena) appears, but she does not look like the goddess at all — her aegis has no power, her armor is dented, her lance broken:

> Mortal! — twas thus she spake — that blush of shame
> Proclaims thee Briton, once a noble name;
> First of thy mighty, foremost of the free,
> Now honour'd less by all, and least by me;
> Chief of thy foes shall Pallas still be found,
> Seek'st thou the cause of loathing? Look around.
> Lo! here, despite of war and wasting fire,
> I saw successive tyrannies expire.
> Scaped from the ravage of the Turk and Goth,
> Thy country sends a spoiler worse than both.
> Survey this vacant violated fane;
> Recount the relics torn that yet remain:
>
> These Cecrops placed, this Pericles adorn'd.
> That Adrian rear'd when drooping Science mourn'd.
> What more I owe let gratitude attest —
> Know, Alaric and Elgin did the rest.
> That all may learn from whence the plunderer came,
>
> The insulted wall sustains his hated name!*
> For Elgin's fame thus grateful Pallas pleads,
> Below, his name; above, behold his deeds![41]

---

*The names of Elgin and Mary Elgin were carved deeply and clearly about halfway up one of the columns of the Parthenon in a place that Hunt had specially reserved. Elgin's name was soon erased, but that of Mary Elgin could still be read in 1826.

Moving deeper into the poem, Venus (Aphrodite) vows to revenge Minerva, and she invokes her own curse upon Elgin:

> Yet still the gods are just, and crimes are cross'd:
> See here what Elgin won, and what he lost!
> Another name with his pollutes my shrine;
> Behold where Dian's beams disdain to shine!
> Some retribution still might Pallas claim,
> When Venus half avenged Minerva's shame.

Minerva now begs the poet to carry her curse home to his native country. Elgin's deed is so abominable, it is not enough that he alone suffer. England, too, has to be punished. She will be plagued by a succession of devastating wars that eventually will destroy her. "Her tyrant empire will be shaken to its base!" Her trade will languish, famine and pestilence will break out over her land, and finally she will be invaded and ravaged. But the main brunt of the curse is to fall on Elgin and his family:

> First on the head of him who did this deed
> My curse shall light — on him and all his seed;
> Without one spark of intellectual fire,
> Be all the sons as senseless as the sire!

The Scottish novelist John Galt was an eyewitness to the sacking of the Parthenon and Erechtheum by Lusieri and his laborers in March 1810 and even intervened in an attempt to prevent a Hydriote vessel from loading still another shipment of Parthenon marbles at Piraeus.

> Two circumstances occasioned this interference on my part: an Italian artist, the agent of Lord Elgin, had quarrelled about the marbles with Monsieur Fauvel, the French Consul. Fauvel was no doubt ambitious to obtain these precious fragments for the Napoleon Museum at Paris; and certainly exerted all his influence to get the removal of them interdicted. On the eve of the departure of the vessel, he sent in a strong representation on the subject to the governor of the city, stating, what I

believe was very true, that Lord Elgin had never any sufficient firman or authority for the dilapidations that he had committed on the temple. Lusieri (the Italian artist alluded to) was alarmed and called on me at the monastery of the Roman Propaganda (Capuchin monastery), where I then resided, and it was agreed that if any detention was attempted I should remonstrate with the governor and represent to him that such an arrest of British property would be considered an act of hostility.[42]

Not to be outdone by Fauvel, Lusieri armed himself with still another firman from the kaimmakam. In addition, he had the support of the HMS *Pylades*, which was dispatched to Piraeus with the explicit purpose of escorting the Hydriote ship and her prize collection of marbles. With this apparently final rejection of Fauvel, Lusieri sent a triumphant message to Elgin. "Covering up all my past woes with eternal oblivion, I wholly give myself up to joy when I see the antiquities on board the *polacca* (HMS *Pylades*). I regret that I cannot follow them as I am obliged to stay here as a surety for paying what I owe and carrying out my promises to the Voivode."[43]

John Galt took passage on this same Hydriote ship, but only as far as Hydra Isle.[44] Before embarking, he wrote to his banker at Malta and instructed him to buy the marbles as soon as the Hydriote vessel reached port. Galt anticipated that Elgin's bankers would allow no further credit, since Elgin was already heavily in debt to them: "Here was a chance of the most exquisite relics of art in the world becoming mine, and a speculation by the sale of them in London that would realise a fortune."[45]

Fortunately for Elgin, Galt's scheme failed when his banker refused to grant him the loan, and thus another collection was on its way to England: forty-eight cases of marbles, including the best of the Parthenon sculptures. Galt meanwhile was itching to strike back at Elgin, and as soon as he returned to Scotland, he wrote a cruel satire that he called "Atheniad." As with Byron's "The Curse of Minerva," Elgin tried to suppress its publication, using the influence of William Richard Hamilton, his former secretary, who now held the position of curator at Elgin's museum in Park Lane.*

---

*Hamilton later became undersecretary at the foreign office.

The "Atheniad" is "an amateurish piece of mock heroics, good-humoured enough on the whole, but where 'The Curse of Minerva' becomes bitter against Lord Elgin, 'the Atheniad' merely shows bad taste."[46] Galt disguises his main characters in the poem. Lusieri is "Dontitos" and Lord Elgin is called "Brucides." The poem begins as Dontitos calls upon Brucides and tells him he must rescue the Parthenon from the Turks. Hoping this would make him famous, Brucides undertakes the task, but in the midst of his endeavors, the gods of Olympus show their wrath and immediately begin to take their revenge. Neptune sinks Brucides' ship at Cerigo, and soon after this, Brucides loses his post at Constantinople, because Minerva has taken his military and diplomatic dispatches and transposed them into garbled nonsense. The goddess then follows Brucides into France, and, disguised as Talleyrand, she persuades Bonaparte to detain all the British prisoners of war. Mars also takes his revenge and stirs up horrible wars in Egypt and Russia. The final act of revenge is left with Athena: Brucides' marriage is destroyed, his children die, and Eros sends a flaming torch into his face, disfiguring him so badly that he becomes a noseless statue.

Although Byron refused to admit it, he borrowed many ideas from the "Atheniad." In one glaring example, Galt calls Eratostratus "the bold youth that fired th'Ephesian dome,"[47] whereas "The Curse of Minerva" has it: "the fool that fired the Ephesian dome."

Elgin's enemies were not confined to poets and novelists. By far, the main brunt of the attack against him in England was leveled by Richard Payne Knight. Knight's influence as a patron of the arts was strongly felt throughout Europe. As a youth, he wrote a diary of a journey to Sicily that so impressed Goethe, immediate arrangements were made to have it published in Germany. Knight's best book, *An Analytic Inquiry into the Principles of Taste*, is a penetrating study of sense, idea, passion, and truth. Claiming that ideal beauty does not exist, Knight did concede to "certain standards of excellence which all cultures have recognised in theory, even though they have departed from them in practice. Accordingly, the precious remains of Greek sculpture afford true beauty, grace and eloquence in the human form. Their perfection can never be questioned."[48]

Elgin's supporters also banded together. Knight, however, one of the first to inspect the Parthenon marbles at the museum in Park Lane, wrongly concluded that they were not Greek but Roman. Benjamin West, the venerable president of the Royal Academy who had tried to find an English artist for Elgin's embassy, came quickly to Elgin's defense. "I have found in this collection of sculpture so much excellence in art, and a variety so magnificent and boundless, that every branch of science connected with the fine arts cannot fail to acquire something from this collection. Your Lordship, by bringing these treasures of the first and best age of sculpture and architecture into London, has founded a new Athens for the emulation and example of the British student."[49]

The leading artists of England praised Elgin for his labors, many of them requesting permission to enter the museum at Park Lane to make sketches and paintings of the sculptures. Included in this select group was the landscape painter Joseph Farington, who saw the sculptures as "the highest quality of Art, a union of greatness and nature."[50] Sir Thomas Lawrence, the British portraitist, was also a frequent visitor, as was the British sculptor Joseph Nollekens, and even the group of painters who were rejected by Elgin at Broomhall in 1799. All of them now admitted that they had missed out on a great opportunity. J. M. W. Turner, in particular, took the time to write Elgin "to pay my homage to your Lordship's exertions for this rescue from barbarism."[51]

Statesmen, foreign dignitaries, and every important name in London society, along with the artists, requested permission to visit Elgin's museum at Park Lane, which was built from his mother's funds. Earlier objections to the presence of the marbles in England were suddenly forgotten. The Elgin Marbles were now the main topic of conversation in London, and their most notable champion was the young historical painter Benjamin Robert Haydon, who up until this time had been unsuccessful in his endeavors to prove that he was predestined to form a new and brilliant school of English historical painting. Through the influence of a friend, a pass was obtained for Haydon, and his impressions were jotted down into a diary, which later was to be his autobiography:

To Park Lane then we went, and after passing through the hall and thence into an open yard, entered a damp, dirty penthouse, where lay the marbles ranged within sight and reach. The first thing I fixed my eyes on was the wrist of a figure in one of the female groups in which were visible, though in a feminine form, the radius and the ulna. I was astonished, for I had never seen them hinted at in any female wrist in the antique. I darted my eye to the elbow and saw the outer condyle visibly affecting the shape as in nature. That combination of nature and idea, which I had felt was so much wanting in high art, was here displayed to mid-day conviction. My heart beat! If I had seen nothing else, I beheld sufficient to keep me to nature for the rest of my life. But when I turned to the Theseus and saw that every form was altered by action or repose — when I saw that the two sides of his back varied: one side stretched from the shoulder blade being pulled forward, and the other side compressed from the shoulder blade being pushed close to the spine as he rested on his elbow with the belly flat because the bowels fell into the pelvis as he sat — and when, turning to the Ilissos, I saw the belly protruded, from the figure lying on its side — and again, when in the figure of the fighting metope I saw the muscle shown under the one armpit in that instantaneous action of darting out, and left out in the other armpits because not wanted — when I saw in fact the most heroic style of art combined with all the essential detail of actual life, the thing was done at once and forever. Here were principles which the common sense of the English people would understand; here were principles which I had struggled for in my first picture with timidity and apprehension; here were the principles which the great Greeks in their finest time established, and here was I. . . .

Oh, how inwardly I thanked God that I was prepared to understand all this![52]

For many months thereafter, Haydon spent every spare moment drawing in Elgin's chilly museum. He drew for ten or fifteen hours at a time, continuing by candlelight until the porter came to close up at midnight:

then often have I gone home, cold, benumbed, and damp; my clothes steaming up as I dried them; and so spreading my drawings on the floor and putting a candle there. I have drank my tea at one in the morning with ecstasy as its warmth trickled through my frame, and looked at my picture, and dwelt on my drawings, and pondered on the change of empires, and thought that I had been contemplating what Socrates looked at, and Plato saw — and then, lifted up with my own high urgings of soul, I have prayed to God to enlighten my mind to discover the principles of those divine things — and then I have had inward assurances of future glory, and almost fancying divine influence in my room, have lingered to my mattress bed, and soon dozed into a rich balmy slumber."[53]

Despite his long hours of labor, Haydon continually fed entries into his diary: "8 September: Drew at Lord Elgin's from ten till half-past two, and from three to three-quarters past five; then walked about and looked at those matchless productions. I consider it truly the greatest blessing that ever happened to this country, their being brought here."[54]

Lord Elgin's original aim in undertaking the Constantinople post must certainly have found gratification with Haydon's entry for 5 November: "Drew at Lord Elgin's — six hours. My taste, thank God is improved wonderfully."[55]

But even with the support of all these artists, Elgin's reputation suffered greatly from the continuing assaults of Richard Payne Knight. As the leading spokesman for the Dilettanti Society, which had come a long distance from its original goal "of meeting once a month in the Star and Garter and drinking toasts to Grecian taste and Roman spirit,"[56] Knight was relentless in his battle with Elgin and even volunteered to write the text of the society's newest publication: "Specimens of Antient Sculpture," which included excellent engravings of at least sixty works of art belonging to various members of the society.

In writing the text for "Specimens of Antient Sculpture," Knight spared no feelings on the issue of the Elgin Marbles, although quite surprisingly, he did not mention Elgin's name.

Of Pheidias' general style of composition, the friezes and metopes of the Temple of Minerva at Athens, published by Mr. Stuart* and since

---

*Stuart was a competent draftsman commissioned by the Society of Dilettanti to make "an accurate and detailed record of the surviving ancient buildings of Athens. The result was the publication in 1762 of volume I of *The Antiquities of Athens*, a magnificent folio work whose beauty and craftsmanship were enhanced by scholarship and accuracy never before attempted in classical archaeology." (William St. Clair, *Lord Elgin and the Marbles*, p. 176.)

brought to England, may afford us competent information, but as these are merely architectural sculptures executed from his designs and under his directions probably by workmen scarcely ranked among artists, and meant to be seen at the height of more than forty feet from the eye, they can throw but little light upon the more important details of his art. The relief in the metopes is much higher, so as to exhibit the figures nearly complete, and the details are more accurately and elaborately made out; but they are so different in their degrees of merit, as to be evidently the works of many different persons, some of whom would not have been entitled to the rank of artists in a much less cultivated and fastidious age.[57]

Despite the great pressure of his marital problems and his heavy debts, Elgin was gratified to know that scores of visitors came daily to view the Parthenon marbles at Park Lane. Above all, he was particularly pleased by the definite revival of Grecian art that he had brought about in England. The foremost painters of the time visited Park Lane and made full-scale drawings of the marbles. Benjamin Haydon was always in attendance and often obliged royal dignitaries and visiting artists with his outward show of enthusiasm over the presence of the Elgin Marbles in England.

Although the decision of the select committee had already been made, Parliament still buzzed over the sale, and many of its members seriously questioned whether Elgin had the right to use his position as ambassador to acquire such a huge collection. The most powerful attack in the select committee came from one of its leading members, Hugh Hammersley. "It was to be regretted that the government had not restrained this act of spoliation; but, as it had been committed, we should exert ourselves to wipe off the stain, and not place in our museum a monument of our disgrace, but at once return the bribe which our ambassador had received, to his own dishonor and that of the country."[58]

In the prolonged debate that ensued, Hammersley proposed the following amendment,

This committee therefore feels justified twenty-five thousand pounds be offered to the Earl of Elgin for the collection in order to recover and keep it together for that government from which it has been improperly taken, and to which this committee is of opinion that a communication should be immediately made, stating that Great Britain holds these marbles only in trust till they are demanded by the present, or any future, possessors of the city of Athens; and upon such demand, engages, without question or negotiation, to restore them as far as can be effected, to the places from whence they were taken, and that they shall be in the meantime carefully preserved in the British Museum.[59]

When Hammersley's amendment was soundly defeated, newspapers throughout Great Britain became furious over the sale. Lord Brougham, a frequent contributor to the *Edinburgh Review*, chided the British government for ignoring the real wants of the people: "If we cannot give them bread, we ought not to indulge ourselves in the purchase of stones!"[60] Cruikshank* used this theme to create one of his most famous cartoons.

On a mild day in March 1817, at the height of all this furor, Haydon brought his young friend John Keats to the British Museum and the poet wrote two sonnets on the occasion:

ON SEEING THE ELGIN MARBLES

My spirit is too weak — mortality
Weighs heavily on me like unwilling sleep,
And each imagin'd pinnacle and steep
Of godlike hardship tells me I must die
Like a sick Eagle looking at the sky.
Yet 'tis a gentle luxury to weep
That I have not the cloudy winds to keep
Fresh for the opening of the morning's eye.
Such dim-conceived glories of the brain

---

*George Cruikshank (1792–1878), the English artist, caricaturist, painter, and illustrator. For one whole generation, his drawings delineated Whigs, Tories, and Radicals with a sharp impartiality. An extreme patriot, he was an outspoken champion of the poor and underprivileged and fearlessly exposed the follies of royalty.

Bring round the heart an indescribable feud;
So do these wonders a most dizzy pain,
   That mingles Grecian grandeur with the rude
Wasting of old Time — with a billowy main —
   A sun — a shadow of a magnitude.[61]

The second sonnet overflows with lavish praise for Haydon and contempt for Richard Payne Knight and his party of connoisseurs:

TO B. R. HAYDON, WITH THE FOREGOING SONNET
ON THE ELGIN MARBLES

Haydon, forgive me that I cannot speak
Definitely on these mighty things;
Forgive me that I have not Eagle's wings —
That what I want I know not where to seek;
And think that I would not be over meek
   In rolling out upfollow'd thunderings
   Even to the steep of Heliconian springs,
Were I of ample strength for such a freak —
Think too, that all these numbers should be thine;
   Whose else? In this who touch thy vesture's hem?
For when men star'd at what was most divine
   With browless idiotism — o'erwise phlegm —
Thou hadst beheld the Hesperean shine
   Of their star in the East, and gone to worship them.[62]

Although these are not Keats's best poems, the Elgin Marbles certainly inspired him to create two masterpieces: "Ode on a Grecian Urn" and "Hyperion." "For the young poet who knew no Greek, the Elgin Marbles opened a vision of the classical world."[63]

Keats visited the Elgin Marbles "again and again, and would sit for an hour or more at a time beside them, rapt in revery. Joseph Severn, the great painter, came upon him on one such occasion. Keats's eyes were shining so brightly and his face so lit up by some visionary rapture that Severn quietly stole away."[64]

Thomas Hardy also visited the museum to view the Elgin Marbles, but his reaction differed sharply from that of Keats. Hardy envisioned the marbles as prisoners sadly conversing on Christmas Day:

> We are those whom Christmas overthrew
> Some centuries after Pheidias knew
> > How to shape us
> > And bedrape us
> And to set us in Athena's temple for men's view.
>
> Oh it is sad now we are sold
> We gods! for Borean people's gold,
> > And brought to the gloom
> > Of this gaunt room
> Which sunlight shuns, and sweet Aurore but enters cold.
>
> "For all these bells, would I were still
> Radiant as on Athena's Hill!"
> > "And I!" "And I!"
> > The others sigh.
> Before this, Christ was known, and we had men's good will.[65]

Among the hordes that visited the museum at Park Lane, it was not an uncommon sight to find a stern riding master instructing his students to sit properly on horseback by studying a certain frieze of the Parthenon. "This same frieze became a common motif of Regency wallpaper; and of the vase in Buckingham Palace Gardens commemorating the Battle of Waterloo."[66]

The Society of Dilettanti soon realized its grave mistake and officially censured Richard Payne Knight by omitting his name from its list of invitations that year. At the same time, the society informed Elgin in writing that he had been elected a member, an honor that had escaped him all these years because of Knight's antagonism. Elgin's reply to the secretary of the society camouflaged the deep pain he had suffered.

> No one knows more intimately than you, that the impulses which led me to the exertions I made in Greece were wholly for the purpose of securing in Great Britain, and through it to Europe in general, the most

effectual possible knowledge and means of improving, by the excellence of Grecian art in sculpture and architecture. My success, to the vast extent it was effected, will never cease to be a matter of the utmost gratification to me. If, when it was first made known to the public, it had been thought that the same energy would be considered useful to the Dilettanti Society, most happy should I have been to have contributed every aid in my power. But as such expectation has long since passed, I really do not apprehend that I shall be thought fastidious if I decline the honor now proposed to me at this my eleventh hour.[67]

Even among the fond sights of her peaceful Archerfield in the winter of 1806, Lady Elgin was overcome by the swift turn of events in her life. No matter how hard she tried, she could not free her mind from the terrible trauma of her husband's wrath. One afternoon she returned from her daily walk to Aberlady Bay and learned that her children had been whisked away to Broomhall. "A court order had been issued in Edinburgh, remanding all four children to Elgin's custody pending the outcome of the divorce proceedings."[68] That same evening she was handed a summons by the constable of Dirleton, instructing her to be at the main courtroom of Parliament House in Edinburgh at ten o'clock the following morning.

The carriage was ready at daybreak. Above Archerfield, the sky was burdened with ominous storm clouds, and a thin blanket of snow had draped itself over the frozen earth. Lady Elgin's stomach churned as the carriage master, Andrew Davidson, helped her into the seat. Her father sat beside her, speechless, his demeanor grave. Mrs. Nisbet had wanted to come along, but she fell ill during the night and was ordered by her physician to remain at home.

Auld Reekie (the fond name for Edinburgh) seemed to be choking under heavy layers of black smoke. Lady Elgin remembered when her father first pronounced the name to her he rolled the *r* until he ran out of breath. Days of peace and happiness, her entire world abundant with love, and not one evil thought in the universe!

A mob of people had already assembled on Princes Street. Off to the east rose Calton Hill, its grotesque gravestones jabbing at the sky, the ancient dead shuddering within its deep and unforgiving bowels.

The snow was falling hard now, and as the carriage approached the General Register House, Williams Nisbet turned to the side and comforted his daughter. Within another few moments, the carriage pulled up in front of Parliament House, where more crowds had gathered on the steps and along both sides of the street. Vendors were everywhere with their carts of hot chestnuts; others waved newspapers high in the air and yelled: "All the details of her Ladyship's private life! Exclusive accounts of her affairs in France and England!"[69]

Robert Fergusson was waiting for them outside the door of Parliament House. Visibly shaken by this entire matter, he nervously introduced them to his chief solicitor, Mr. Topping, a small balding man who suddenly changed features when he put on his wig and robe. The great hall was exactly as Lady Elgin remembered it when the parish schoolmaster of Dirleton had brought his class here on an annual visit to Edinburgh's ancient sites: the massive oak-timbered ceiling, the stained-glass windows, the solicitors in their solemn wigs and robes, the statues of each lord president dating back to the year 1685. As she entered the advocates' library behind Mr. Topping, she could hear the resounding echo of the schoolmaster's voice: "This great library houses every book published in Scotland from the time of Charles III."[70]

Topping only had a moment to tell her that Elgin had retained a firm of expensive London solicitors and was bent on winning the case at any cost. She only half listened, and after taking her chair in the main courtroom, she didn't dare lift her eyes toward the sea of inquisitive faces staring at her. A few meters to her right, a large coal stove belched out sickening waves of heat.

In the dull silence, the main door of the courtroom noisily swung open and an austere lord president walked in, followed by four equally stern lord judges.

Part 3

The Trial[1]

THE TRIAL
OF R. J. FERGUSSON, ESQUIRE
FOR ADULTERY
WITH THE COUNTESS OF ELGIN
COMMISSARY COURT OF EDINBURGH
MARCH 11, 1808

The defendant, Mr. Fergusson, having suffered a previous judgment to go by default, a jury was this day summoned for the purpose of assessing the quantum of damages:

A LIST OF THE JURY

William Weston, Esq.	William Page, Esq.
Francis Dutton, Esq.	William Robertson, Esq.
John Townsend, Esq.	John Sherrard, Esq.
James Rogers, Esq.	John Sanderson, Esq.
Thomas Bates, Esq.	David Dean, Esq.
John Johnson, Esq.	Major Rhodes, Esq.
Joseph Oake, Esq.	William North, Esq.
Samuel Moody, Esq.	John Crawford, Esq.
John Anderson, Esq.	George Brown, Esq.
Thomas Baylis, Esq.	Thomas Gordon, Esq.

Samuel Gordon, Esq.

COUNSEL FOR THE PLAINTIFF

Messrs. Garrow, Dampier, Stewart.

COUNSEL FOR THE DEFENDANT

Messrs. Topping, Nolan, Adam, Horner.

Mr. Garrow addresses the Court:

"My Lords and Gentlemen of the Jury, I have the honour of attending you on behalf of my noble plaintiff, the Seventh Earl of Elgin and Eleventh of Kincardine, for the purposes of ascertaining the damages to be allowed him for the misconduct of the defendant who permitted a previous judgment to go by default.

"Of the many melancholy cases with which my practice for twenty years in the Courts of Westminster has led me to become acquainted, this by far exceeds them all. I bring to your attention that the noble plaintiff is the representative of one of the most ancient and respected families of Scotland. He was solemnly joined in marriage to Lady Elgin, then Mary Nisbet, who was also of a very respectable and opulent family. She was then at the age of twenty-one and possessed every accomplishment of mind and person which could make her the object of the warmest attachment. His Lordship was a dozen or so years her senior, but there was no such disparity as could make the match in the slightest degree unequal. A short time before the marriage, Lord Elgin had been appointed Ambassador to the Sublime Porte at Constantinople, and such was the ardour of his attachment to his bride that he proposed to abandon all those splendid prospects which this appointment held out for him, and to retire to scenes of domestic happiness and endearment — if such a course should be more agreeable to her. However, she agreed to accompany him in his embassy to Constantinople, where they spent several years.

"My Lord and Gentlemen, it is my intention to prove that throughout this whole period Lord and Lady Elgin exhibited an example of the strongest mutual affection and regard, affording a true picture of perfect conjugal felicity. Their well-regulated family revealed a pattern of the best English manners and the most regular attention to domestic and religious duties. Lady Elgin resisted the batteries of ridicule and never gave card parties on a Sunday; nor did she indulge in the fashionable follies of dissipation. Quite to the contrary, she adhered strictly to the practice of those virtues in which she had been educated by her respectable parents. During this interval, three children were born, a son and two daughters, and they found within themselves and in the endearments of their children all those means of pure and unmixed happiness which life can bring.

"The work of his embassy completed, Lord Elgin left Constantinople with his family and, after passing through Italy, arrived at France. We all recollect that breach of diplomatic courtesy which took place in France at that time, in consequence of which all the English then resident in that country were detained prisoners of war. Mr. Fergusson was also in Paris at this time. In Lord Elgin, he recognized a friend and a neighbour of his family, and thus their relationship was fixed upon terms of the greatest respect and honour.

"Shortly after this period, Lord Elgin was seized with an indisposition which made it necessary for him to seek the waters of Barèges for the recovery of his health. Here a fourth child was born, a male who was given the name of William. Several months later, Lady Elgin travelled to Paris and was unceasing in her efforts to procure Lord Elgin's liberation from prison. But, my Lords and Gentlemen, was this her only purpose in visiting the infamous capital of France? And was her fourth child in fact the offspring of Lord Elgin?

"Upon the untimely death of that infant son, Lady Elgin was permitted to return to England while his Lordship remained confined in France. She resided for a short period with her parents in Portman Square, London, with whom her children then lived, but soon after her arrival there, and while in a state of pregnancy, she left the house of her parents and took a house for herself at Number 60 Baker Street, near Portman Square. And here, my Lords and Gentlemen, she had an adulterous intercourse with the said Robert Fergusson, being carnally connected with him in London, both before and after her delivery in the month of January, and until she left London for Scotland on the following June.

"It is now my duty to submit proof of this criminal correspondence. I hope not to dwell long on this part of the subject because I do not mean to bring more pain upon the heart of that Lady whom Lord

Elgin once revered; nor can I inflict any new wound on those most respectable parents who already have suffered so much from their daughter's indiscretion. My Lords and Gentlemen, before calling upon the noble plaintiff's witnesses, permit me to bring certain facts to your attention. In order to maintain an action for a case of adultery, it is necessary to establish two points: that a valid marriage exists between two spouses, and that there is sexual intercourse between the defendant and the guilty spouse.

"Adultery, as a ground for divorce, may be proved by a preponderance of evidence. However, the proof must be sufficiently definite to show the appropriate time, the place of the offense, the circumstances under which it was committed, and the conclusion that the libellee was a party to the illicit act. Here I must remind you that it is a fundamental rule of English jurisprudence that it is not necessary to prove the direct act of adultery, since there could not be one case in a hundred in which such proof might be attainable. It is rare indeed that the parties are surprised in the direct act. In almost every case, the fact is inferred from circumstances that lead to it, otherwise no protection could be given to marital rights. Thus the two parties need not be caught in the very act of adultery; the crime may be sufficiently established by indirect or circumstantial evidence, or by evidence consisting in part of both.

"Secondly, my Lords and Gentlemen, I submit to you that in order to amount to adultery, a completion of sexual intercourse is not required; nor is the birth of a child essential. For the purpose of divorce, the most important element of adultery is a guilty intent. Furthermore intercourse must be voluntary. An act accomplished by force or fraud is not sufficient grounds for divorce. Therefore an adulterous disposition between two persons is usually of gradual development, and even if it can be shown to exist with comparatively light proof or perhaps with negligible circumstantial evidence, nevertheless this shall be sufficient to justify an inference that adultery has taken place.

"I shall now proceed to furnish you with such proof. My Lords and Gentlemen, I submit that the defendant, Mr. Fergusson, in fact seduced by degrees and in such a way as to especially suit the innocent and naive character of Lady Elgin. The behaviour, the views, and the objects of Lord Elgin were all to be misrepresented. His public and private conduct were to be attacked; he was to be brought down from being the object of her Ladyship's love and adoration, and be made a victim of scorn and disgust. Amidst all such exhortations, the defendant was considered to be a friend of the family. Demon is a more appropriate name! His one object was to prevail upon Lady Elgin to despise her husband and alienate him by the coolness of her conduct. For this reason did the defendant volunteer to convey the bier of her dead child to Scotland. Unhappy woman! How little did she foresee her fate that her own husband's friend should be the means of making her children orphans and entailing upon them such miserable consequences!"

Mr. Topping objects.

"My Lords and Gentlemen, such theatrics as these may be appropriate in the Courts of Westminster, but surely not here in Edinburgh."

The Lord President advises Mr. Garrow to call upon his first witness, upon which Mr. Garrow states: "On behalf of my noble client, I call Mr. William Richard Hamilton to the witness chair."

Kneeling, and with his right hand on the Holy Evangil, the witness is sworn and purged of malice.

"Your name is William Richard Hamilton?"

"It is."

"What is your age?"

"I have just turned thirty."

"And your situation?"

"I am an Under Secretary in the Foreign Office."

"You held a situation under Lord Elgin?"

"I did."

"What exactly was this situation?"

"I acted as private secretary to his Lordship when he was at Constantinople."

"Did you sail with him on his embassy?"

"I did."

"At what time was that?"

"Upon the third day of September 1799, shortly after his Lordship was appointed to the post."

"Was Lady Elgin with him during all this time?"

"She was."

"Did you observe their demeanor as man and wife?"

"I did."

"During your residence at Constantinople, were you constantly at their table?"

"I was."

"And during the whole time of your being with them, did they conduct themselves toward one another as man and wife?"

"Indeed. His Lordship was an affectionate and tender husband."

"And Lady Elgin?"

"A most dutiful wife."

"Tender and affectionate also?"

"Yes."

"Mr. Hamilton, in what manner was the household conducted as to regularity in the offices of religion?"

"With great propriety. There was a chaplain attached to the embassy, Reverend Philip Hunt, and his prayers were attended by the household on the Sunday with the greatest regularity."

"And was the service of the Church of England?"

"Yes."

"Now then, Mr. Hamilton, had you the opportunity of observing whether Lady Elgin's affections remained to his Lordship with regard to his public as well as his private concerns?"

"Her Ladyship appeared to take a lively interest in everything that concerned Lord Elgin, either of a public or of a private nature."

"Were any children born to them while you were at Constantinople?"

"A son, the name of Bruce."

"Had you an opportunity of observing Lady Elgin's conduct toward the child?"

"She was quite patient at first."

"And later?"

"She became withdrawn. I suspect it was —"

Mr. Topping interrupts.

"My Lords, must we subject ourselves to the suspicions of the witness?"

Mr. Garrow continues: "Mr. Hamilton, would you say that this withdrawal on the part of Lady Elgin was due to a definite reason?"

"Yes, while in Constantinople, his Lordship contracted a severe ague, which consequently resulted in the loss of his nose."

There is a muffled murmur in the courtroom, which the Lord President permits.

"Mr. Hamilton, would you say that her Ladyship's interest in Lord Elgin began to wane at this point?"

"Yes."

"In your observations, did you see any outward manifestations of her Ladyship's waning love?"

"I did. It was first brought to my attention by his Lordship."

"What did he say to you?"

Upon the hesitation of the witness, the Lord President advises him to answer the question.

"His Lordship said that, because of her tender age, Lady Elgin often fell prey to unusual behaviour while in the presence of handsome men."

There is a second commotion in the courtroom before Mr. Garrow proceeds:

"Were you able to substantiate this statement of his Lordship?"

"Yes, while in her Ladyship's presence one day, I heard her remark of Signor Lusieri: 'What a handsome devil he is!' "[2]

"Who is Signor Lusieri?"

"A painter, whom his Lordship assigned to supervise the work in Athens."

"Are you referring to the taking down of the Parthenon marbles?"

"Yes."

"And was Signor Lusieri in fact handsome?"

"I should believe so."

"Were there any other men to your knowledge, for whom Lady Elgin may have expressed a similar remark?"

"Count Sébastiani."

"Who is he?"

"The personal agent of Bonaparte. He visited with the household upon several occasions in Constantinople, and also at Pau."

"Would you say that he too was of handsome countenance?"

"Yes."

"Were they any others, Mr. Hamilton?"

"Mr. Fergusson, of course."

"The defendant?"

"Yes."

"I ask you now to impress upon your memory, Mr. Hamilton, and tell this Court if you ever saw Mr. Fergusson in the company of Lady Elgin?"

"I did."

"Were they alone?"

"Yes."

"Do you remember where these meetings occurred?"

"In a house at Number 60 Baker Street in London."

"Did you come upon them by chance?"

"No, I was instructed to observe them."

"By whom?"

"Lord Elgin."

"For what reason?"

"His Lordship nourished strong suspicions about Lady Elgin's demeanour where men were concerned. These suspicions were intensified when his Lordship learned that Lady Elgin was to leave France on the same ship as Mr. Fergusson."

"You were not on board this vessel yourself?"

"No, I was residing in England at the time."

"Then how could you keep them under surveillance?"

"Lord Elgin entrusted a letter to the Captain of the vessel and, upon the ship's arrival in England, the Captain delivered it to my residence. Her Ladyship was residing at this time in the house on Baker Street, near Portman Square."

"And you assumed the watch from that moment on?"

"Yes."

"Were you not detected?"

"I took every precaution."

"Mr. Hamilton, will you tell the Court how long Lady Elgin remained at 60 Baker Street?"

"Approximately twelve months or so."

"And was a child born to her there?"

"Yes, a female of the name of Lucy."

"Did you at any time observe Mr. Fergusson entering the house at Baker Street?"

"Yes, both before and after the birth of the child. Indeed, Mr. Fergusson was a frequent visitor."

"For how long a period would he remain?"

"Until the early hours of morning."

"After leaving London, did Lady Elgin go directly to the home of her parents in Dirleton?"

"No, she lodged herself at a hotel in Edinburgh."

"Do you remember the name of that hotel?"

"Fortune and Blackwell's."

"Was your assignment now finished, Mr. Hamilton?"

"It was. Soon after I compiled this information, I wrote immediately to his Lordship in France."

"And you swear again that your testimony is true?"

"Entirely true."

Mr. Garrow now picks up a packet of letters from the table and displays it to the Court. "My Lords and Gentlemen, I have here certain letters which fell into the hands of my noble plaintiff over a period of time, and with your kind permission I shall now read from them — but before doing so, let me say that when one seals a letter with wax and seals also its envelope, this operation melts the wax of the letter and causes it to open. Thus when Lord Elgin took off the envelope he found these letters already open inside, discovering meanwhile that they had been written by Mr. Fergusson to Lady Elgin, and conceived in such high terms of affection that Lord Elgin could not doubt they were meant as an advance to criminal intercourse. While Lady Elgin was at Paris, she bore a son who died soon thereafter. Its body being embalmed, the child was then committed to the care of Mr. Fergusson, who procured liberty to return to Scotland and then personally attended its being deposited in Lord Elgin's family vault at Dunfermline. In the various letters which Mr. Fergusson wrote, no allusion to the surviving children can be found, but to this boy we find numerous allusions. At one time, Lady Elgin expresses the desire to visit her dear William's tomb, but Mr. Fergusson begs her to resist the temptation. 'I know,' says he, 'you will obey me and I entreat you to remember who placed that infant's head to rest.'[3]

"Yet, prior to Mr. Fergusson's appearance on the scene, Lady Elgin's conduct was exemplary as proven from the following extracts of letters which she wrote to her husband while he was in confinement in France: 'Dearest Elgin: Keep up your spirits. I will be with you. Willy is a darling infant. If I can be but with you even in confinement, I would not mind anything. I am well this morning, though I was very ill last night. I have written to Mr. Talleyrand.'[4]

"In another letter, she says, 'I have again written to Mr. Talleyrand and have begged him to receive me. I have also written to the First Consul (Bonaparte), which if he approves, I hope we are now in a fair way of procuring your exchange. May God bless my dearest Elgin. I am much more comfortable, now that I am perfectly persuaded that this is no ways personal against you. It is only a reprisal. Pray, write to me. Monsieur Talleyrand has been most polite to me. God bless you, my dear Elgin. I have written again to the First Consul and now to you. I have not lost time, have I? Pray, take the greatest care you can of yourself, my dear Elgin. For heaven's sake, we have not had much comfort in our marriage. But we have got over the worst. The good is yet to come. And it will come, my dearest Elgin. To be sure, it will!'[5]

"My Lords and Gentlemen, if only this poor woman could see that she was soon to be separated from her devoted husband; that Mr. Fergusson would be answerable for breaking this domestic happiness and that one day he would deprive her of a son and three daughters! If only she realized that this same Mr. Fergusson, by a very artful and subtle seduction, was to destroy her happiness forever! And for this, Mr. Fergusson today is to be accountable.

"I had proposed to read to this Court further extracts from Mr. Fergusson's letters to Lady Elgin which show that he was perfectly well-acquainted with the character of her Ladyship and that she had been educated in the best principles of morality. He knew that she was not a person to be taken by storm; that any rash attempt upon her virtue would only alarm her and put her on guard; and that it was to be done solely by artifice. However I now feel considerable difficulty in having this task imposed upon me and therefore I shall burden you only with this last extract which Mr. Fergusson wrote to Lord Elgin while his Lordship was imprisoned in France: 'I have wrote [*sic*] a few lines to you, my Lord. Your letters to Lady Elgin acquainted her of your impression of mind. Let us hope the best that in this act of severity you will get away and see your Lady Elgin. I have to inform you that Mr. Talleyrand says he will permit that Lord Elgin should be exchanged for General Boyer. I am in hopes of your being liberated. Keep up your spirits; and endeavour to be as comfortable as you can.'[6]

"This clearly marks the confidential situation in which Mr. Fergusson was placed. I could go on, my Lords and Gentlemen, but I wish to spare the feelings of others whose names are herein mentioned. Therefore I shall not burden you further. Allow me instead to call upon my noble plaintiff's next witness, Mr. John Morier."

John Morier, aged thirty, unmarried and residing in London, is solemnly sworn and examined by Mr. Garrow:

"Did you also accompany Lord Elgin to Constantinople?"

"I did."

"In what capacity?"

"As his Lordship's second private secretary. I stayed at Constantinople until January, two years following."

"Did you live in the same house with Lord and Lady Elgin?"

"I did."

"Then you had the same opportunity as Mr. Hamilton, the previous witness, of observing their conduct as husband and wife?"

"Lord Elgin was a tender and considerate husband. . . ."

The Lord President cautions the witness to answer only the question put to him, after which, Mr. Garrow rephrases the question:

"Mr. Morier, what were your personal observations of Lord Elgin's conduct toward Lady Elgin?"

"His Lordship was a tender and considerate husband."

The Lord President momentarily permits the laughter in the courtroom.

"And what were your personal observations of Lady Elgin's conduct toward Lord Elgin?"

"In the beginning, her Ladyship was a most affectionate wife and mother."

"Do you mean to say that her conduct changed?

"Yes."

"When exactly?"

"As Lord Elgin's affliction became more serious."

"You are referring to the loss of his Lordship's nose?"

"Yes."

"Mr. Morier, were you able to discern any actual manifestations of her Ladyship's change of conduct at Constantinople?"

"Yes, her Ladyship became quite abrupt whenever she was alone with his Lordship."

"Go on."

"Her Ladyship also left the house early each day."

"For what purpose?"

"I cannot truly say. However, not a day passed without an afternoon tea or a stroll through the gardens at Pera. Her Ladyship also loved to read a great deal."

"And what of the evenings?"

"When not reading or playing at cards, her Ladyship often chose to retire early."

"She had her own bed chamber?"

"Yes."

"Separate from his Lordship's?"

"Entirely."

"Mr. Morier, I want you to think carefully before answering this next question: did Lady Elgin in fact have a weakness for men?"

"Her Ladyship is a very beautiful woman. Men find her quite attractive. Yes, I would say that she indeed had a weakness for men."

"Can you recall any actual incident of such weakness?"

"Many times I observed a certain look in her Ladyship's eyes whenever a man, particularly a strikingly handsome man, visited the household."

"What sort of look was this?"

"One of admiration, I think."

"Nothing more?"

"Of attraction too."

"Sexual attraction?"

Mr. Topping protests, and the Lord President concurs, advising Mr. Garrow that he is on direct examination and the Court will not permit him to lead his witnesses. Mr. Garrow then begs the Court's forgiveness and states that he has no further questions to ask of this witness. Mr. Topping, choosing not to cross-examine, Mr. Garrow then calls Mr. Richard Sterling to the witness chair, where he is sworn and examined.

"Mr. Sterling, when did you first become acquainted with Lord and Lady Elgin?"

"In Paris, during the time of our detention there."

"Was the defendant, Mr. Fergusson, also in Paris at this time?"

"He was."

"Did you have a friendly relationship with Lord and Lady Elgin?"

"I did."

"What was your impression of their attachment?"

"I found it rather strained."

"How so?"

"They were seldom together."

"Did you ever see Mr. Fergusson alone with Lady Elgin?"

"No, they were always in the company of the others."

"Others?"

"The Cockburns, Mrs. Fitzgerald, and Colonel Craufurd."

"They were *détenus* also?"

"Yes."

"Where did these meetings occur?"

"At the Hotel de Richelieu in Paris; also at Barèges and Pau."

"Mr. Sterling, can you tell us anything further about the relationship between Mr. Fergusson and Lady Elgin?"

"Lady Elgin seemed quite interested in Mr. Fergusson from the outset. She was constantly inquiring as to his whereabouts. In my view, their relationship went beyond mere friendship."

"Please be more specific, Mr. Sterling."

"I would say that Lady Elgin was infatuated with Mr. Fergusson."

"Were you able to observe Mr. Fergusson's feelings toward her Ladyship?"

"Yes, he too appeared to be enamoured of her."

"Thank you, Mr. Sterling."

Again Mr. Topping does not cross-examine the witness. Charles Duff, aged forty-five years and married, is next to be sworn and examined by Mr. Garrow.

"I believe that you too were in the employ of Lord Elgin?"

"I was."

"Where do you reside, Mr. Duff?"

"At Number One Weymouth Street, Portland Place, London."[7]

"Did you remain with Lord and Lady Elgin throughout their stay at Constantinople?"

"I did."

"What was the impression on your mind as to the manner in which Lord and Lady Elgin conducted themselves?"

"I never saw a happier couple in my life."

"Did you attend the funeral of their child who died in France?"

"I did."

"Who else was in attendance, Mr. Duff?"

"Mr. Fergusson, Lord Elgin's mother, the Rector of the church at Dunfermline, and a few relatives and friends."

"Where was the child interred?"

"In Lord Elgin's family vault at Dunfermline."

"Now then, Mr. Duff, did you receive any instructions from Lady Elgin after she returned to England from France?"

"Her Ladyship asked me to hire a house for her, which I did accordingly."

"Why should she ask you to do this? Did not her parents have a town house in London where she could stay?"

"Precisely. Mr. Nisbet visited with me one day and said both he and Mrs. Nisbet were sorry to learn that Lady Elgin had chosen to reside at Number 60 Baker Street. Mr. Nisbet, in particular, expressed his disapprobation of her Ladyship's refusal to stay at the Nisbet household in Portman Square."

"Mr. Duff, did you have any occasion to visit with Lady Elgin's servants while she was residing at Baker Street?"

"Yes, I had frequent conversations with Mrs. Sarah Gosling; also with Miss Nonweiler and Mr. Robert Draper."

"What was the subject of your conversations?"

"Lady Elgin's conduct."

"In what regard?"

"Mr. Fergusson's daily visits there."

"Can you elaborate, Mr. Duff?"

"Mr. Fergusson often came to the house as late as twelve and one in the morning, and went away at three or four in the morning, sometimes even later. Mrs. Gosling disapproved of this very much, but never expressed to me that there was any criminal connection between Lady Elgin and Mr. Fergusson."

The Lord President advises the witness to answer only the questions put to him.

"Mr. Duff, do you recall any conversations you may have had with Lady Elgin during this time?"

"Yes, I was assisting her Ladyship in packing up, previous to her setting out for Scotland, and she seemed much agitated. 'Oh, Duff,' she said to me, 'I am quite miserable. If they continue to plague me, I shall go off with Fergusson.'"[8]

"To whom was she referring?"

"Lord Elgin and her parents."

"And what was your response?"

"I said to her Ladyship: 'God forbid I should ever see that day, my lady, as you would be looked upon as not better than a girl of the Town if you go off with Fergusson.'"[9]

"Mr. Duff, were you aware of a correspondence by letters being carried on between Lady Elgin and Mr. Fergusson?"

"I was. Lady Elgin applied to Mrs. Duff by letter, to be allowed to enclose a letter to Mr. Fergusson. I disapproved of her being engaged in this matter and by my desire Mrs. Duff wrote immediately to Lady Elgin and informed her Ladyship that she refused to receive or deliver any such letter."

"What did your wife do with this letter?"

"She destroyed it."

"And that was the end of the matter?"

"Hardly. Mr. Fergusson came to my house about a fortnight later and demanded her Ladyship's letter, but I told him it had been destroyed."

"That is all, Mr. Duff."

In cross-examination, Mr. Topping asks:

"Mr. Duff, is it correct to say that most of your testimony here does not arise from any personal observations regarding Lady Elgin's conduct in London, but in truth results from hearsay information of servants and chambermaids?"

"I have known Mrs. Gosling for a long time; also Mr. Draper. They are respectable persons."

"Prior to your leaving for England, what were your actual observations of Lady Elgin's conduct at Constantinople?"

"Most commendable."

"And her Ladyship's behaviour toward Lord Elgin and her children?"

"Equally so."

"Would you say that Lady Elgin was that type of mother who abandons the needs of her children for selfish pursuits?"

"Decidedly not."

"Thank you, Mr. Duff. You may step down."

Here, the Lord President announces a recess of one hour.

When court resumes, Mr. Garrow moves that the deposition of Mrs. Sarah Gosling, which formerly was made to "lye in retentis" until a proof was allowed, should now be opened and made a part of the proof in the noble plaintiff's cause. Mr. Topping brings up an objection but is overruled by the lord judges, and the deposition is permitted to be read.*

---

*Mrs. Gosling had been assigned by Mrs. Nisbet to be a servant to Lady Elgin at Number 60 Baker Street, and Elgin's solicitors expected her to be the key witness until she fell ill. The Commissaries at Edinburgh therefore agreed to grant a deposition commission to James Chalmer, confirming Mrs. Gosling's state of health and allowing Chalmer to examine her in the presence of William Moncur, a clerk of the court. Mrs. Gosling died shortly after giving the deposition.

Knightsbridge*

Appeared Sarah Gosling, now residing at Knightsbridge in the County of Middlesex, married, age thirty-three, and being solemnly sworn according to the form directed by the Commission, and the usual questions of a preliminary nature being put to her, hereby swears that she holds no malice or ill toward either of the parties in this Cause; that she has neither received nor been promised any money or good deed for being a witness; that Mr. Bichnell now present did apply to her and enquire what she knew concerning the conduct of the Countess of Elgin, to which the deponent answered, and Mr. Bichnell then told her that he was acting for Lord Elgin, asking her several questions with regard to an intercourse between Lady Elgin and Mr. Fergusson; that the deponent brought pen and ink to Mr. Bichnell and answered these questions to the best of her knowledge and conscience.

Mr. Spottiswood, acting on the part of Lady Elgin, here objected to this proceeding, in respect that the witness having furnished Mr. Bichnell with a statement of facts relative to the Cause, is thereby, according to the Law of Scotland, disqualified from being a witness therein. The Commissioner repels the objection, and the witness, being then especially interrogated:

DEPONES that she was one of the defender Lady Elgin's servants, lived with her in London in the year 1806, her Ladyship then residing at Number 60 Baker Street.

DEPONES that she knows Robert Fergusson Esquire of Raith, and that he used to visit Lady Elgin in her house at Baker Street during the time of Lord Elgin's imprisonment in France; that Mr. Fergusson called frequently in the daytime and often in the evenings; that Lady Elgin was in the habit of going out many nights; that her Ladyship returned home sometimes at ten, eleven, or twelve o'clock.

DEPONES that Mr. Fergusson at different times visited Lady Elgin after she had thus returned home from her evening engagements; that she observed Lady Elgin more than once, after she came from her evening engagements, take off her dress and put on a loose gown; and that it was her general custom to do so.

DEPONES that she saw Lady Elgin admit the visits of Mr. Fergusson after her Ladyship had changed her dress; that at these visits there was no person with Lady Elgin except Mr. Fergusson; that she has known

*A suburb of London.

Mr. Fergusson to remain alone with Lady Elgin at these visits for an hour at a time and even longer; that when Mr. Fergusson retired from these visits the deponent has found Lady Elgin in bed; that she recollects Mrs. Nisbet calling on her daughter at Baker Street one night at twelve o'clock when Mr. Fergusson was then in the house.

DEPONES that Lady Elgin received Mrs. Nisbet on this occasion in the drawing room, but Mr. Fergusson was not in the drawing room while Mrs. Nisbet continued with Lady Elgin; that Mr. Fergusson was in Lady Elgin's bedroom during Mrs. Nisbet's visit and did not leave the house till after Mrs. Nisbet was gone; that Mr. Fergusson, when leaving the house after these evening visits, was sometimes let out by the deponent and sometimes by Lady Elgin's maid and not by any of the Footmen; and that at different times the men servants had gone to bed when Mr. Fergusson retired.

DEPONES that she has known Mr. Fergusson to continue with Lady Elgin till four and five o'clock in the morning; that there were no other persons in the house on these occasions except Mr. Fergusson and Lady Elgin; that it was Lady Elgin's general custom to direct the curtain of the Window which was behind the Sopha in the drawing room to be let down; that she generally gave this order in the morning when she came into the room, and it remained down all day; that she never made any observations on the state of the Sopha after Mr. Fergusson had been with Lady Elgin as to its being rumpled or otherwise, since this Sopha was of such a construction as a person sitting upon it could make no impression; and that, being interrogated by Mr. Bichnell as to what she means by a loose gown which she has said that Lady Elgin put on in the evenings, describes it as a loose wrapping gown which Ladies wear when they have their hair combed and which Lady Elgin used to put on every morning and evening.

All this is truth, as the deponent shall answer to God.

(Signed) Sarah Gosling
James Chalmer, Commissioner
William Moncur, Clerk[10]

Following the reading of the deposition, Miss Ann Crerar, now residing in Edinburgh, unmarried, aged twenty-two years, is sworn and examined by Mr. Garrow:

"What was your most recent occupation, Miss Crerar?"

"I was formerly Chambermaid in Fortune and Blackwell's Hotel."

"Here in Edinburgh?"

"Yes."

"Where exactly is the hotel located?"

"At the southernmost end of Princes Street."

"Were you ever acquainted with the defendant Mr. Fergusson?"

"I was Chambermaid to Lady Elgin when she resided at the hotel during the month of August, 1806. Mr. Fergusson took residence there at the same time."

"Will you tell this court everything you know regarding their residence at the hotel?"

"On the very day that Lady Elgin registered at the hotel, another woman came also. Her name was Lady Harvey. She remained only a short time and as soon as she left, Mr. Fergusson took her lodgings, which consisted of a Parlour and bedroom, on the same floor with those occupied by Lady Elgin. The room numbers were Seven and Eight, and they had a communication with each other, being separated by a door between the two Parlours. I went into Mr. Fergusson's bedroom the morning after he came to the Hotel and I observed that his bed had not been slept in, and that it remained in the same state as when it had been made down by myself the preceding evening. I then went into Lady Elgin's bedroom and from the appearance of the bed, I was satisfied that two people had slept in it, being convinced of this from the appearance both of the pillows and the sheets. The pillows had the mark of two people having lain on them, and the sheets were marked in the same manner. That same morning, I saw Mr. Fergusson in Lady Elgin's Parlour. I went directly to John Fraser, who is a waiter in the Hotel, and told him that two people had slept in Lady Elgin's bed, and I wondered if Lord Elgin had come and slept there. Mr. Fraser said that he had not, and warned me to hold my tongue as Lady Elgin might get into a scrape."

"That is all, Miss Crerar. You may step down. Thank you."

Mr. Topping does not cross-examine. John Fraser is called, waiter in Fortune and Blackwell's, married, aged thirty-eight years, residing in Edinburgh, confirming the testimony of Miss Crerar, and adding,

"Mr. Fergusson was personally known to me, having lodged at the Hotel many times previously. A few days after Lady Harvey left the

Hotel, Mr. Fergusson came and was shewn into Lady Elgin's apartments, where he continued with her Ladyship for about a quarter of an hour. Upon his coming out, he enquired whether he could be accommodated with lodgings on the same floor, and being told by myself that he could, he engaged those lodgings which had been occupied by Lady Harvey. Mr. Fergusson passed the next day entirely in Lady Elgin's company, and even invited himself to tea, continuing with her Ladyship till about half past ten, at which time I lighted him to his own Parlour. He then desired the candles there to be lighted, as he had letters to write. Miss Crerar later came to me and said that Mr. Fergusson had not slept in his bed, and that from the appearance of Lady Elgin's bed, two people had slept in it. When Mr. Fergusson finally took leave and had paid his bill, he requested that his arrival should not be put in the newspapers, mentioning that from his short stay in town he would be plagued with acquaintances calling on him. He had no servant or baggage with him; and I did not see him have a night cap."

Again, there is no cross-examination by Mr. Topping. Mary Ruper is summoned to the witness chair: servant at Broomhall, unmarried, aged twenty-five years, served Lady Elgin while she resided at Number 60 Baker Street, entering her service on the fifteenth of November, 1805, and continuing till the twenty-second of June following, concurring with the testimony of Sarah Gosling's deposition:

"When Mrs. Nisbet came to visit her daughter one night, Mr. Fergusson hid behind a screen which stood in the drawing room, and after Mrs. Nisbet left, Mr. Fergusson remained in the house till a late hour in the morning. The next day, I mentioned to Mrs. Gosling that Lady Elgin's dog had dirtied a green cushion which was on the Sopha. Mrs. Gosling shook her head and said it was not the dog who had dirtied the cushion, but that rogue, Mr. Fergusson."

"Miss Ruper, did you and the other servants of the house form any opinion of this situation?"

"Indeed we did. We all agreed that there was an improper connection between Mr. Fergusson and Lady Elgin."

The evidence against Fergusson and Lady Elgin being overwhelming, Mr. Topping places their cause upon the court's mercy as the last wit-

ness for the plaintiff is called to the chair: Thomas Willey, formerly
Lady Elgin's footman, discharged by Lord Elgin "for having got
drunk, now servant to his Royal Highness, the Duke of Kent,"[11] wid-
ower, aged thirty-three years, and bearing no malice or evil against either party, affirms that he "was in Lady Elgin's service while she
resided at Number 60 Baker Street, Portman Square, London, coming
to her service from Scotland about two or three months after her Ladyship took residence at Baker Street. I was well-acquainted with Mr.
Fergusson of Raith. He was frequently in the practice of calling for her
Ladyship, both through the day and during the evening while she
resided at Baker Street. Occasionally Mr. Fergusson called at twelve
and till half past one in the morning according as her Ladyship returned from her evening parties. Lady Elgin was always at home to Mr.
Fergusson, and I hardly recollect one night that Mr. Fergusson did not
call sooner or later. Sometimes he stayed till three or half past three in
the morning, and I was told by Sarah Gosling that she had let him out
of the house even after four o'clock in the morning. Indeed, Mr. Fergusson was shewn more attention by Lady Elgin than any other person
who came to visit there. She seemed happier when in Mr. Fergusson's
company than when in the company of any other person. Everytime
they met they held hands and shewed great familiarity. I recollect one
day about noon, six weeks after Lady Elgin had delivered her child, I
went up to the drawing room and opened the door without knocking.
I saw Lady Elgin at full length on the Sopha, and upon my coming in,
Mr. Fergusson took hold of a shawl and in great confusion threw it
over Lady Elgin's legs."

"Were her Ladyship's petticoats up?"

"I could not positively say."

"Why not?"

"A little writing table stood in front of the Sopha and I was prevented from seeing exactly whether her Ladyship's legs were uncov-
ered or not before the shawl was thrown over them. However, from
the hurry and confused way in which the shawl was thrown over her
Ladyship's legs, I would say that indeed her petticoats were up."

"And what did Mr. Fergusson do at this time?"

"He tried to calm her Ladyship. Her face was much flushed. He then walked towards the fire with his back toward me and, turning only his head, said, 'It is only Thomas.'"

"Were you able to observe whether Mr. Fergusson's breeches were buttoned or unbuttoned?"

"I could not see any part of him in front. He continued at the fire in the same position with his back to me during all this time."

"Mr. Willey, why did you enter the drawing room without knocking?"

"It was always my custom to knock before going in, but on this occasion, I was in a hurry to deliver a message to her Ladyship."

"That will be all, Mr. Willey. Thank you."

Mr. Topping, again showing no inclination to cross-examine, Mr. Garrow now asks Mr. Hay Donaldson to step forward — writer to the signet, practicing in Edinburgh, duly sworn and examined.

"Mr. Donaldson, have you any information regarding the entailed estate of the defendant's father?"

"I have."

"Upon whom is the estate entailed?"

"It is entailed upon Mr. Robert Fergusson, after the death of the father, without division."

"Is Mr. Robert Fergusson the only son?"

"To my knowledge."

"In your professional opinion, would you consider this estate to be substantial?"

"Quite so."

"Have you ascertained its real value?"

"No."

"But in your opinion, it is opulent?"

"Yes, very much so."

Here, Mr. Topping comes forward to cross-examine:

"Mr. Donaldson, when did you last see the defendant's father?"

"Only a few days ago."

"And what was the state of his health?"

"Mr. Fergusson's father is a hale and stout man; and very strong for his years."

"Do you honestly believe that this estate can produce twenty thousand pounds per year?"

"I cannot rightfully say."

"Thank you, Mr. Donaldson. You may step down."

Mr. Garrow again faces the Court:

"My Lords, the noble plaintiff's case is closed."

At this point, Mr. Topping steps forward to address the Court:

"My Lords and Gentlemen, I have the honour of attending before you as the counsel for the unfortunate defendant in this cause. I am well-warranted in using this epithet, after hearing the manner in which my learned friend from London presented his client's case to you. He would venture to have you believe that this indeed is one of those melancholy examples of human frailty, where a man has been placed in the way of temptations that are impossible to resist. Perhaps this is true. I need only remind you that the defendant was twenty-seven years old when the supposed criminal intercourse took place.

"Certainly I should not complain of my learned English friend. To the contrary, I commend him. Furthermore, I hope and trust that each man on this Jury shall give due consideration of the whole circumstances in this case when called upon to arrive at a verdict. I trust that in your judicious and discerning minds, my client's interests shall lose nothing by my own inexperience in advocating cases of this description; or suffer by that comparison which you might make between the greater and more extensive experience of my learned English opponent. My feeble efforts cannot be contrasted with his superior and towering eloquence, for he brings here an incomparable learning and noble breeding, while I, like yourselves, am but a simple Scotsman residing in a humble abode beneath Auld Reekie's soiled skirts."

The Lord President permits the laughter.

"Nevertheless, my Lords and Gentlemen, I feel that I am required to make certain observations on my part, which I hope to impress briefly but strongly upon your minds. Much has been said of the defendant's crime and yet no real evidence was offered here today in respect to Lady Elgin's unfaithfulness to her matrimonial bed. We listened to the testimony of many witnesses, during which not a few deplorable charges were made against the honour and good name of Lady Elgin and the defendant. However not one of these witnesses could honestly admit that Mr. Fergusson was actually seen in criminal conversation with Lady Elgin.

"As for the letters that fell into Lord Elgin's hands, let me say that they furnish no conclusive proof that adultery was indeed committed. Bear in mind that Lady Elgin's health was seriously impaired at this time, both physically and emotionally. My learned English friend feels that it is your duty to scourge the defendant in punishing an offense of this nature. Thank God, it is not within the province of this jury to scourge. If there is an injury here, it is of a civil nature, and the compensation, if any, must be a requital by a civil remuneration. It pleases me to say that the laws of Scotland know of no vindictive return for an injury such as this. 'Vengeance is mine, saith the Lord!'

"When my learned English friend talks of twenty thousand pounds as a requital, I feel great surprise. On the one hand, he admits that no pecuniary reimbursement can repay his noble client's injury, yet he seeks precisely this. And more, for he would convert this civil transgression, if such it is proven to be, into a criminal case. But it is my strong conviction that the courts of Scotland will never permit such an innovation in the law.

"With respect to the financial condition of Mr. Fergusson, I am free to disclose that in fact he is not worth one shilling. He exists merely upon the bounty of his father. He is not an only child, but the eldest son of a large family. His father may live many additional years, and thus Mr. Fergusson can be but a life-tenant, without the power of raising twenty shillings, let alone twenty thousand pounds. He may also be burdened with provisions for relatives, which would preclude the possibility of his ever paying heavy damages, should they be imposed upon him today. This is exactly his state and condition.

"I am persuaded that his cause is now in honourable and sympathetic hands. Furthermore, I entertain no doubt but that you will deal with him in mercy and consideration. My Lords and Gentlemen of the Jury, I thank you."

At this point, the jury is charged by the Lord President:

"Gentlemen, I call your attention to the importance of this case, which involves an injury, perhaps the greatest injury that one can inflict upon another. In all actions of this description, it is the task of the plaintiff to make out his title to a claim and to show that such claim is well-founded. It remains now for you to say if this claim should be granted. You must act with caution, deliberately considering if there is an offense here, and if so, its appropriate punishment. I am fully persuaded that your verdict will also afford public gratification. Retire then, into your chamber. This case is left entirely in your hands."

Within the hour, the jury returns "with a Verdict for the Plaintiff: damages of ten thousand pounds."[12]

In the civil action held at London, Fergusson had claimed that no adultery took place in France, "especially in the voluptuous and fascinating capital of the French Empire, where temptation is ever busily at work. But when Lady Elgin arrived in England, without the protection of her husband, and possessing sweetness that might rivet an anchorite, charms that could command and fascinate the coldest heart, he — all alive to such unequalled excellence and beauty — fell a devoted victim to such a shrine."[13]

This admission was brought to the attention of the commissaries when the divorce decree was heard shortly after the adultery trial against Fergusson:

At Edinburgh, anent the action and cause for divorce, raised, intended, and pursued before the Commissary at the instance of the Right Honourable Thomas, Earl of Elgin and Kincardine, against Mary, Countess of Elgin and Kincardine, by virtue of the said Commissary, his libelled summons raised there anent which maketh mention that where the said Thomas, Earl of Elgin and Kincardine, pursuer; and where the said Mary, Countess of Elgin and Kincardine, defendant, were regularly married and cohabited together as husband and wife, owned and acknowledged each other as such and were holden, treated, and reputed married persons by their friends and neighbours, of which marriage five children were procreated, and of whom four are alive today.

And although Mary, Countess of Elgin and Kincardine, stood bound and obliged to preserve the marriage bed inviolate, yet true it is that she, regardless of her marriage vows and of the whole attachment which ought to subsist between married persons, and of her duty as wife and mother, has for sometime past had carnal intercourse with a man or with men known not to be the said Thomas, Earl of Elgin and Kincardine, and has been guilty of an act or acts of adultery.[14]

Throughout the long proceeding, Lady Elgin felt that she was back at Palermo harbor on board the *Phaeton*, weak and nauseous, frightfully alone, while Masterman kept wringing her hands and weeping: "Her poor Ladyship, a fine honeymoon is this!"[15]

And more particularly, the said Mary, Countess of Elgin and Kincardine, has had such carnal conversation and intercourse, and committed such an act or acts of adultery with Robert Fergusson Esquire of Raith, in all or one of the nights or days during their journey together from France to London, and also in the city of Edinburgh. And therefore concluding that in law, equity and justice, the said noble pursuer ought and should have the said Commissary, his sentence and decreet, finding and declaring that the pursuer is free of marriage contracted, solemnized and completed between him and the said defender. And that the said pursuer may marry when and whom he pleases in the same manner as if the defender were naturally dead, or as he might have done if he had never been married to her.

It ought finally to be found and declared that the said Mary, Countess of Elgin and Kincardine, has forfeited and lost all manner of right, interest, or benefit by the said marriage — either legal or conventional. And that the noble pursuer has a just right and title to the provisions made in his favour, which shall include the care and upbringing of the surviving children. And thus the said Commissary gives and pronounces his sentence and decreet in the aforesaid manner — divorcing, separating, finding and declaring.[16]

In the months that followed, *The Times* and other English publications steadily wrote of Elgin's misfortunes, referring in detail to his enormous debts and scores of creditors. Foreseeing a life of humiliating poverty, Elgin wrote again to Prime Minister Spencer Perceval, repeating his long list of expenses and once more requesting "a mark of Royal approbation as a Scotch Peer. I need hardly add that such an arrangement would be in the highest degree gratifying to my feelings, and if such a Peerage is conferred, I shall be prepared to accept payment by installments, or partly by annuity, if this would be more convenient."[17]

Perceval's answer came quickly and sharply: "I must candidly say that I should feel it quite impossible to recommend any arrangement of that nature!"[18]

Elgin's income from his estates in Scotland totalled only two thousand pounds a year. By the usual standards of nobility, he was never a wealthy man, nor "easy in his circumstances"[19] as Dundas had suggested to King George III when recommending Elgin for the embassy at Constantinople. Although Elgin's salary at Constantinople was almost seven thousand pounds, it was hardly enough when compared to the domestic expense of more than eight thousand pounds for maintaining the embassy his first year alone. This did not include the salaries and expenses of his large staff, the maintenance of his house in the suburb of Pera, the cost of postage, couriers, and other sizable expenses of an actively large embassy. But beyond all this, he spent close to twenty thousand pounds of his own money to buy tents, horses, medical supplies, gunboats, and military equipment "for the British Expeditionary Forces in Egypt."[20] The government stolidly refused to pay him this amount, and in the end, Elgin had no other choice but to settle for only ten thousand pounds.

The Elgin Marbles were moved to the British Museum in August 1816, and under the terms of the act passed by Parliament, which transferred their ownership to the English government, Elgin and his heirs were to be made trustees of the British Museum. From the purchase price of thirty-five thousand pounds, the government put a claim on eighteen thousand, "In payment for a debt cunningly transferred to them by one of Elgin's creditors."[21] The balance of the money was then dispersed among those creditors who were fortunate enough to get their share before it ran out, and thus Elgin himself did not receive one penny from the sale.

Nevertheless he refused to give up. Several months later, he wrote to Perceval's successor, Lord Liverpool,* and once more recounted the

---

*Perceval was assassinated on May 11, 1812, in the lobby of the House of Commons.

many disasters on his journey from Constantinople and the expected return to England, only to be seized in France and persecuted with the most vindictive animosity by Bonaparte. He also informed Lord Liverpool about the Tweddell affair:

> It was while suffering under these severities and separated from all but the most constrained communications from my family in England, that the foulest and most insidious intrigue was darkly at work here, preparing the ruin of my domestic peace, creating prepossessions in regard to my official conduct, which however I had subsequently the good fortune to remove at least from Mr. Perceval's mind; nor were the true motives of this undefined, unavowed, yet most injurious persecution brought home to its real source in disappointment and jealousy till Mr. Spencer Smith, finding a willing instrument in Mr. Robert Tweddell to distort one of the most ordinary incidents in foreign stations, could not refrain from standing prominently forward in the publications that then appeared against me. And presuming upon the ill will against my operations in Greece, in which some late travellers had indulged, he actually transmitted anonymous abuse against me to the newspapers at the moment when the House of Commons was entering upon the subject of my marbles.[22]

The last line of Elgin's letter was an outright plea for mercy: "All the money I had drawn upon public account, the whole proceeds of my patrimonial estate, my dowry, and every private fund at my disposal, have been entirely absorbed!"[23]

Lord Liverpool sympathized with Elgin's plight, but once again his request for peerage was not granted. During these negotiations, he suffered yet another setback: his son Bruce fell gravely ill, and his physicians in Edinburgh were unable to diagnose the sickness or cure it. Fighting desperately to save his only son and heir, Elgin brought the boy to London, where he was examined by the finest physicians of the time. They all concurred that Bruce was a hopeless epileptic:

> First on the head of him who did this deed,
> My curse shall light, on him and all his seed;
> Without one spark of intellectual fire,
> Be all the sons as senseless as the sire![24]

Elgin tried to ignore these cruel attacks of Byron, and despite his mounting reversals, he was still hopeful "of bequeathing something to his children besides his debts."[25] Doggedly, he made a final appeal for a British peerage, but again it was denied. Whatever assets he possessed were now put immediately into trust. To add to his embarrassment, the disfigurement of his face brought on such a deep depression, he began avoiding people, even those who were closest to him. It was not long before his beloved Broomhall became the target of his creditors, and although the title of the estate was protected by ancient English law, he could no longer maintain it properly. Most of the rooms remained unfurnished, and the large force of servants had to be discharged.

In 1820, Elgin returned to the House of Lords as one of the representative peers for Scotland. A year later he was, with the long-despised Byron, one of the first to subscribe to the Philhellenic Committee to support the revolutionary forces in Greece, who were now on the verge of defeating the Turks and expelling them from their country.

Elgin felt no sorrow when he learned that Lord Byron, after a series of feverish attacks, had died in the small Greek village of Missolonghi on April 19, 1824. He had gone there to train some peasant troops whom he himself had subsidized. For three and a half months he lived a Spartan existence, but the village was infested with unclean swamps, and the young poet eventually succumbed to fever. He regarded himself a complete failure at Missolonghi. Sir Harold Nicolson thought otherwise: "Lord Byron accomplished nothing at Missolonghi except his own suicide. But by that single act of heroism, he secured the liberation of Greece."[26]

It was no surprise to the people of Edinburgh when Elgin married again. His second wife was Elizabeth Oswald of Dunnikeir, daughter of a neighboring landowner from Fife. Immediately after the marriage, Elgin departed for France with her, leaving the care of the children to his mother, the dowager countess of Elgin. For the rest of his life, "he was obliged to live in France to escape his creditors."[27] He died in abject poverty in Paris on November 4, 1841, and his enormous debts "were not finally paid off by his family until another thirty years had passed. The affair of the marbles had left a bitter legacy."[28]

* * *

As for Lady Elgin, after the furor and sensationalism of the trial had abated, she and Robert Fergusson were quietly married and for a brief time lived at Raith, Fergusson's ancestral home. When Fergusson entered political life as a member of the Whig Party, Lady Elgin accompanied him to London, and they took residence in the Nisbet house at Portman Square until Fergusson's untimely death shortly thereafter.

Lady Elgin's last years were spent at Archerfield. The stain and disgrace of the adultery trial would hound her for the rest of her life. Her days were now mostly taken up with reading and with walking her dog along the jagged cliffs overlooking Aberlady Bay. As she stared at the pounding sea one day, she was obsessed by the raw sight of a mortally wounded Parthenon, the spidery scaffolds clutching its west pediment as Lusieri and the sweating laborers tugged on ropes and pulleys. Even after all these years, she could still hear the deafening echo of chisels eating into the veins of the first marble frieze, the haunting sound of that exquisite cornice falling to the ground in a thousand pieces, Elgin's wild voice staining the Attic sky with eternal shame, the Turkish disdar angrily throwing his arms upward and crying: "Telos!"[29]

Yet this was not the end.

That same pull of the sea now tugged her back to those wretched marbles lying on a cold museum floor. In the shrouded distance, she could hear Athena's vengeful curse as she stood there paralyzed, terrified by the relentless surge of time, the fierce growth of grass under her feet, the thunderous pulse of the firth on Scotland's ribs.

It was a terrible augury: "What a desperate horrible idea that nothing but death can make us free!"[30]

In 1855, Lady Elgin was put "to rest in a tomb not only unkempt and forlorn, but nameless too. It was not until 1916 that her name was finally inscribed on the hideous stone."[31]

Epilogue

*A*LMOST TWO HUNDRED YEARS AFTER Elgin's pillage, the question of the Parthenon marbles continues to be heatedly debated. Within the past decade, the British government has rejected the Greek government's formal request for their return to Greece, the official response of the House of Commons being delivered by Mr. Ray Whitney, undersecretary at the foreign office: "The collection secured by Lord Elgin, as a result of transactions conducted with the recognized legitimate authorities of the time, was vested by Act of Parliament to the Trustees of the British Museum in Perpetuity."[1]

The Greek government, of course, rejected this decision and strongly vowed to continue in the pursuit of its rightful claims. According to documents recently opened to the public, however, the British attitude had been quite different during World War II, when Greece was considered a strategic ally of Britain: "In the eyes of British strategists, then as now, Greece was an essential part of the defensive complex of the eastern Mediterranean. Equally, a British presence in Greece presented no less dangerous a threat to German interests in the Balkans."[2]

In an effort to secure Greece's cooperation on this matter, several senior officials in the foreign office suggested that once the war was over, Greece should be given back the Elgin Marbles. Subsequently, on December 30, 1940, Mr. S. H. Wright of the Treasury Chambers, Whitehall, sent a letter to Mr. Philip B. B. Nichols, head of the South-East European Department of the Foreign Office:

We have to provide an answer to the following Parliamentary Question:

MISS CAZALET (Thelma Cazalet-Keir, a National Conservative MP): To ask the Prime Minister, whether he will introduce legislation to enable the Elgin Marbles to be restored to Greece at the end of hostilities as some recognition of the Greeks' magnificent stand for civilisation. We have asked the British Museum for their observations on the lines on which they think this question should be answered. The Foreign Office will no doubt also be interested and we should accordingly be grateful for the observations of your Department also.[3]

Miss E. Welsford, librarian of the Courtauld Institute, discussed the matter with several university authorities and wrote back to the foreign office:

I have consulted my Professors, who agree that, provided they are not exposed to weather, scholarship would not suffer if the Elgin Marbles were returned to Greece. So much for a direct answer. Indirectly, however, scholarship could obviously suffer from a number of considerations which are political. The Balkans are likely to continue being the cockpit of Europe, and though London is not as inviolate as it was, probably they are safer kept here, within easy and immediate access to vaults than they would be in Athens, whence they might be stolen for Turkey for instance! Then, so long as they are here, they provide a focus for western Europe for interest in Greece and Greek art; both the Professors feel that probably it is, for that reason, in Greece's best interest to have them here — though in all probability Greece would not take that view. A set of the best possible casts to be put up on the Parthenon is the ideal from the Professors' point of view, leaving the originals here. To erect the originals there (in Athens) would be disastrous as they would be destroyed by weather, and also they would be too far off to be studied. If they do go back to Greece, a special museum must be built for them.[4]

On January 8, 1941, Mr. R. James Bowker, deputy head of the South-East European Department of the foreign office, was given a memorandum on Miss Cazalet's question about the Elgin Marbles:

I enclose a copy of the British Museum memorandum of the 31st ultimo as you requested. You will, I take it, be sending us the comprehensive memorandum you propose to write, as Treasury is the intermediary between the British Museum and Parliament, and we shall accordingly have to see that the Museum's standpoint is also considered by our Ministers.[5]

Legal Considerations: Even if the acquisition of the Elgin Marbles had not been made by Parliament, an Act of Parliament would be necessary to remove them from the British Museum, since the Trustees have no power to alienate material of this kind.

Moral Considerations: There is no doubt that Lord Elgin's action was right in every way. It was a good thing to get the sculptures out of Greece, and a good thing to bring them to London; it was done with proper authority, and all the technical operations were expertly performed, but the Greeks regard it as a Foliation of their national heritage under Turkish tyranny. It is beside the point that the export of antiquities is now prohibited in Greece and Italy and all of Near Eastern countries. The principle of tying works of art to their places of origin is not recognised by Western nations, and the frequent claims that such as have got out shall be returned, have never been admitted and seem to be preposterous. The point is that the Acropolis of Athens is the greatest national monument of Greece, and that the buildings to which the Marbles belonged are still standing or have been rebuilt.

Practical Considerations: There can be no question of replacing the sculptures on the buildings, even if enough of the Parthenon were left to carry all that belongs to it. Exposure of the weather would not be contemplated by the Greek authorities, or if it were, would be opposed by expert international opinion. The pieces that are now in London would be placed in a museum, probably not on the Acropolis, where there is hardly room to enlarge the present building and certainly not room enough inside it. The return of the Marbles would therefore not improve the appearance of the Parthenon or the Acropolis, though it would gratify Greek sentiment. But Greek pride may be reasonably offended by the patronage (assumed in recent newspaper correspondence and in this Parliamentary Question) which proposes the return as a favour rather than a right.

Mr. W. L. C. Knight, chief official on the Greek desk at the foreign office, sent a draft reply to the Treasury on January 24, 1941:

THE ELGIN MARBLES

The perennial question of the return of the Elgin Marbles to Athens has now cropped up again in a rather acute form, as a Parliamentary Question by Miss Cazalet.

Miss Cazalet's question has already been postponed once, but she insists on asking it in view of the "pressure to which she is being subjected by English and Greek friends." It is therefore necessary to consider urgently the nature of the reply to be returned to Miss Cazalet, and less urgently, the nature of the decision on the general question which His Majesty's Government should eventually arrive at. That they should reach such decision in the fairly near future seems clear in the light of our present relations with Greece, and the interest now being taken in the question by the British public, as shown by the recent correspondence in the *Times*. Of the letters published, the great majority were in favour of the Marbles being restored to Greece.

In view of the time which may be required for a decision on the general issue, it would seem necessary therefore to return a non-committal reply to the Parliamentary Question. The reply might be to the effect that the present moment is inopportune for a final decision on a subject which raises several important issues, and has given rise to much controversy in the past; but that His Majesty's Government will not fail to give the matter their careful and sympathetic consideration. The Treasury, who are the intermediary between the British Museum and Parliament, have obtained from the former and communicated to the Foreign Office an interesting memorandum on the Elgin Marbles and the part taken by Parliament in their acquisition for the nation. The return of the Elgin Marbles, if decided on, should be in the nature of a gesture of friendship to Greece, and not based on the principle that antiquities should be put back where they came from, which would be a most awkward and dangerous precedent. The best time for the gesture would be after the war, when transport would again be safe. It would thus set the seal on Anglo-Greek friendship and collaboration in the way that would most appeal to Greek patriotic sentiment. We should, however, presumably ensure for ourselves, in perpetuity, a share in the control of the arrangements to be made for the preservation of these treasures, e.g., permanent British representation on the committee. For the gift to be complete and completely acceptable, it should comprise, in addition to the Parthenon friezes, the Caryatid and the column from the Erechtheum, and all the other sculptures that constitute the Elgin Marbles.[6]

RECOMMENDATIONS

1. That the reply to Miss Cazalet's question should be to the effect that the present moment is inopportune for a final decision on a subject which raises several important issues, and has given rise to so much controversy in the past; but that His Majesty's Government will not fail to give the matter their careful and sympathetic consideration.
2. That, subject to the views of His Majesty's Minister at Athens, it should be decided in principle to return to Greece the Elgin Marbles, including the Caryatid, the column from the Erechtheum, etc. on the following conditions:
   a. It should be made clear that the decision to return the Marbles is in the nature of a gesture of friendship to Greece and is not based on any recognition of the principle that antiquities should be returned to their place of origin.
   b. The Marbles should not be returned until after the war.
   c. Before they are returned, adequate arrangements should be made for their proper housing, exhibition, and preservation.
   d. His Majesty's Government should be assured of a share, in perpetuity, and in the control of the arrangements to be made for their preservation.

Sir Stephen Caselee, a classical scholar as well as a government official, offered his opinion on Knight's memorandum: "I am personally very much against the whole project, but since the British Museum has receded to a certain extent from its former rigid position, I suppose we must go as far as is now suggested."[7]

Others, like Sir Orme Sargent, deputy undersecretary of state, voiced strong reservations:

It may well turn out that if we make one gift to satisfy Greek archeological sentiment, Greek ethnographical imperialism will demand that it should be similarly rewarded. As regards the conditions under which the Marbles should be returned, I would deprecate condition (d), to the effect that His Majesty's Government should be assured of a share in perpetuity in the control of the arrangements to be made for the preservation of the Marbles. This would be all right if an offer to this effect came spontaneously from the Greeks, but for us to demand it, would certainly offend Greek amour propre and undo a good deal of the psychological value of the gift. Besides, from the technical point of view, I should say it was quite unnecessary.[8]

In reply, the Honourable Sir Alexander Cadogan, permanent undersecretary of state, wrote, "I don't know where all this is going to end. Whose is the Bellini portrait of the Sultan which, unlike the Elgin Marbles, was obtained by direct fraud on the part of our Envoy? Public attention has been focused on the Elgin Marbles, but they were actually acquired in a manner no more disreputable than many of the contents of European and American museums. I hope we shall think twice before taking a final decision."[9]

Sir Anthony Eden, secretary of state, wrote on January 15, 1941: "I am prepared to advise reply to the Parliamentary Question as suggested, but we should not go further at present. With much else, both artistic and political, this is something that can well be decided after the war."[10]

These recommendations, however, were not even sent to the Treasury, and a few days later, Mr. M. L. C. Clarke dispatched a note to Knight, the official on the Greek desk at the foreign office:

The German propagandists not infrequently refer to the Elgin Marbles, which the British "stole" from Greece and refuse to return to her. As usual, the material for the propaganda comes from English sources. It was Byron who, at a time when everyone thought it right that the treasures of Greece should be transferred from a country where they were ignored and neglected to western European countries, attacked Lord Elgin as vandal and despoiler; and since the time of Byron there have been, and still are, many Englishmen who feel that the marbles should be in Athens rather than in London. Counter propaganda, if thought necessary, should be on these lines; Elgin was inspired by an enthusiasm for ancient Greek art which was shared by the educated of other European countries, not least by Germans, e.g., Stackelber and

Haller, who were active in excavation, and Ludwig of Bavaria, who secured the Aegina sculptures for the Munich Glyptothek. The genuine philhellenism of the eighteenth- and nineteenth-century German scholars and literary men might be contrasted with the unsympathetic attitude which Germans are now forced by their propagandists to adopt. Reference might also be made to the notorious freedom with which Nazi leaders appropriate works of art from public and private collections.[11]

The whole matter was put to rest on January 23, 1941, with this final exchange in Parliament:

ELGIN MARBLES

Miss Cazalet: asked the Prime Minister whether he will introduce legislation to enable the Elgin Marbles to be restored to Greece at the end of hostilities as some recognition of the Greeks' magnificent stand for civilisation.

Mr. Attlee: His Majesty's Government are not prepared to introduce legislation for this purpose.[12]

Since then, the argument that the Parthenon marbles should be restored to Greece "has been reopened every five years, and on each occasion, the debate on either side of the question has been emotional and ill-informed."[13]

In the 1980s, the former actress and culture minister Melina Mercouri launched a vigorous battle, charging the British with "vandalism." After her death, her husband, internationally known film director Jules Dassin, announced on March 30, 1994, a worldwide campaign for the return of the Parthenon marbles to Greece. Dassin was elected chairman of a foundation whose prime aim was to seek, in cooperation with the state and the Culture Ministry, the return of the Parthenon marbles to Greece, where they would be housed in the new museum at the foot of the Acropolis. The foundation's nine-member board of film directors and producers, architects, scientists, scholars, and lawyers met in London on September 18, 1994, and reiterated their demand for the return of the marbles.

On June 6, 1996, "thirty-three Labour MPs submitted a draft

resolution in the House of Commons favouring the return of the Elgin Marbles to Greece." The resolution called on the British government to begin immediate negotiations with the Greek government on the issue. The Labour deputies also congratulated the Channel 4 television stations of Britain for the quality and success of its recent documentary on the Parthenon marbles, and noted that a telephone poll conducted after the program revealed that 92.5 percent of the 100,000 viewers who participated in the poll voted in favor of the return of the marbles to Greece. Although there had been good arguments in the past for keeping the Parthenon marbles in the British Museum, the MPs remarked that "the poll clearly shows that public opinion in England is now overwhelmingly in favour of their return to Greece."[14]

Finally, the Greek culture minister announced on January 4, 1997, that an official request had been sent to the British government asking for the return of the Parthenon marbles to Greece.

Amidst all these discussions and reverberating furor, the current Lord Elgin has made it known that he dared not visit Greece under his real name, "and that indeed he was sorry his great-great-grandfather [had] ever [seen] the bloody stones!"[15]

Notes

PROLOGUE

1. William St. Clair, *Lord Elgin and the Marbles*, 16.

Sicily

1. Mary Nisbet, *The Letters of Mary Nisbet, Countess of Elgin*, 7.
2. Historical Manuscripts Commission, "Report on the Manuscripts of J. B. Fortescue," vol. 2: 603.
3. Lord Grenville Leveson Gower, *Private Correspondence*, vol. 1: 262.
4. Robert Walpole, *Memoirs Relating to European and Asiatic Turkey*, sec. 15: 82ff.
5. Arthur Hamilton Smith, "Lord Elgin and His Collection," *Journal of Hellenic Studies* (1916): 180.
6. St. Clair, *Marbles*, 24.
7. Ibid., 6.
8. Nisbet, *Letters*, 7.
9. Historical Manuscripts Commission, "Fortescue," vol. 5: 91.
10. Joseph Farington, *Farington Diary*, 21 April 1799.
11. Ibid., 22 April 1799.
12. Hunt Papers, 17 July 1799.
13. Nisbet, *Letters*, 30.
14. Ibid., 20.
15. A. Michaelis, *Ancient Marbles in Great Britain*, 109.
16. Nisbet, *Letters*, 24.
17. Ibid., 22.
18. Ibid., 23.
19. Foreign Office, *British Foreign and State Papers*, 78/22.
20. J. Christopher Herold, *The Age of Napoleon*, 67.
21. Ibid., 68.
22. Ibid., 69.
23. Nisbet, *Letters*, 20.
24. Michaelis, *Ancient Marbles*, 111.
25. Nisbet, *Letters*, 23.
26. Ibid., 25.
27. Smith, *Elgin*, 169.

28. H. W. Williams, *Travels in Italy and Greece*, vol. 2: 331.
29. Nisbet, *Letters*, 23.
30. Ibid., 25.
31. Ibid., 26.
32. John Barrow, *Life and Correspondence of Admiral Sir William Sydney Smith*, vol. 1: 378.
33. St. Clair, *Marbles*, 21.
34. Smith, *Elgin*, 168.
35. Ibid., 169.
36. Robert Tweddell, *Remains of John Tweddell*, 49ff.
37. Nisbet, *Letters*, 75.
38. William Richard Hamilton to Lord Elgin, 4 February 1800, Smith, *Elgin*, 174.
39. Foreign Office, *British Foreign and State Papers*, 78/22.
40. Nisbet, *Letters*, 45.
41. Barrow, *Life and Correspondence*, vol. 1: 381.
42. Nisbet, *Letters*, 39.
43. Smith, *Elgin*, 182.
44. William Wittman, *Travels in Turkey, Asia Minor, and Syria*, 65.
45. Ibid., 65.
46. Nisbet, *Letters*, 45.
47. Smith, *Elgin*, 182.

Turkey

1. Nisbet, *Letters*, 56.
2. William Richard Hamilton to Lord Elgin, 1 March 1800, Smith, *Elgin*, 172.
3. Historical Manuscripts Commission, "Fortescue," vol. 6: 89.
4. Lord Elgin to Lord Grenville, 16 February 1800, Foreign Office, *British Foreign and State Papers*, 78/28.
5. Ibid., 78/25
6. Ibid., 78/24.
7. Ibid., 78/20.
8. Ibid., 78/29.
9. Nisbet, *Letters*, 147.
10. Smith, *Elgin*, 176.
11. Nisbet, *Letters*, 59.
12. John Sloane, *Notebooks*, 13 August 1816.
13. Nisbet, *Letters*, 119.
14. Smith, *Elgin*, 184.
15. Walpole, *Memoirs*, 162.
16. Joseph Dacre Carlyle, *Poems*, 13.
17. Ibid., 14ff.

18. Nisbet, *Letters*, 119.
19. Foreign Office, *British Foreign and State Papers*, 78/33.
20. Ibid., 78/32.
21. Ibid., 78/33.
22. Ibid., 78/33.
23. Admiral Viscount Keith, *Keith Papers*, vol. 2: 406.
24. Lord Elgin to Lusieri, 10 July 1801, Smith, *Elgin*, 207.
25. Lusieri to Lord Elgin, 20 September 1801, St. Clair, *Marbles*, 62.
26. St. Clair, *Marbles*, 74.
27. Smith, *Elgin*, 205.
28. Lacy to Hunt, 8 October, Smith, *Elgin*, 204.
29. Ibid., 230.
30. Ibid., 190.
31. Nisbet, *Letters*, 141.
32. Ibid., 97.
33. *Select Committee Report of the House of Commons on the Earl of Elgin's Collection of Sculptured Marbles*, 41.

Greece

1. St. Clair, *Marbles*, 60.
2. Ph. E. LeGrand, "Bibliographie de Louis-François-Sebastien Fauvel," Revue Archéologique, 3rd ser., 30 and 31, 1897.
3. Smith, *Elgin*, 207.
4. St. Clair, *Marbles*, 109.
5. Smith, *Elgin*, 172.
6. Ibid., 173.
7. Ibid., 191ff.
8. Plutarch, *The Lives of Noble Grecians and Romans*, ed. J. and Wm. Langhorne.
9. *Select Committee Report*, 40.
10. Patrick Leigh Fermor, *Mani*, 27.
11. Ibid., 214.
12. Edward Daniel Clarke, *Travels in Various Countries of Europe, Asia, and Africa*, sec. 2, pt. 2: 483.
13. Edward Dodwell, *A Classical and Topographical Tour through Greece*, sec. 1: 322.
14. St. Clair, *Marbles*, 94.
15. Ibid., 104.
16. R. Chandler, *Travels in Greece*, 191.
17. Edward Daniel Clarke, *Greek Marbles*, 32.
18. W. Otter, *The Life and Remains of the Reverend Edward Daniel Clarke*, 505.
19. St. Clair, *Marbles*, 115.

20. Ibid., 115.
21. Admiral Viscount Keith, *Keith Papers*, vol. 2: 402.
22. Ibid., 405.
23. Nisbet, *Letters*, 184.
24. Ibid., 187.
25. Ibid., 189.
26. Ibid., 207.
27. Ibid.
28. Ibid., 209.
29. Foreign Office, *British Foreign and State Papers*, 78/36.

Constantinople

1. Nisbet, *Letters*, 215.
2. Smith, *Elgin*, 232.
3. Ibid., 233.
4. Ibid., 237.
5. Nisbet, *Letters*, 217.
6. Walpole, *Memoirs*, 98.
7. Nisbet, *Letters*, 217.
8. St. Clair, *Marbles*, 85.
9. Foreign Office, *British Foreign and State Papers*, 78/33.
10. Smith, *Elgin*, 234.
11. Nisbet, *Letters*, 233.

Athens

1. Smith, *Elgin*, 240.
2. St. Clair, *Marbles*, 119.
3. Smith, *Elgin*, 239; also William Falconer, *The Shipwreck*, 207, which contains Captain Clarke's personal account of the incident.
4. Ioannes Gennadios, *Lord Elgin and the Previous Archaeological Invasions of Greece, Especially Athens*, 2.
5. John Cam Hobhouse, *A Journey through Albania and Other Provinces of Turkey, in Europe and Asia, to Constantinople*, 347.
6. F. S. N. Douglas, *An Essay on Certain Points of Resemblance between the Ancient and Modern Greeks*, vol. 1: 85.
7. T. S. Hughes, *Travels in Sicily, Greece, and Albania*, sec. 1: 266.
8. Peter Edmund Laurent, *Recollections of a Classical Tour*, 110. The destruction of the caryatids at the Erechtheum is also mentioned in Williams, *Travels in Italy*, 316.
9. Williams, *Travels in Italy*, sec. 2: 307.
10. Nisbet, *Letters*, 204.

11. Smith, *Elgin*, 258.
12. St. Clair, *Marbles*, 149.
13. Nisbet, *Letters*, 234.
14. An excerpt from the French newspaper *Moniteur*, 130.
15. Edward Gibbon, *The Decline and Fall of the Roman Empire*, 686.
16. Robert Burns, *The Jolly Beggars*, 63.

Paris

1. Smith, *Elgin*, 347.
2. Nisbet, *Letters*, 286.
3. Lady Blennerhasset, *Talleyrand*, 117ff.
4. Charles Maurice de Talleyrand-Périgord, *Mémoires*, vol. 1: 33ff.
5. St. Clair, *Marbles*, 122.
6. Nisbet, *Letters*, 240.
7. Colonel Craufurd was quoting a popular remark of the time, probably attributed to Lord Byron.
8. Nisbet, *Letters*, 248.
9. Smith, *Elgin*, 360.
10. Nisbet, *Letters*, 250ff.
11. Michael Lewis, *Napoleon and His British Captives*, 183.

Barèges

1. Nisbet, *Letters*, 263.
2. St. Clair, *Marbles*, 125.
3. Smith, *Elgin*, 360.
4. LeGrand, "Biographie de Fauvel," 92.
5. *Bulletin de la Société Nationale des Antiquaires de le France*, 1900, ser. 6: 245.
6. Farington, *Diary*, 5 December 1806.
7. Nisbet, *Letters*, 242.
8. Ibid., 242.
9. Ibid., 244.
10. From the French newspaper *Moniteur*, no. 131.
11. St. Clair, *Marbles*, 129.
12. Nisbet, *Letters*, 290.
13. Ibid., 146.
14. A Cierval, *Chartres, sa cathédral, ses monuments*, 87.
15. G. Michaud, *Talleyrand: Histoire politique et vie intime*, vol. 2: 77ff.
16. Nisbet, *Letters*, 247.
17. St. Clair, *Marbles*, 129.
18. Nisbet, *Letters*, 245.
19. Ibid., 247.

20. Foreign Office, *British Foreign and State Papers*, 27/68.
21. British Museum, Additional Manuscripts 38266 F 5.
22. *Correspondance de Napoléon Premier Publiée par Ordre de l'Empereur Napoléon III*, vol. 8: 315.
23. Lord Elgin to Sir Spencer Perceval, 6 May 1811, British Library, Additional Manuscripts 38246 F 119.
24. Nisbet, *Letters*, 296.
25. *Select Committee Report*, vii.
26. Ibid., 43.
27. Lord Elgin, "Memorandum on the Subject of the Earl of Elgin's Pursuits in Greece," 91.
28. Ibid., 95.
29. *Select Committee Report*, 43ff.
30. St. Clair, *Marbles*, 130.

Pau

1. Nisbet, *Letters*, 321.
2. Ibid., p. 330ff.
3. Lord Byron, "Written after Swimming from Sestos to Abydos."
4. Byron, *Correspondence*, sec. 1.
5. Andre Maurois, *Byron*, 139.
6. Ibid., 140ff.
7. Byron, *Correspondence*, sec. 1.
8. Maurois, *Byron*, 125.
9. Byron, *Correspondence*, sec. 1.
10. Maurois, *Byron*, 128.
11. Ibid., 130–31.
12. Lord Byron, "Maid of Athens, Ere We Part."
13. Byron, *Correspondence*, sec. 1.
14. Maurois, *Byron*, 143.
15. St. Clair, *Marbles*, 189.
16. Lord Byron, "Childe Harold's Pilgrimage," canto 2.
17. Smith, *Elgin*, 295.
18. Nisbet, *Letters*, 354.
19. Ibid., 324.
20. Ibid., 351.
21. Lewis, *Napoleon*, 183.
22. *Select Committee Report*, 43.
23. Philip Hunt, *A Narrative of What Is Known Respecting the Literary Remains of the Late John Tweddell*, 4; also in the National Library of Scotland, 5645 F 210.
24. Farington, *Diary*, 20 June 1808.
25. *The Trial of R. Fergusson, Esq.*, 6.

26. Ibid., 5ff.
27. St. Clair, *Marbles*, 134.
28. Ibid., 134ff.
29. Ibid., 135.

Scotland

1. Lusieri to Lord Elgin, 20 June 1804, St. Clair, *Marbles*, 138.
2. Lord Byron, *Childe Harold's Pilgrimage*, canto 2, n. 2.
3. Lusieri to Lord Elgin, 26 June 1805, St. Clair, *Marbles*, 208.
4. British Library, Additional Manuscripts 38266 F 5.
5. Robert Fergusson to Lady Elgin, 10 December 1806, *The Trial of R. Fergusson*, 10.
6. Ibid., 11.
7. Ibid., 11ff.
8. Commissary Court, Scottish Records Office, Edinburgh, Scotland, "Decreet Divorce, Thomas, Earl of Elgin and Kincardine, against Mary, Countess of Elgin and Kincardine," 1808: 6.
9. *The Times* (London), 16 December 1805.
10. The chief source on the Tweddell case is a quarto volume published in 1816 by Tweddell's brother, the Reverend Robert Tweddell, *The Remains of John Tweddell, Late Fellow of Trinity College, Cambridge, Being a Selection of His Correspondence, a Republication of his "Profusiones Juveniles," an Appendix Containing Some Account of the Author's Collections, Manuscripts, Drawings, etc., and of Their Extraordinary Disappearance, Preceded by a Biographical Memoir of the Deceased, and Illustrated with Portraits, Picturesque Views, and Maps*. The volume was priced at three guineas, and 225 pages of its appendix were devoted entirely to vicious accusations against Lord Elgin. Elgin's defense in this matter appears in a long letter to the editor of the *Edinburgh Revue*, no. 50, 1815.
11. Hunt, *A Narrative*, as quoted from an article in the *Christian Observer*, August 1815.
12. Clarke, *Travels in Various Countries*, pt. 2, sec. 2: 533.
13. Philip Hunt to Robert Liston, 20 June 1817, St. Clair, *Marbles*, 246.
14. H. J. Todd, *An Account of the Greek Mss. Chiefly Biblical*, v.
15. Ibid., 38.
16. National Library of Scotland, 5645 F 210.
17. St. Clair, *Marbles*, 220.
18. Lord Elgin, "Memorandum on the Subject of the Earl of Elgin's Pursuits in Greece," 78.
19. *Select Committee Report*, E. O. Visconti, "Two Memoires Read to the Royal Institute of France on the Sculptures in the Collection of the Earl of Elgin," *Memorandum*, 78.

20. Ibid., 135.
21. *The Trial of R. Fergusson*, 23.
22. Benjamin Robert Haydon, *Autobiography and Memoirs*, ed. Aldous Huxley, 207.
23. Ibid., 232.
24. Ibid., 233.
25. Michaelis, *Ancient Marbles*, 148.
26. Haydon, *Autobiography*, 233; also quoted in the *Select Committee Report*, 92.
27. *Select Committee Report*, xvii.
28. Robert Walsh, *A Residence at Constantinople*, sec. 1: 122.
29. Lord Byron to John Cam Hobhouse, 31 July 1811, *Byron's Correspondence*, sec. 1: 43.
30. Smith, *Elgin*, 313.
31. St. Clair, *Marbles*, 187.
32. Clarke, *Travels in Various Countries*, pt. 2, sec. 2: 484.
33. Douglas, *An Essay on the Ancient and Modern Greeks*, 89.
34. Dodwell, *A Classical and Topographical Tour*, sec. 1: 324.
35. Hughes, *Travels*, sec. 1: 261.
36. J. C. Eustace, *A Classical and Topographical Tour through Italy*, sec. 2: 20.
37. François-August-René Chateaubriand, *Travels to Jerusalem*, sec. 1: 187.
38. Sloane, *Notebooks*, 13 August 1816; also Gennadios, *Invasions*, 77.
39. St. Clair, *Marbles*, 194.
40. "The Malediction of Minerva," *New Monthly Magazine*, April 1815.
41. Lord Byron, *The Curse of Minerva*.
42. John Galt, *The Life and Studies of Benjamin West, Esq.*, sec. 2: 75.
43. Foreign Office, *British Foreign and State Papers*, 78/68.
44. Smith, *Elgin*, 280.
45. John Galt, *Autobiography*, sec. 1: 159.
46. St. Clair, *Marbles*, 198.
47. John Galt, "Atheniad," *Monthly Magazine*, no. 49 (1820).
48. Richard Payne Knight, *Analytic Inquiry into the Principles of Taste*, in Smith, *Elgin*, 322.
49. St. Clair, *Marbles*, 167.
50. Farington, *Diary*, 27 February 1808.
51. St. Clair, *Marbles*, 168.
52. Haydon, *Autobiography*, 66.
53. Ibid., 69.
54. Haydon, *Diary*, 8 September 1808.
55. Ibid., 5 November 1808.
56. St. Clair, *Marbles*, 176.
57. Richard Payne Knight, *Specimens of Antient Sculpture*, vol. 1: xxxix.
58. Hansard, *Parliamentary Debates*, 7th ser., 34 (1816): 1008–26.
59. Ibid., 1027–40.
60. St. Clair, *Marbles*, 182.

61. John Keats, *Poetical Works*, ed. H. W. Garrod.
62. William Sharp, *Life and Letters of Joseph Severn*, 32.
63. St. Clair, *Marbles*, 267.
64. Sharp, *Joseph Severn*, 32ff.
65. Thomas Hardy, *Winter Words: Christmas in the Elgin Room*.
66. *Report of the Select Committee on Arts and Manufacturers*, Parliamentary Papers, v, 1835. Also Cornelius Vermeule, *European Art and the Classical Past*, 141.
67. St. Clair, *Marbles*, 271.
68. Commissary Court, Edinburgh, "Decreet Divorce."
69. *The Trial of R. Fergusson*, 19.
70. Robert Miller, *The Municipal Buildings of Edinburgh*, 7.

The Trial

1. The chief sources for this part are:
   The Trial of R. Fergusson, Esq., published in 1807, in London, by T. Marshall and kept in the National Library of Scotland, Edinburgh.
   The Trial of R. Fergusson for Adultery with the Countess of Elgin, Wife of Earl of Elgin, a subsequent edition, which was published in 1808 by J. Day and is also kept in the National Library of Scotland.
   "Decreet Divorce, Thomas, Earl of Elgin and Kincardine, against Mary, Countess of Elgin and Kincardine," the complete record of the divorce proceedings before the Commissary Court of Edinburgh, 11 March 1808, pp. 1243–1473, which is preserved in the Scottish Records Office, Edinburgh.
2. Nisbet, *Letters*, 76.
3. Robert Fergusson to Lady Elgin, 4 March 1808, *Trial of R. Fergusson*, 10.
4. Ibid., 19.
5. Ibid., 32.
6. Commissary Court, Edinburgh, "Decreet Divorce," 1622.
7. Ibid., 1624.
8. Ibid., 1625.
9. Ibid., 1625ff.
10. Mrs. Gosling's deposition was written and signed on July 14, 1807.
11. *Trial of R. Fergusson*, 31.
12. Ibid., 33.
13. Ibid., 19.
14. Edinburgh, "Decreet Divorce," 1273–80.
15. Nisbet, *Letters*, 9.
16. Commissary Court, Edinburgh, "Decreet Divorce," 1275.
17. British Museum, Additional Manuscripts 38246 F 119.
18. Ibid., 38191 F 197.
19. Historical Manuscripts Commission, "Fortescue," sec. 2: 184.

20. Smith, *Elgin*, 312.
21. Ibid., 313.
22. Lord Elgin to Lord Liverpool, 18 April 1817, British Library, Additional Manuscripts 38266 F 3.
23. Ibid.
24. Lord Byron, *The Curse of Minerva*.
25. National Library of Scotland, 1055 F 118.
26. Harold Nicolson, "Byron Curse Echoes Again," *New York Times Magazine*, March 27, 1949, 12.
27. St. Clair, *Marbles*, 270.
28. Ibid.
29. Clarke, *Travels*, sec. 2, pt. 2: 483.
30. Lady Elgin to Robert Fergusson, 18 December 1806, in Commissary Court, Edinburgh, "Decreet Divorce," 1634.
31. Nisbet, *Letters*, 352.

Epilogue

1. Act of Parliament 47, Geo 3, cap. 36.
2. Michael Howard, *The Mediterranean Strategy in the Second World War*, 10ff.
3. Foreign Office, *British Foreign and State Papers*, 371/33195.
4. Ibid.
5. This memorandum was signed by John Edgar Forsdyke, keeper of Greek and Roman antiquities in the British Museum from 1932 to 1936, Foreign Office, *British Foreign and State Papers*, 371/33195.
6. St. Clair, *Marbles*, 272.
7. Foreign Office, *British Foreign and State Papers*, 371/33195.
8. Ibid.
9. Ibid.
10. Ibid.
11. Ibid.
12. *Hansard Parliamentary Debates* (1941): 319; also in John Torode, "The Day the FO Lost Its Marbles," *Guardian* (London), 21 March 1984; also in Gavin Stamp, "Keeping Our Marbles," *Spectator* (London), 10 December 1983, 14–17.
13. George Karo, "The Problem of the Elgin Marbles," in *Studies Presented to D. M. Robinson, 1951–1953*; also St. Clair, *Marbles*, 272–73.
14. As reported by Cosmos News Agency, Athens, Greece, June 6, 1996, on the Internet.
15. Donald Dale Jackson, "How Lord Elgin First Won—and Lost—His Marbles," *Smithsonian*, December 1992, 146.

Bibliography

PRINCIPAL SOURCES

Commissary Court, Scottish Records Office, Edinburgh, Scotland. "Decreet Divorce, Thomas, Earl of Elgin and Kincardine, against Mary, Countess of Elgin and Kincardine." 1808, pp. 1273–1472.

Farington, Joseph. *Farington Diary*. Edited by James Grieg. London: British Museum, 1922.

Gennadios, Ioannes. *Lord Elgin and the Previous Archaeological Invasions of Greece, Especially Athens 1440–1837*. Athens: (privately printed), 1930. Published in Greek, this book is devoted entirely to the reaction of travelers to Lord Elgin's taking down of the Parthenon marbles.

Herold, J. Christopher. *The Age of Napoleon*. New York: American Heritage Publishing, 1963.

Nisbet, Mary. *The Letters of Mary Nisbet, Countess of Elgin*. London: John Murray, 1926.

St. Clair, William. *Lord Elgin and the Marbles*. London: Oxford University Press, 1967. A thorough and accurate work, this book strongly supports Lord Elgin's position.

Smith, Arthur Hamilton. "Lord Elgin and His Collection." *Journal of Hellenic Studies* (British Museum), 1916. This long article, published on the one-hundredth anniversary of the acquisition of the Elgin Marbles by the British Museum, is the chief source of Lord Elgin's endeavors in Greece. Smith was a relative of the Elgin family and had access to many important letters and documents.

The Trial of R. Fergusson. Edinburgh: J. Day Publisher, 1808.

GENERAL SOURCES

Barrow, John. *Life and Correspondence of Admiral Sir William Sydney Smith*. London: R. Bently, 1848.

Blackstone, William. *Commentaries on the Laws of England*. London: Oxford University Press, 1765.

Blennerhasset, Lady Charlotte Julia, *Talleyrand*. London: J. Murray, 1894.

British Museum. Additional Manuscripts. London.

Brown, William J. *Syphilis and Other Venereal Diseases*. London: Cambridge University Press, 1970.

Burns, Robert. *The Jolly Beggars*. Edinburgh: Anderson, 1905.

Byron, Lord. *English Bards and Scotch Reviewers*. London: John Murray, 1809.

———. *The Curse of Minerva*. London: John Murray, 1812.

———. *Childe Harold's Pilgrimage*. Cantos 1 and 2. London: John Murray, 1812.

———. *Byron's Correspondence Chiefly with Lady Melbourne, Mr. Hobhouse, the Hon. Douglas Kinnaird, and P. B. Shelley*. Edited by John Murray. London: John Murray, 1922.

———. *Byron: A Self-Portrait, Letters and Diaries, 1798 to 1824*. Edited by Peter Quennell. London: John Murray, 1950.

Carlyle, Joseph Dacre. *Poems*. London: Cadell and Davis, 1805.

Chandler, R. *Travels in Greece*. London, 1776.

Chateaubriand, François-August-René. *Travels to Jerusalem*. London: H. Colburn, 1835.

Choiseul-Gouffier, Comte de. *Voyage Pittoresque de la Grece, 1782–1809*. Paris: J. P. Aillaud, 1812.

Cierval, Alexandre, *Chartres, sa cathédral, ses monuments*. Paris: Selleret, 1896.

Clarke, Edward Daniel. *Greek Marbles*. London: Cambridge University Press, 1809.

———. *The Tomb of Alexander*. London: R. Watts, 1805.

———. *Travels in Various Countries of Europe, Asia, and Africa*. London: Cadell and Davis, 1823.

Cockerell, C. R. *Travels in Southern Europe and the Levant, 1810–1817*. London: Longman, Green, 1903.

Creasy, E. S. *History of the Ottoman Turks*. London: Colonial Press, 1878.

Cust, Lionel, and Sidney Colvin. *History of the Society of Dilettanti*. London: Macmillan, 1898.

Description of the Collection of Ancient Marbles in the British Museum. London: British Museum, 1861.

d'Hauterive, E. *La Police secrete du premier empire, bulletins quotidiens, adressées par Fouche à l'empereur*. Vol. 1. Paris: Perrin and Company, 1908.

Dodwell, Edward. *A Classical and Topographical Tour through Greece*. London: Rodwell and Martin, 1819.

Douglas, F. S. N. *An Essay on Certain Points of Resemblance between the Ancient and Modern Greeks*. London: John Murray, 1813.

Elgin, Lord. *Memorandum on the Subject of the Earl of Elgin's Pursuits in Greece*. Edinburgh: Balfour Kirkwood and Co., 1810.

———. Letter to the editor in response to "The Remains of John Tweddell" (in *Edinburgh Review*, No. L). *Edinburgh Review*, Mawman, 1815.

———. Postscript to a letter to the editor. *Edinburgh Review*, Mawman, 1815.

Eustace, J. C. *A Classical and Topographical Tour through Italy*. London: Mawman, 1813.

Everett, Edward. *Journal*. Library of the Massachusetts Historical Society, 1839.

Falconer, William. *The Shipwreck*. London: Cadell and Davies, 1803.

Fellows, C. *Excursion in Asia Minor.* London: John Murray, 1839.

Fermor, Patrick Leigh. *Mani: Travels in the Southern Peloponnese.* New York: Harper and Row, 1958.

Foreign Office Papers, Public Record Office, London.

Fortescue, J. B. *Historical Manuscripts Commission Report Preserved at Dropmore.* A copy is in Foreign Office Papers 78 series in the Public Record Office, London.

Furtwangler, A. *Masterpieces of Greek Sculpture.* London: W. Heinemann, 1895.

Galt, John. *Autobiography.* London: Carey, Lea, Blanchard, 1883.

———. *Letters from the Levant.* London: Cadell and Davis, 1813.

———. *Life and Studies of Benjamin West, Esq.* London: Nichols, Son and Bentley, 1816.

———. *Life of Byron.* London: Colburn and Bentley, 1830.

Gardner, E. A. *Ancient Athens.* London: Macmillan, 1915.

———. *Handbook of Greek Sculpture.* London: Macmillan, 1915.

———. *Six Greek Sculptors.* London: Duckworth, 1915.

Geldart, William H. *Elements of English Law.* London: Williams and Norgate, 1911.

Gibbon, Edward. *The Decline and Fall of the Roman Empire.* New York: Viking, 1952.

Gillies, John. *History of Greece.* London: A. Strahan, 1786.

Gower, Lord Grenville Leveson. *Private Correspondence*, London: J. Rivington, 1810.

Hardy, Thomas. *Winter Words: Christmas in the Elgin Room.* Dorchester, Dorset: Henry Ling, 1927.

Haydon, Benjamin Robert. *Autobiography and Memoirs.* Edited by Aldous Huxley. London: Oxford University Press, 1926.

———. *Correspondence and Table Talk.* London: Chatto and Windus, 1876.

———. *The Diary of Benjamin Robert Haydon.* Edited by W. B. Pope. Cambridge: Harvard University Press, 1960.

Hertslet, E. *Treatise Regulating the Trade etc. between Great Britain and Turkey.* London: Butterworth, 1875.

Historical Manuscripts Commission. "Report on the Manuscripts of J. B. Fortescue, Esq., Preserved at Dropmore." London, 1892–1927.

Hobhouse, John Cam. *A Journey through Albania and Other Provinces of Turkey, in Europe and Asia, to Constantinople.* Philadelphia: M. Carey and Son, 1817.

Holdsworth, W. S. *History of English Law.* London: Methuen, 1909.

Homer, *The Odyssey.* Translated by Alexander Pope. London: W. Bowyer, 1752.

Howard, Michael. *The Mediterranean Strategy in the Second World War.* London: Weidenfeld and Nicholson, 1968.

Hughes, T. S. *Travels in Sicily, Greece, and Albania.* London: J. Mawman, 1802.

Hunt, Philip. *A Narrative of What Is Known Respecting the Literary Remains of the Late John Tweddell.* London: (private printing), 1816.

Hunter, John. *Treatise on Venereal Disease.* London: Royal Society of London, 1786.

Karo, Georg Heinrich. "The Problem of the Elgin Marbles." In *Studies Presented to D. M. Robinson 1951–1953.* Cambridge, Mass.: Harvard University Press, 1948.

Katsainos, George M. *Syphilis* (in Greek). Athens: (private printing), 1939.

Keats, John. *Poetical Works.* Edited by H. W. Garrod. London: Oxford University Press, 1939.

Keith, Admiral Viscount. *Keith Papers* (1927–1955). Navy Records Society. London.

Knight, Richard Payne. *Specimens of Antient Sculpture.* London: Dilettanti Society: 1809 and 1835.

———. *An Analytic Inquiry into the Principles of Taste.* London: Dilettanti Society, 1805.

Larrabee, S. A. *English Bards and Grecian Marbles.* New York: Columbia University Press, 1943.

Laurent, Peter Edmund. *Recollections of a Classical Tour.* London: G. and W. B. Whittaker, 1822.

Leake, W. M. *Journal of a Tour in Asia Minor.* London: John Murray, 1824.

Lechevalier, J. F. *Voyage de la Troade.* Paris: Dentu, 1802.

LeGrand, Ph. E. "Biographie de Louis-François-Sebastien Fauvel." *Revue Archéologique,* 3rd ser., 30 (1897).

Lewis, Michael. *Napoleon and His British Captives.* London: Allen and Unwin, 1962.

Maitland, F. W., and F. Pollock. *History of English Law.* London: Cambridge University Press, 1898.

Marshall, T. *The Trial of R. Fergusson, Esq.,* in the National Library of Scotland.

Maurois, Andre. *Byron.* New York: D. Appleton, 1929.

Medwin, Thomas. *Conversations of Lord Byron.* Edited by Ernest J. Lovell Jr. London: H. Colburn, 1824.

Menzies, Sutherland. *Turkey, Old and New.* London: W. H. Allen, 1880.

Michaelis, A. *Ancient Marbles in Great Britain.* London: Cambridge University Press, 1882.

———. *Der Parthenon.* Leipzig: Breitkopf and Hartel, 1883.

Michaud, Louis Gabriel. *Histoire politique et vie intime.* Paris: Bureau de la Biographie Universelle, 1853.

Miller, Robert. *The Municipal Buildings of Edinburgh.* Edinburgh: Town Council, 1895.

Moore, T., editor. *Letters and Journals of Lord Byron with Notices of His Life.* London: (private printing), 1830.

Morritt of Rokeby, J. B. S. *Letters Descriptive of a Journey in Europe and Asia Minor in the Years 1794–1796.* London: John Murray, 1914.

Murray, A. S. *Sculptures of the Parthenon*. New York: E. P. Dutton, 1903.

Nicolson, Harold. *Byron: The Last Journey*. London: Constable, 1940.

Otter, W. *The Life and Remains of the Reverend Edward Daniel Clarke*. London: G. Cowie, 1825.

Paton, A. A. *History of the Egyptian Revolution*. 2nd ed. London: Trubner, 1863.

Phillips, O. Hood. *The Principles of English Law*. London: Sweet and Maxwell, 1939.

Plutarch. *The Lives of Noble Grecians and Romans*. Edited by John and William Langhorne. London: T. Longman, 1795.

Pullan, R. P. *Principal Ruins of Asia Minor*. London: Texier and Pullan, 1865.

Russell, Jack. *Nelson and the Hamiltons*. London: Blond, 1969.

Schliemann, H. *Troy*. London: John Murray, 1875.

Select Committee Report of the House of Commons on the Earl of Elgin's Collection of Sculptured Marbles. London: John Murray, 1816.

Sharp, William. *Life and Letters of Joseph Severn*. London: Sampson, Low, Marston Ltd., 1892.

Sicilianos, D. *Old and New Athens* (in Greek). Athens: Aetos, 1953.

Sloane, John. *Notebooks*. London: Sir John Sloane Museum, 1816.

Smith, Arthur Hamilton. *The Sculptures of the Parthenon*. London: British Museum, 1910.

——. *Catalogue of Sculpture in the Department of Greek and Roman Antiquities*. London, British Museum, 1892.

Smith, Edward. *Life of Sir Joseph Banks*. London: J. Murray, 1911.

Stevens, G. P. *The Erechtheum*. Cambridge, Mass.: Harvard University Press, 1927.

Talleyrand-Périgord, Charles Maurice de. *Mémoires*. Paris: Napoleon Society, 1895.

Todd, H. J. *Catalogue of the Archepiscopal Manuscripts in the Library of Lambeth Palace*. London: Law and Gilbert, 1812.

——. *An Account of the Greek Mss. Chiefly Biblical Which Had Been in the Possession of the Late Professor Carlyle, the Greater Part of Which Are Now Deposited in the Archepiscopal Library at Lambeth Palace*. London: Law and Gilbert, 1820.

Tweddell, Robert. *Remains of John Tweddell, Late Fellow of Trinity College, Cambridge, Being a Selection of His Correspondence, a Republication of His "Profusiones Juveniles," an Appendix Containing Some Account of the Author's Collections, Mss, Drawings etc., and of Their Extraordinary Disappearance, Preceded by a Biographical Memoir of the Deceased, and Illustrated with Portraits, Picturesque Views and Maps*. London: J. Mawman, 1816.

Vermeule, Cornelius. *European Art and the Classical Past*. Cambridge, Mass.: Harvard University Press, 1964.

Waldstein, C. *Essays on the Art of Pheidias*. London: Cambridge University Press, 1885.

Walpole, Robert. *Memoirs Relating to European and Asiatic Turkey*. London: Longman, Hurst, Rees, Orme, and Brown, 1817.

Walsh, Robert. *A Residence at Constantinople.* London: Westley and Davies, 1836.

Williams, H. W. *Travels in Italy, Greece, and the Ionian Islands.* Edinburgh: (private printing), 1820.

Wittman, William. *Travels in Turkey, Asia Minor, and Syria.* London: R. Phillips, 1803.

Index